MOLLY KEANE

A LIFE

Sally Phipps

virago

VIRAGO

First published in Great Britain in 2017 by Virago Press
This paperback edition published in 2018 by Virago Press

1 3 5 7 9 10 8 6 4 2

A CIP catalogue record for this book
is available from the British Library.

ISBN 978-0-349-00754-0

Typeset in Goudy by M Rules
Printed and bound in Great Britain by
Clays Ltd, St Ives plc

Papers used by Virago are from well-managed forests
and other responsible sources.

Virago Press
An imprint of
Little, Brown Book Group
Carmelite House
50 Victoria Embankment
London EC4Y 0DZ

An Hachette UK Company
www.hachette.co.uk

www.virago.co.uk

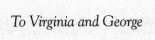

To Virginia and George

PREFACE

The arrival of *Good Behaviour* on my desk when I was senior editor at André Deutsch Limited was less simple than it should have been. Gina Pollinger, Molly's agent, who before her marriage had been one of our editors, had called me to say that she was about to send us a novel she thought I would love, but the person whose desk it landed on was not me but Gina's ex-colleague, Esther Whitby, and she, having read it, passed it on to me, fully expecting to get it back. In our firm, the person who first read and loved a book usually became its editor. In this case, however, I said 'I'm sorry, Esther, but I am going to pull rank. I am going to edit this novel.' I knew I was being mean.

Esther kept her mouth shut, so I failed to realise that I was just losing one of my best friends. She was furious, and not a person who made light of being offended. I don't know how long her resentment lasted, but it was for a considerable time. Luckily for me, another aspect of her nature is great generosity and kindness. It was only after that aspect finally prevailed that I learnt how nearly I had lost her.

What had moved me to such bad behaviour was not only the novel's quality. It was also the extent to which I shared Molly's background. East Anglia and Ireland are chalk and cheese but there are still resemblances between big-house families (particularly if short of cash) and both of us came from such families. Both of us started out 'horsey', and both had learnt to flinch at the word 'brainy'. 'Oh, you're the brainy one, aren't you?' said one of my partners at a hunt ball – and he might as well have accused me of reeking of halitosis. 'Brainy' was why Molly published all her early novels under a pseudonym. How I sympathised!

But with *Good Behaviour* it was instantly clear to me that she ought to step forth as herself, and her own hesitation about it was very slight. Molly was essentially modest, but like all good writers, she knew deep down that she was good. I think the shape her modesty took was simply not feeling that being a very good writer was all that important. You did it as well as you could – of course you did! – but so what?

With *Good Behaviour* she achieved something quite extraordinary. She makes Aroon, her narrator, tell a whole long and complicated story *without ever understanding what that story is about*. This is so clever, it's mind-blowing – and the best thing about it is that it is never clever for the sake of cleverness. There are moments when the reader pauses to congratulate him or herself for being astute enough to twig what is really going on – but never any when he or she is exclaiming 'Clever Molly'. But clever Molly has used her 'distancing' technique to turn us into something nearer watchers than story-readers. It is as though we are seeing events unfold which we can then interpret for ourselves, and the effect of this is *much* more poignant than explication would be.

Her two subsequent novels – *Time After Time* and *Loving and Giving* – were less brilliant than *Good Behaviour*. Although, *Time after Time* was wonderfully entertaining and *Loving and Giving* was perhaps the most amazing thing she ever did considering her age and frailty at the time she wrote it.

Because it is many years since I last read *Good Behaviour* I thought, when asked to write this preface, that I ought to read it again. This turned out to be unnecessary. I only had to pick the book up and there it all was in my head. I could move about in the story as easily as I can move about in memories of my own past. I think I can say that such an experience is true of no other novel I ever published.

As for Molly herself – her personality: well, I liked and admired many of 'our' authors, but Molly . . . Molly I loved.

We communicated mostly by letter, not seeing much of each other – just brief meetings on her infrequent visits to London, on one of which I took her to the Booker Prize-giving dinner. We kept telling each other to suppress excitement, 'because that damned Indian is going to get it' – which he did. Molly kept her cool, but judging by my own disappointment, hers must have been horrible.

There was just one occasion when I spent real time with her, and it was then that admiration turned into love.

To celebrate the publication of *Good Behaviour* we gave a party in Dublin, and it was agreed that after it I would drive Molly back to her home in Ardmore. My idea was that I would spend the night there, then seize the chance for a few days' holiday exploring southern Ireland. It was only about halfway down our long drive together that it dawned on me that plans had been made: plans for parties. Six of them. A whole week of parties. And I was to stay with Molly at Dysert all that week. Help! Actually *staying* with someone ... it was not something I liked doing. It seemed, however, to be taken so firmly for granted that I had the distinct impression that I must have been told about it in advance – only I knew that had not happened. But what could I do now except sit back and let it happen – which, of course, I did. And that week was the most wonderful fun.

Molly was a perfect hostess, not just because of the kindness and care she put into it, but because of how brilliantly open she was. At once we might have known each other for years. We could talk about anything – we could even understand things unsaid. For example, Molly disapproved of the fact that I lived with a black man – a Jamaican. Not a word was said about it – of course not! – but there it was, *and it didn't matter.* It was none of her business, and so many other things between us were acceptable – were amusing – were important – were *fun.* Molly's astonishing gift for giving and taking pleasure filled our days together.

And it was not just her. Those parties ... It struck me that if I had been condemned to six Norfolk drinks parties with complete strangers, all of whom shared the interests of my dear parents and other relations – hunting, shooting, fishing, plus sailing and gardening if you were lucky – it would have been stupefyingly boring, but here it was not. Generalisations about nationalities are usually silly, but it is perfectly true that the Irish are *much better* at talking than the English. Those parties were full of surprises and laughter. They sparkled. All the more so for the brief sketches of the people we were about to meet, rarely unkind but always funny, provided by Molly on the way to each party. I shall go on laughing till the day I die at her quotation from one rather grand old woman, spoken in the voice of someone with ill-fitting dentures: 'I read your book, Molly. I absolutely hated it, but I must say it's well written – I didn't find a single spelling mistake.'

One thing I enjoyed slightly less than the rest was the night we spent staying with Molly's old and valued friend Stephen Vernon. He was by then very ill, paralysed and wholly dependent on a carer. Molly was accustomed to his condition, but to me it came as a shock, and so did the state of his house. That house's famous elegance was only just still perceptible. Molly, whose perfectionism embraced domestic detail, could not possibly have failed to notice this, but she gave no sign of having done so. I came to the conclusion that she was responding to the situation with a more serious version of her attitude to my Jamaican partner: there was nothing she could do about it, so wipe it out. Indeed she went further: she boosted whatever was good. That seemed to be wise as it was kind.

The dazzle of Molly's charm sometimes made people suspect it did not go deep. Her relationship with Stephen was only one of the many which proved this to be utter nonsense. This marvellous book by her daughter Sally will reveal how complex she was, full of uncertainties, anxieties, even fears, capable of striking out in anger and of little streaks of prejudice and snobbery, but with every page it becomes clearer that in spite of all of this, Molly's *essential essence* was in the generosity, lovely kindness and wisdom which won her so many instant friends. It was almost as though there were two of her, one shaped by class and family circumstances, against which she often rebelled but from which she would never quite escape, and the other which stirred into life whenever she worked her way through to writing-level, and this Molly became able to see through her first self with calm amusement. That second Molly, the more 'real' of the two, was as responsive to love as she was to the challenges of her art, so was dominant in her friendships as well as her books. That was why so many quickly made friends remained bound to her for life.

Not long before she died, when guiding a pen over paper had become difficult, she wrote me a little goodbye letter (and I know she did the same to Gina). In it she thanked me for publishing *Good Behaviour*, with the most emphatic declaration of how much it had meant to her – how it had given her a new life. It was a deeply sad letter to get, being such a clear indication that the end was near, but it was also a wonderfully generous gift. I am not a letter-keeper. Nothing would have made me throw that one away.

Diana Athill
London, August 2016

PROLOGUE

After Molly Keane's death in 1996 the novelist Clare Boylan wrote of her, 'If the best should be kept till last then it is fitting that Molly Keane, the very best of the Anglo-Irish ascendancy writers, was also the last of them. Molly's death last month closed the pages on Anglo-Irish literature. There are no more big houses. There will be no more big-house writers.' She quotes Molly ascribing what she called her 'limited talent to amuse' to having been brought up as a Protestant in Ireland. 'All the Protestants were poor and had big houses,' Molly said. 'We entertained a lot but we had poor food, bad wine and no heat. It was an absolute duty to be amusing.' Molly cultivated this art in a literary, personal and social sense. She could use it abrasively and wickedly but she also felt that the gift of seeing things as funny was a blessing and a healing bridge across life's pain.

When talking to Clare, Molly was referring to the 'big house' in a social sense. This phrase also had a political meaning which impinged on her life when her family home was burned during the civil war of 1922–3. For the sake of readers who are not Irish it is perhaps necessary to say that the civil war had been preceded by the Easter Rising (1916) and the War of Independence (1919–21). The Treaty (brokered by Michael Collins and Fine Gael) ending this conflict with England gave most of Ireland independence but kept the six Northern counties (largely Protestant) with Britain. Civil war broke out between supporters of the Treaty and those who disagreed with it (De Valera and Sinn Fein). From January 1922 to July 1923 about two hundred Ascendancy houses were burned by 'irregulars' associated with Sinn Fein; the reasons for this were complex and connected to the Protestant history of the families concerned and to their interconnection with English rule. It can also be said that, over the decades, a number of Irish Patriots came from these houses. The position of the Anglo-Irish was ambivalent – they did not think of themselves as English, they were rooted in the land of Ireland and few of them chose to look at the uneasy nature of this Irishness – Elizabeth Bowen has described them as only being truly at home when they were on board the boat between England and Ireland.

When Molly suggested that I should write about her she gave me no instructions except to say 'make it as much like a novel as possible'. I knew that one of her reasons for asking me was simply practical: she wanted to push the work my way but she also knew that I understood the very peculiar Anglo-Irish world in which we all grew up and she liked my essay-like way of writing.

I accepted her request with some misgivings. I was uncertain of my ability to bring her to life as she really was, enchanting and troubled, courageous and fearful, warlike and compassion-ate – a lover of life and a pessimist. As a child I was swept up in all these paradoxes, exhilarated and sometimes engulfed by them. She was my mother and she was also an artist – a fact which greatly interested me – and I hope it has given me the necessary detachment to write about her with truth and love.

Torn by opposing currents, her stiletto sharpness and her infinite kindness, she was a person both beguiled by the beauty of the world and besieged by dark forces, fascinated and sharp-eyed concerning human nature and above all amused. Her writing reflects this; she knows her world to the bone in an almost Jane Austen manner, and, like her, she transcends her conversational mode and small social scene and reaches out to all her readers. She sometimes said that she only wrote for the money. In fact, she was a serious writer and perfection-ist in this as in all things. She had pity for her people 'trapped in the human condition' – victims of jealousies, yearnings and willpower – she relished their absurdity and also their courage and humanity.

A child of nature and of the drawing-room, she observes both with the poetic exactness of her profound sense of place. The rooms of houses long gone continue to exist in her novels where the sun still bleaches a hall table and silk curtains rot slowly in the windows, or a master cook lifts a perfectly risen soufflé from her sulky kitchen range. Outside a character tend-ing his garden is 'bent like a reed in a cold wind' and azaleas pour out their scent of 'pepper and honey'.

Her world was impinged on by its fuller, immediate past, and the losses of the future, but beyond that she did not see things historically or politically. She blamed this on her lack of education. It was as much a question of temperament. She was not drawn to the overall view, but to the luminosity of detail (in the Proustian way). She filters her writing sensuously and emotionally, and then structures and calms it with the measure and craftsmanship of her language.

Her long life almost spanned the century. She has to be the last of the Anglo-Irish writers, because she bore witness to the dying away of her world. It is partly this, running parallel with her own fading, and its unreconciled sense of life's splendour, which gives to her late books their fierce autumnal colours.

CHAPTER I

Aged ninety, Molly Keane lay on the sofa in her home at Ardmore, surrounded by the driftwood of her life at the time: sewing, which she found increasingly hard to see, a letter half written, and a copy of the *Spectator* through which she was slowly proceeding. Pleasurable tasks had become marathons. The flowers and the fire in the room were tended by other hands in ways she did not quite approve of, and felt obliged to show gratitude for. It was a dark evening, and the sea from which she drew solace was invisible through the window. Although she did not speak of it, I knew that all day her inner state had been vertiginous. She longed for life and she longed for death, and she felt cheated of both. She struggled with sadness, impatience and a blanketing tiredness that drained her of humour and the small residue of vitality on which she relied. It was six o'clock and the contest was nearly over for that day. She began to relax and to take a few sips from a tiny glass of whiskey. Her eyes, which had the distant, luminous look of old age, changed slightly and recovered a little of their former brightness. She began to talk about the idea of my writing her biography, something that had been said and unsaid between us for years. She was shy of pushing it on me and I was shy of thinking of her as a subject and not as a person, as well as being doubtful of my ability to bring her enchanting and troubled personality to the page. I was fifty-five, she was my mother, fossiled into my psyche by her love and by the happiness and difficulty which this had brought me over the years. We loved each other, but had long wrestled with the dream character we wished the other to be. As well as being my mother, she was an artist, a fact that interested me deeply and I hoped would give me the necessary distance. A sort of deal was done between us that evening as we sipped whiskey in the room, which like every drawing-room she had ever had, smelt in February of hyacinths and turf smoke.

'I trust you completely,' she said; 'the only thing I'm afraid of is that you won't be nasty enough.' She spoke as a writer and with generosity because she hated it when people were nasty about her in real life. She knew my weakness, my fear of the scalpel (which she wielded so fruitfully in her own work) and my desire for a serenity which is not always there. She was not averse to serenity herself, but she felt it to be a rare occurrence often tainted by complacency and illusion. I wish I had seen her then as I see her now. Writing about her has given me a synthesis of what she conquered and suffered and enjoyed. Her character was passionate, excitable and easily moved to amusement and anxiety. Her talent was a very personal matter. She wove her writing out of her own colour and bleakness, and very directly from the world immediately about her.

She was born on 20 July 1904 in Co. Kildare. She died at her home in Ardmore, Co. Waterford, ninety-one years later. Ireland encompassed her life, which occupied most of the century. She was the child of a small, vivid world which has ended. Her writing is prismatic, a celebration and a critique of the world she lived and died with, and was entirely enmeshed by.

She was the third child of Agnes and Walter Skrine, born after Susan (1900) and Charlie (1902), and before Walter (1907) and Godfrey (1909). She thought of herself as the cuckoo in the nest. In some respects the Skrine family was the wrong one for her because she had a Latin temperament and a need for drama and demonstrative love. In fact, they were all people of passion but with the others it took the form of a strong, submerged current, whereas in her case it was the mainstream. Yet if she had not been very much a Skrine and a rebel against certain aspects of being one, she would not have written the extraordinarily original books she did. Her family gifted her and wounded her, as families often do. Her reaction to this state of affairs was extreme and voluble. She preferred not to understand or analyse it, but she put it into words all her life, and made it a cornerstone of her art.

Even as a little girl with a longing for involvement she told me she felt apart. In one of the few family photographs which exist, she looks different from the others. Aged three or four, she stares boldly into the camera, as though seeking its attention. Her thick hair is cut in a fringe. Her hair itself was a source of otherness. Red hair was not looked on favourably. It symbolised hoydenishness, Irishness, wildness. Their cook in Kildare referred to her as 'that right red rip', and she seems to have lived up to this title in childhood. She was light-boned, thin with a translucent complexion. Her dark eyes were expressive and flashed with amusement or fury. Most of these physical attributes stayed with her into old age including her youthful skin. She inherited the long nose of her father, and complained always that it spoilt any aspirations she might have had to beauty. All the children were stamped with this Skrine nose.

Molly's mother, Agnes Nesta Shakespeare Higginson, was born into a family from Antrim, Northern Ireland, many of whose sons became soldiers and colonial administrators. She was one of seven children and when she was twenty-nine, in 1895, she married an Englishman, Walter Skrine, and went to live with him at his ranch in Alberta, Canada. She was a published writer before her marriage, a poet and a contributor to *Blackwood's Magazine*. On a visit to her parents she wrote a poem telling of her love for Ireland, for her husband and for the prairie:

> I dreamt of gentle Ireland beneath the Northern
>   Light
> The waves that broke on Ireland were callin' me
>   by night
> Till back across the salt sea, back against the sun
> I took the way the birds know, and woke in
>   Cushenden
>   Not with you.
>
> Oh what about the roses then, and what about the
>   strand!

For now 'tis wantin' back I am to that lone land;
'Tis the other house I'm seein' on the green Hill's
    breast
An' a trail across the prairie that's goin' south an'
    west
        Back to you.

Susan was the only child born in Canada but they all had a romantic feeling for the Bar S Ranch and spoke about the prairie in a particular tone as though it was something familiar, revered and free. This must have been an attitude learned from their parents. Walter seems to have been a natural rancher. He loved and understood land and was a good stockman and horseman. Since he put the acres of the Bar S together it has only had three owners in total. He is still a hero among those who work his ranch today. Despite being so happy there, the Skrines sold up in 1902. When they began to have children they felt, like most of the Anglo-Irish, that it was their duty to give them an English education (ironically, in the Dotheboys Hall establishments which damaged their sensibility and contributed to the odd melancholy and asceticism afflicting most of them in later life).

Also people of their caste, unlike many Irish immigrants, tended to live abroad for a limited period only, and then come home to the relations, hunting fields and trout streams of their youth. In their case, neither returned precisely to their roots but they came back to familiar ground, settling first in Kildare and later moving to Ballyrankin House, Ferns, Co. Wexford. Nesta was within a train journey of Antrim, and

Walter belonged to that species of Englishman who falls in love with Ireland.

He grew up in Somerset where his family lived in elegant houses of Bath stone presided over by chatelaines, some of whom made his Irish children feel like mountainy poor relations when they stayed with them in later years. He was the youngest of twelve. Molly had the Bath Skrines in mind when she mentioned younger sons of limited means with graceful names from the mother's side such as Vivien, Sholto or Hyacinth. Walter's middle name was Claremount. There were not enough Bath stone mansions to go round, so younger sons were expected to join the forces, or the Church or to travel, as he did. Prior to his generation the Skrines had been a rich landed family, their property passing from father to eldest son in an unbroken line from the fifteenth century to the end of the nineteenth, when it began to be dispersed by an abundance of daughters. After the Canadian prairies, Walter Claremount was drawn to Ireland, perhaps by the hunting and certainly by his Irish-born wife and his own cousins who lived in Kildare.

Molly described her first memory thus: 'Life in early youth is not amusing, events are either tragic or dramatic. I think my very earliest memory might be classed as a drama. I can't explain why at the age of about three, I was left unattended on a grass lawn with a view of the stable yard. I only know I saw my father crucified against the door of the saddle-room, with his hunting boots legless standing on the cobbled verge beneath him ... ' This hallucination induced by the sight of his empty hunting clothes airing in the sun shows perhaps that the dark aspect of her imagination was present from an early age.

Molly's childhood was frightening. She was not shielded from fear as much as is possible, as children are today. A Victorian ideal of courage was held up to the little Skrines. 'Fortune favours the brave,' they were told, especially in matters of horsemanship. She was a very courageous person, but she was intrigued by fear. She mentioned it, understood it and wrote about it often, perhaps because it was a taboo subject in her family.

Fear was also present, together with many delights, in the almost unlimited freedom to roam which she experienced from a very early age. Children were parked out of doors at all seasons, among insects, birds and beasts in a perpetually seeding and dying universe of gardens, fragrant flowers and smoking manure heaps, soft grasses and stinging nettles. Frequently alone, or accompanied only by a small dog, she absorbed this universe as a child does, until it became indelibly part of her inner landscape. This was really her chief education. Although she was very bright she was not much drawn to thinking, but to learning through feeling, perceiving and doing things in the world around her. This was the foremost influence on her sensuous style of writing and the reason why she so frequently intertwined the deepest feelings and moods of her characters with the landscape in which she placed them. Except for short sessions with governesses (brief compared to the times she spent wandering) she had almost no abstract schooling whatever.

Her love of words crept up on her later. Wordsmithing was possibly in her genes. It came from both sides of the family. The Skrines, particularly during the nineteenth century, were men of letters, extensively quoted in the

Oxford English Dictionary. Her mother published *Songs of the Glens of Antrim* in 1901 to huge success. It sold sixteen thousand copies, far more than Yeats could aspire to at the time. These poems are written in a misty, romanticised dialect which seems somewhat patronising today, but in that era it was an acceptable convention used by many poets. In keeping with her dialect, her nom de plume was Moira O'Neill. Her poems have a deep, gentle feeling for landscape and sea. They were frequently set to music and they possess their aficionados to this day, especially in Ulster. Her prose lacks the sentimental aspect of the Victorian convention she utilised in her verse. It is simply and elegantly expressed with a certain sharpness reminiscent of her daughter's own sharpness, although she did not possess Molly's mastery, the deadly accuracy and witty, exquisite preciseness in matching feelings to words.

Relations between the two of them were complex. When *Good Behaviour* made Molly for a time the grand old lady of Irish letters, she was much interviewed by young feminist journalists anxious to hear about her mother. The line she had adhered to over the years – 'I was the unloved, unattractive child, and I was often sick. My mother hated me and I hated her' – did not quite stand up. By then she was seventy-eight and had long reflected on the pains and joys of her own motherhood and could not hold to an opinion forged when she was a young thing in rebellion. In some ways she never ceased to be a young thing in rebellion but the truth was ambiguous. There are indications of love in their attitude to one another. They are both attracted and repelled. In time they settled for being mutually disappointed while displaying signs of an awareness that there was something extremely special about the other which fascinated them, and on rare occasions drew them close. Mrs Skrine came to expect the worst and expressed her feelings in quiet disapproval. In time Molly embarked on a witty loquacious 'hatred' which fuelled her funny stories, influenced her writing and masked her hurt at her mother's view of her. A little girl in search of passionate affection and attention, she grew up in an era when, as Molly said, children were there 'to field tennis balls with sulky diligence' and to serve the adult world not vice versa. When she was small they seem to have been on friendly terms. They kissed when she went to wake her mother, accompanying the maid who carried in the early morning tea tray with bread and butter 'cut thin as veils' on it. They kissed at night after the children's evening visit to the drawing-room. Molly remembered the misery of being forbidden to partake of the grown-up delicacies on the tea table, but she relished her drawing-room dress of blue velvet and lace, and the romance of the children sometimes being allowed to take lanterns and rush around the dark garden with them. She was a sensuous connoisseur of childhood kisses. The cheek of an elderly cousin searched for through lace veiling and silver strands of hair was soft and slack, her father's was a little prickly, but her mother's cheek was delicious, 'filled like a peach to the skin'.

It is not surprising that the tiny Molly liked to dress up in her blue velvet, seize a lantern and have fun. She was born with a serious love of fiesta and a talent for creating it. In a sense what she most reproached her mother for was a lack of celebration. 'When I was very young, Christmas was not at all that glamorous. Although we lived in what today would be considered an unmanageably large house, perfect for parties, my mother, for all her other wonderful merits, was a determined recluse, indifferent to food or drink, and averse to parties in her own or other people's houses.' This need of Molly's included parties, but went beyond them into the more modest celebrations of everyday existence which put a softness and warmth into living. She credits her mother with taste in the arrangement of her rooms and with being a good gardener but she was 'stringent', with little interest in comfort or treats; fires went out, bath water was chilly, food was seldom delicious and flowers in the house were 'a rare occurrence'. A small silver goblet stood, as permanent decoration, at the centre of the dining-room table in lieu of flowers. Her mother's disinterest in such matters nourished Molly's tendency towards them. In adulthood, the sensuous, consoling, celebratory attributes of domestic life were deeply important to her; she was always making a champagne cocktail to enhance some victory or anaesthetise some sorrow, filling a hot-water bottle, piling driftwood onto the fire or brewing barley water and beef tea to soothe an ailing body. She offered people those things with love. Her mother did not go about life in that way. 'She had an enormous distaste for housekeeping. She did not really like children – she did not like dogs either and she had no enjoyment of food.'

This critique of the mother in *Good Behaviour* could fit Mrs Skrine except in its harshest detail. She did like children. She was not cold as Mrs St Charles in the novel was cold, but she could not show love as Molly wanted it to be expressed.

When fumbling for memories of her childhood and making belated efforts to be fair, Molly said, 'She was a star. I loved her to distraction, and she loved me in an abstracted sort of way.'

Later their mother said to Susan, 'I made so many mistakes with Molly.' They clashed and tried to change each other by the wrong means. Disapproval was a disastrous alloy with Molly's emotional make-up. Coaxing might have worked better. Mrs Skrine was not a coaxer, she was an Ulsterwoman, direct, low key and possessed of Victorian certainties about right and wrong. As a child, Molly was undoubtedly an actress and a show-off. She said of herself: 'I was born dishonest and a social snob' and 'I always knew how to flatter and yearn'. Mrs Skrine was bound to find such traits undesirable. For her, modesty was the important thing. This meant modesty of mind, or *amour propre* and, above all, of the person. Despite her mother's efforts, Molly retained through life a rather free view of the body, characteristic of her twenties generation. Mrs Skrine's point of view was utterly Victorian. Molly described an incident in which her youthful sense of justice is outraged and her older self makes a real effort to understand.

'I was lying on the grass kicking my legs in the air and exposing my navy blue knickers with elastic around the knees when my mother saw me from the window and summoned me inside, we had the most awful row. I was very embarrassed . . . Neither could I understand my mother's reaction to my childish abandon. I queried my sister on this much later in life, and she simply said, "Well you know Mother's generation just felt that modesty could not be instilled at an early enough age."'

She referred to this behaviour in uncharacteristically patient terms as 'not quite Puritanism', yet she is right. Mrs Skrine's poetry bears witness to the fact that she was not a Calvinist. She partook of the sensuous world just as Molly did, but they did so in completely different circumstances for different reasons.

Mrs Skrine was comely, the shape of a slender pigeon. She wore Henry Heath hats out of doors and favoured muted colours and touches of lace. All her children could adopt the tone of quiet chilling acerbity which she sometimes used to devastating effect. She was a social recluse and given to reverie. Molly, while being extremely social, also needed – like most writers – a certain amount of reverie but she feared it as laziness. In adulthood, all the Skrines deplored laziness; this fear was connected psychologically with their mother. In old age her mother succumbed entirely to reverie; wrapped in gossamer shawls and sustained by egg flips with a whiff of cognac in them, she took to her bed for years. Her younger grandchildren, my cousins, who had never seen her on her feet, called her 'Our Granny-in-bed'. She spoke little and depression overtook her. This was the burden of melancholy which her children inherited, and with varying degrees of victory battled by means of their diligence, passion and high standards.

If she was not quite a puritan, she was not quite an intellectual either. She would not have wished to think of herself as such, although she translated Dante and, apart from gardening, all her inclinations were cerebral or inward, writing, reading, music and prayer. She was born into an extroverted colonial age and her real life, that of the mind and the imagination, was carried on quietly as a sort of subtext to the booted and spurred country life going on around her, which she would have considered more important and real than any of her own concerns. She refused an invitation from Lady Gregory asking her to stay at Coole at Yeats's behest. The Republican movement may have thought of them as Protestant grandees, but she felt that Lady Gregory and Yeats were dangerous Sinn Feiners themselves.

The Victorian emphasis on form and surface was impenetrable in some ways. This powerful surface was bulwarked by axioms. Two of them frequently quoted by Molly in her early writings were 'Mother knows best' and 'Father says so'. An affectionate obedience to that situation came naturally to her mother's generation, together with an adroitness, in some cases, for doing as one wished within it. Most of the Skrine children accepted the status quo, but Molly questioned it, and almost from the beginning kicked against it. Her mother could not understand her passionate refuting of something she herself considered right and natural. There is no doubt that childhood was easier for boys. Her mother admired and indulged them; you could hear it in the voices of the Skrine men when they mentioned the word 'Mother'. When they said the word as grown-ups, they were looking back on something magic. Molly envied the love she saw going out to the boys. She wrote about it in *Mad Puppetstown* – 'He loved his mother to the edge of romance. Hardly ever did he sulk at her, hide from her or keep her waiting for his pleasure.

'"Time for milk and nap," she said. "Time for chocolate," amended Evelyn. Easter was given one too before she climbed back into the dim room that would be her own some time. She envied Evelyn with a sudden flashing envy because he was a boy and could presume with so much grace and success over matters like chocolate. That was to be a boy. Easter felt a girl, and out of it as her lagging feet carried her up again to the nursery.'

Feeling out of it was something which troubled Molly. As a child she was like a magpie on the watch for something bright and special all the time. This displeased her mother but rather intrigued her father. He showed a softness towards Molly which she could have benefited from if she had not been so preoccupied with her mother. She used to tell the story of her father's apples. These did not grow in his orchard, but arrived in a crate from New Zealand via the Army & Navy Stores catalogue (this all-purpose cornucopia of provisions for Anglo-Irish households of that date was one of their strongest colonial links). The older children descended to the smoking room to chat with their father and watch him eating his pre-breakfast apple after their own miserable repast of lumpy porridge and milk with skin on it. 'You must not ask' was a cardinal rule. 'We would stand, eyes glued on the apple as he stripped it with a silver knife, making small conversational openings about bantams or rabbits or the pony . . . On my fatal day, I longed so ardently for that instant of satisfaction that I stepped forward, as it were to the footlights, and recited from *Reading Without Tears* what I thought was an appropriate and tactful suggestion – "'A' stands for apple, so juicy and sweet, which when ripe in autumn we all like to eat!" Here followed a dreadful pause when Daddy's face took on its sternest and least approving expression. "So that is what you children are here for," he said. Everything in his tone implied condemnation of greed, and I knew what the retribution could be. I was wrong. When he turned his back, as I thought in disgust, it was to stoop over the crate of delights and take out another, an entire apple, to be divided into 3 fair parts between us.'

It was his habit also to take them on a Sunday outing in the pony trap. In summer they went to the woods where he read aloud from *The Jungle Book* or *Tales of the Blackfoot Indians*, and sometimes lit a campfire. Molly referred to these trips as 'a dreadful chore for him ... A task, a duty he had to do.' Her brother Godfrey did not agree with her interpretation. He had warmer recollections of picnics in the 'Wild Wood' and said he thought his father was particularly charmed by Molly. If that was so, it is hard to tell why she did not respond. She often wrote about the 'absolute distance' between parents and children. In her case, it was an emotional distance more than a lack of love. There was always strong covert feeling in the Skrine family but unspoken feelings never suited Molly. She craved the words of love and (untypically of her time and caste) spoke them throughout her life, to her children, her dogs, and to all the people she cared about. Her brothers called each other 'old chap' and looked into one another's eyes and shook hands when they parted or met. For Molly, that was inadequate, smoke signals instead of flesh and blood. This is perhaps why she misread her father's feelings for her. She looked for an intimacy which was not possible (or only very rarely) between parents and children in her milieu. Intimacy came obliquely through shared interests, specially sporting ones. Here, too, the boys had the advantage. 'Charlie got on marvellously with my father. He was terribly good on the pony, and a very good shot, so he had much more in common with him than the rest of us had.'

Although she may have exaggerated, being good at things was important. All the children grew up to be perfectionists, to be competitive, and to be unself-forgiving if they fell short of their own high standards. Although this was a generalised Victorian notion, it was very strong in their father. He was a beautiful horseman but he did not really teach his children to ride. He believed that horsemanship was God-given. You were born with a correct seat, light hands and burnished courage. His offspring displayed these attributes to varying degrees, when he mounted them on obstinate donkeys, headstrong ponies and horses that were too much for them. He expressed quiet appreciation of their triumphs and disappointment at their failures. Charlie inherited his grace in the saddle, and his fearlessness. Molly, with her embryonic writer's imagination, knew about fear and struggled very successfully with the secret shame of it. She genuinely believed that the only way to please her father was to be good at things. His fostering of competitiveness bit into her psyche a little too deeply, in a way that could not be softened by his gentleness when she asked for the apple, nor his affection in the 'Wild Wood'.

Throughout her life she suffered from occasional but painfully deep feelings of loneliness and exclusion. This became a constant theme in her writing and it forms part of a secret armoury of feelings not quite acknowledged by her or her characters which sometimes exploded like tiny subterranean bombs rippling the finely focused, nuanced surface of her narratives. She described an episode which perhaps encapsulates the seed of this harrowing emotion in herself. Miss Bell, a charming, youthful governess, had told the children in 'a fascinatingly awful way' the facts of sex and birth. Molly, intrigued and troubled, turned to her mother: ' . . . I tried to confess to my mother after the bedtime prayer recital at her knee. I tried. Bedtime drew near and very near and still I could not get it out. She urged me to tell, but without giving a hint on the subject to help in this terrible unveiling. She was sitting on the low window sill of her bedroom, and I knelt on it, a guilt still locked inside me. She must have been close to exasperation, when from her window she saw the sweeping arrival of the dog-cart drawing up at the hall door to dislodge my father, home from a grouse shoot, and his pointer dog, Romulus. He got down and gave the reins to the groom who was waiting to take the horse round to the stable yard.

I knew the opportunity was nearly lost. I was going to lose her. Between sobs I blurted out, 'It's awful, things we shouldn't know.'

'What things, Molly?'

More sobs, then, 'Things like how babies are born!'

'You mustn't pay any attention. It's not true. Bedtime now.'

She gave me a quick kiss and ran out of the room and on down the corridor and the long stairs. I could hear her hurrying across the hall and through the window I saw them meet on the flight of steps and kiss, not quickly.'

She sees this scene through the telescope of her adult artist's eye as a tragedy ransomed by humour (always for her the supreme healer). Yet the raw pain of the child is still sharp. How does such a child of such parents survive? Molly, like many others, was saved by the servants in the household. She did not often speak about her rescuers but her work is full of tributes to them, and to 'the divine endless patience, wherein the servants of Ireland are, with rare exceptions, steeped and endowed – at any rate insofar as their employers' children are concerned'.

Mad Puppetstown (1931) was the first of her novels to be published by William Collins and the first concerned with childhood. She manoeuvred the powerful story of her early life more skilfully perhaps in later books, but here it is at its rawest and truest because it is fresh in her consciousness and closest to its actual time. One cannot pretend that the relationship with the workforce was equivalent to the parental one, but it was an ongoing love always there to be visited, a secure bulwark against the emotional reticence in the family, which was abhorrent to her, and even a healing antidote to it. There is a direct portrait of Paddy Fortune, the real stud groom at Ballyrankin, in *Puppetstown*. He had the awkwardly broken nose, and eyes 'blue as a crow's' of an ex-steeplechase jockey, and 'he was an intimate friend and ally of the children. The grass swished smartingly around their bare legs as they ran towards him.' The real Paddy Fortune had plenty of time to talk as he worked with the horses. He was quite strict and his authority was accepted by Molly because he was calm, and she trusted him completely. She did not have similar feelings for her nanny, whom she left behind in the nursery busy with Walter and Godfrey when she was no longer a baby, and whom she suspected thereafter of being 'a spy and a reporter'.

Governesses were emotional abysses. The fascinating Miss

Bell was a case in point when she told the children about sex, and sometimes laughed at their mother. Molly was attracted to her – 'I suppose all children like a rebellious person' – but she did not have confidence in her. Although she often identified with the plight of the governesses when she came to write about it later on, in childhood she regarded them as risky creatures, either seductive and dangerous, or, more usually, pathetic and lonely.

Mary-Josie, the young maid with whom she took in her mother's morning tea, cuddled and embraced her and sometimes brought her home secretly to the gate lodge to play with her younger brothers and sisters. She learned, like Basil and Evelyn in her book, to hide this friendship: 'You smiled and you made a face at her and she smiled back secretly – you knew that it did not do for mother in her bed to realise the depth of your intimacy with Mary-Josie.' Mrs Skrine's position was partly rooted in the caste system, and partly due to a genuine fear of the nits, fleas, diphtheria and other diseases deemed to proliferate in the homes of the lower classes. The space between two worlds was often where real life happened for an Anglo-Irish child.

Molly's talent for subversiveness and her talent for diplomacy were both fostered by a childhood spent skirting the frontiers between two worlds. The austerity which maddened her in her family made her feel, albeit subconsciously, that in an emotional sense the world of the poor had a richness about it that was grander than the drawing-room. It is a strange thing to say about someone who became such a connoisseur of the nuances of snobbery, but in the long run her own snobbery, strong as it was on the surface, was shallow-rooted compared to the language of the heart she learned in her second world. That is why when she describes the back-door shrubberies, the boot-rooms, the haylofts – 'the regions screened by laurel and flowering currant from the sensitive eyes of the gentry', she endows them with the glamour of trysting places. They represented an escape from the difficulties of both ways of life, and freed people to express something impossible in their regular existence, an unspoilt affection – like that of strangers meeting in a foreign country.

While still very young in Kildare, the Skrine children spent hours in the yard with Joe, the stable boy. 'He was our dearest friend,' Molly said when she was eighty. He was scarcely older than Susan and Charlie but much more self-sufficient. He protected Molly from the peacocks when they fanned their tails into a swaying forest and strutted around her, almost taller than she was. He drove them off, and sometimes tortured them by snatching an exotic tail feather to make into fishing flies with Charlie. 'They frightened me so much that I loved to see them suffer,' she said, speaking as one who never quite lost the terror and savagery of childhood. The children were attracted to the hay barn, a sheltered oasis that smelt of summer when they were turned out for hours during the cold months. Joe was king here. He took them on rat hunts with the dogs, led them to caches of kittens, and to nests where the hens had just laid, so they could carry warm eggs in to the cook, and sometimes be rewarded with bacon rinds or a freshly baked scone, destined for the drawing room not the nursery tea.

Molly was being pulled into an upper loft by Charlie when her small wrist slipped through his grasp and she fell into a stable where Joe found her lying half stunned, being warmed by the soft breath of a horse. He consoled her and carried her into the house. When the doctor came to set her broken arm she had to be cut from the new coat of which she had been very proud, and anaesthetised with chloroform on a clean handkerchief. She remembered awaking to the scrunch of pain when the anaesthetic wore off.

Although he is a more sophisticated version, the essence of Joe is encapsulated in her wonderful portrait of Patsy in *Mad Puppetstown*. Patsy is her type of hero. 'Whatever he did had about it the stamp of artistry.' The children were drawn irresistibly to the boot-room where he presided, a bare-foot, gracious host, over his copulating ferrets, bunches of rabbit snares, shoes, oil lamps and feathers. In the novel Easter identifies with his violent, poetically expressed hatred of Mrs Kelly the cook, because it mirrors her personal sense of 'subservient animosity towards authority'. Easter's feelings echo Molly's own. She deeply resented the expected serfdoms of childhood and quickly became subversive when forced to go along with them.

She could sometimes compromise in this respect towards her parents, but never with the Aunts. At a lecture in Paris in 1985, she said: 'There were five of us. Life should have been an idyll, but we had these two rather tricky Aunts ... ' She was over eighty at this time and by then she had written the Aunts almost out of her system (aspects of them appear in almost all her works) and she could afford to take a tone of sophisticated mildness towards them. In childhood, it seems to have been all-out war. At times the children appear to have held the upper hand; staying at Rockport, the family home in Antrim, for months in the summer they disrupted the 'quietly occupied lives' of Lou, a gardener, and May, a painter. Drunk on sea air and the long sandy beach, even the virtuous ones like Charlie and Susan succumbed to wildness. Unused to the young, and in an attempt to follow instructions from Wexford, the embarrassed Aunts whispered after breakfast. 'Have you been?' The children would answer in the affirmative and rush headlong to their private loos among the rock pools. They spent the morning by themselves roaming the strand. They chatted with a few nuns who strolled by, and with John of the Rocks, a fisherman. They were forbidden to speak to either on religious grounds. Lou and May were staunch Unionists. John of the Rocks was a particular anathema to them for political as well as religious reasons. He is the model for Nick in *Full House* who is the most idolised man Molly ever put on paper, being almost completely happy with his life, in tune with nature and full of unspoken understanding for the troubles of others. The children went fishing with him at dawn before the household woke up. It was a heady cocktail, the magic hour, the first disobedience of the day, and helping him to draw in the brimming, glittering net, 'undismayed by pity'.

One year Molly, used to supplementing poor nursery fare with treats she found growing out of doors, ate a great deal of seaweed, sucking out the jelly. She nearly died of the results, causing the ladies deep anxiety.

When the Aunts came south on long visits they bullied their nephews and nieces, with parental backing, although they, too, favoured the boys. They stood, watch in hand, by the strawberry beds, allowing the children precisely five minutes to stuff themselves. Like Nicandra in *Loving and Giving*, Molly was inclined to squint through her fingers during family prayers. When Lou, acting as chief reader, made the mistake of asking the children to contribute, Molly solemnly prayed, 'Please God, send us strawberries and cream.' She was hauled from the room and thereafter frequently cautioned for her greed as well as her lack of modesty. 'You are far too fond of your own hot breakfast, Miss', they would tell her. The position of Maiden Aunts was very strong in families, and 'they felt no dishonour in their dependence'. When her sisters arrived, Mrs Skrine handed over the domestic reins of the house to them, and took thankfully to Dante, or some other literary endeavour. The servants hated them as much as the children did. Although they were nasty to people, they loved plants and were knowledgeable and tender gardeners. In her 1992 introduction to *The Knight of Cheerful Countenance*, Molly wrote, 'My Aunt Lou, a tough lady in all things, grew the poppy *Mecanopsis baileyii* where its blue flowers could float in the shelter of a hazelnut walk, and would go out on the coldest nights to put a stable lantern near some delicate darling, while the woman in the gate-lodge might die in child birth for all she knew or cared.'

Molly felt that most children are born with a sense of guilt and without a sense of humour, which has to be acquired later. There is no doubt that the Aunts fostered both these attributes in her, the first deliberately and the second unconsciously. Her struggles with them helped to make her a highly tuned observer of human nature, because they left room for a third eye. They were not the emotionally engulfing struggles she experienced with her mother. Looking back, in Paris, she acknowledged her debt to her Aunts: 'I have written, and I expect I shall going on writing, about people like them. I find their manner of getting through life, their grip to the last on the fantasies that support them, absorbing, interesting, even dramatic.'

Certainly the role of Bijou in *Spring Meeting*, which gave pleasure to many, and launched Margaret Rutherford's comedy career, was unmistakably drawn from Lou. Molly remembered that the zany character who took flight in the play upset Mrs Skrine. She felt it was a cruel caricature of her sister, when she attended the first night, dressed in a lace fichu pinned with a rose.

Molly's position as the spitfire in the middle of the family was isolating and detrimental to her craving for a soulmate. The situation with Susan was hopeless. She was four years older and not Molly's type. They did not become friends until late in life. Molly was an explorer and Sue was a diligent child not keen on the 'adventure of disobedience'. She was good at things. She wrote plays and sewed beautifully. Molly loved acting in the plays and dressing up her dolls in the clothes Sue made for them but her 'teaching manner' stopped the rare moments of intimacy between them. They shared a bed and frequently fought. The nursery maid brought them a supper of warm milk and biscuits and carried in the canary, its cage draped with a shawl, to sleep in their room. There were mice living under the floorboards and 'between the bird-seed and the biscuit crumbs they had a royal time', adding to the general unease of the girls' night.

Susan was even lighter boned than her sister and she did not have Molly's determined lust for enjoyment. She was dark with an attractive olive complexion. In later life she came to love India, where she lived for some years, and worked as a teacher. Her light, gentle voice could become shrill as a high violin chord when she was nervous or passionate about something. She was intellectual like her mother, elegant, neat, critical and self-critical. Molly said, 'I had an awful time with Sue, and I used to team up with Charlie against her.' Teaming up with someone against someone else seems unfortunate grounds for friendship, but it is a fairly common trait in Anglo-Irish life, which Molly appears to have picked up on quite soon.

Although it may have started with them ganging up against Susan, Molly looked back on her intimacy with Charlie in almost romantic terms. 'Before the Great War,' she wrote, 'when my brother and I were 7 and 5, life was static. The freedom of the day belonged to us, we moved into a different world. I had a donkey called Moth and he had a pony. We would start off with him leading me on a rein and when we were out of sight he'd let me go. No one knew where we were.' Their honeymoon was brief but never forgotten by her, because in it she first experienced the sweetness of friendship with another child, and the pain of its betrayal. Charlie went off to prep school and came back too grand to play. He only wished to ride and fish and shoot, and instruct his brothers in these matters. Her imagination had been full of schemes for his return, and he repulsed her, leaving her like Nicandra 'alone with her shaken heart and rejected gifts'. This common occurrence in families was a particularly devastating blow to her because of her longing for intimacy. She retold the story several times. *Mad Puppetstown* reflects the good times as well as the betrayal of her relationship with Charlie. The intensity and instability of childhood friendship is vividly evoked in this book. Brothers are a leitmotif in Molly's work and they are frequently idealised by the girls. Charlie remained a hero to her. In later life she kept a photograph of him in her room. His picture shows him seated, wearing his uniform, with his sword of honour and naval cap resting on a table beside him. He looks handsome and benign, his dark head sleek as an otter's, with a twinkle in his eye. Charlie had a tremendous twinkle and a tremendous sadness. He honed his character by being hard on himself. This maddened Molly who sought enjoyment and fun, although she, too, could be hard on herself. She admired him always. Charlie was so good in adulthood that one wonders where the naughtiness which never left Molly and Godfrey went in his case. It became the twinkle in his eye and also went into the passion and occasional recklessness of his horsemanship. He was sometimes referred to as the best horseman in Ireland. Molly's friendship with Godfrey and Walter came later. They were too young for her to treat them seriously in youth. She took Charlie very seriously. He exerted the power of ignoring her. She always found being ignored extremely hard. She could not let it pass. It chipped into her psyche and hurt. He represented what she loved about the Skrines, the courage, the sporting brilliance, the twinkle, the self-discipline and the search for God. He also embodied the 'tightness' as she called it, against which she rebelled.

Even after leaving the nursery for the school room, there were still daily walks with Nanny, collecting sticks and piling them onto the wheel carriage of the pram, for the nanny was much better at keeping a good fire going than the governesses were. In the pram were Walter and Godfrey, the baby brothers. Walter, who became almost insanely brave when he grew up, was an anxious baby who cried a lot and suffered from eczema until it was cured by the magic Miss Bell with applications of buttermilk. The older children teased him. Once when he was a toddler they put him in a cardboard box harnessed to a sturdy spaniel, and drove them across summer lawns and paths until the floor of the box and the seat of his pants were quite worn out and he wept in agony. When Molly told this story, one felt she was ashamed of her cruelty and sorry for it, and yet still a bit exhilarated by the chase.

His parents were shocked when Walter later took to motorbikes instead of horses. He eventually converted to horsemanship and pursued it with passion and courage. He was the most sensitive of the children. The family ethics damaged him. His schools also contributed to his lifelong asceticism and sense of undeserving. At the second string English prep schools attended by the Skrine boys, they were often struck and always hungry. It is hard to imagine in the present era of overfed children that our grandparents, without actually meaning to, almost starved them.

Godfrey, the youngest, was a charming, sanguine child with large brown eyes which gazed calmly on the world. When the nanny's attention was diverted, Molly enjoyed lifting him out of the cot and dressing him up in the spare bonnets and frocks, which boy infants wore then. He was a sunny child and adult, who almost escaped the burden of melancholy affecting the others. In old age it crept up on him a bit and he kept it at bay by reading Thomas à Kempis and practising yoga. They were all very attached to him and in later life turned to him when they were in trouble. The sense of being on a secret spiritual journey experienced by all of them (Molly the least, perhaps because of her worldliness and creative work) was very strong in him. His Skrine devotion to duty was combined with an affectionate nature and a certain light-heartedness. He was a great enjoyer. When they were older, the brothers and sisters had deeply forged feelings of loyalty and service to each other in difficult times. Molly went through phases of intimacy with each of them, the longest being with Godfrey (particularly during youth), with Charlie and Walter in her middle years, and with Sue when they were both old.

Apart from her honeymoon with Charlie, she never maintained a lasting closeness to any of the others during childhood. Her passionate desire for a soulmate probably frightened them off, or maybe what she wanted was not possible in the volatile, egocentric context of children's relationships. In old age she was wistful about what Isabelle Allende calls 'the myth of a happy childhood'. There were moments when the dream came true. She wrote a description of a glamorous Edwardian tea party at the house of the Fanshawe cousins in Kildare. She and her siblings, surrounded by 'vapours of sweet peas and cooling scones', are stunned by the sight of an opulent cream cake as they line up to kiss an ancient Aunt. After the banquet, they appear untypically united and cosy: 'As is so often the way with parties the drive home was the best part of the affair. Snuggled together in the back seat of the dog-cart, with no hesitation now about crushing the life out of our starched coats and dresses, we munched dear Uncle Harry's present of a box of chocolate biscuits.' The criss-crossed longings for intimacy and for something delicious to eat, which haunt Molly's perception of childhood, seem to be fulfilled here.

At other times she was a small, solitary traveller walking down the avenue which swept grandly away from her house through parkland with a view over the River Slaney to the Blackstairs Mountains. One could deviate from this route in various directions. The park meadow was full of mature trees, creating for a child tented, secretive worlds, some with sweeping branches to the ground ready to be bounced on. There were many beech trees where one could search in the soft leaf mould for tiny angular nuts in fairy cups. One could stand on the plank bridge looking down on a hidden stream. In autumn Molly visited the orchard in search of a Beauty of Bath apple with its magic rose-tinted flesh. She went to the nut walk to look for hazelnuts until frightened off by a tramp, Old Nettle, wheezing on the other side of the hedge. Tramps were a feature of the landscape. They had their familiar circuits to which they returned. They knocked on the back door and the cook, who often refused the children, never left them without sustenance. Tramps cursed those who failed to put tea or milk into their billycans. Behind the road was Hand Hill where their father took them to the Glen on Sundays. The river dominated everything and Molly had a great respect for it. In winter it was full of streaming green weed and frightening currents that could drown you. In summer it became a gentle paradise with miniature cliffs and bays and saltless sand to play on. Shoals of minnows swam over her feet when she paddled and butterflies and thistledown floated past.

The gift of this landscape to Molly's imagination had

another side. 'The hours of liberty were long' and they could sometimes fill with boredom and loneliness. One does not recognise depression in childhood but one knows it. She certainly did. It was part of her heritage. *Loving and Giving*, her darkest and one of her best books, much of it written in her eighties after she had recovered from a stroke, revisits childhood. Nicandra, the good little girl of eight, is surrounded by a household in turmoil because of her mama's reckless love affair. Existing in an atmosphere of pain and unease, she has been told no facts. She is about to experience a child's worst scenario, the disappearance of a mother: 'What now? She knew a miserable distaste for the day that loomed ahead. Nicandra could not name Depression, but she had a cure for it, teasing Silly Willy at the West Gate Lodge.' He was her perfect victim. Nicandra, usually so sweet and eager to please, savagely taunts the handicapped boy and lashes his shins with a small whip to make him dance. Afterwards she feels strangely better. 'She was back in the proper life. Magic had fallen from the air. She felt purged of the morning's unfortunate happenings.'

Unusually for her, Molly makes an overt psychological link in this sequence, and it illuminates a mystifying aspect of her own personality, which was her tendency (shocking in a person who was also very kind) to find a cure for depression in attack. It brought her instant relief. One could feel her vitality resurging. Assaults, verbal, of course, in adulthood, launched by the sharpest of wordsmiths, left her victims withered and breathless. In the long term she was sorry, but she could seldom admit it. This situation had entangled roots into her childhood where she found herself sometimes 'living on the edge of some nasty secret', and where the gale-force emotions which her small frame encompassed could seldom find direct expression. The code of behaviour in her family was extreme. Feelings were corralled, existing in poetry, in the cry of the hounds or the last post being sounded over a dead soldier's grave, but not acknowledged in their primitive form inside oneself. Ignoble feelings were punished or repressed (they were not allowed to exist). One of the strengths of her work is her understanding, sometimes humorous, sometimes angry and stark, of this side of human nature in herself and others, and her desire to write about it. Goodness sometimes bored her, although she needed it, and indeed loved it when it came without didactics.

Molly was ten in 1914. The war which had such a devastating effect on the society into which she grew up seemed dream-like to her when it was actually going on. Her father was too old and her brothers too young to fight. The children were summoned to the drawing-room to be told when a young cousin had died in battle. 'One put on a face of black tragedy but you didn't really know these cousins, and you didn't really know what war was like ... The whole thing was very much played down anyway ... The real story came out afterwards. What the young poets and others wrote, and what one heard much later ... but at the time there was nothing like that ... They all died heroes.'

The real story did not become known for a long time; certainly she did not hear it from the young survivors with whom she later danced or hunted. They were bent on forgetting and her generation of girls was determined to help them forget. She was haunted by a scene she witnessed at Warleigh, her father's home near Bath. When she was widowed in 1915, her formidable English aunt, Lady Mary Jane Skrine, forced her maid to model her new wardrobe of mourning clothes. The girl wept as she paraded in her mistress's dresses and cloaks and elegant black veils and hats because her husband was in the trenches at the time and she was afraid of bringing him bad luck by dressing in widow's weeds. This incident influenced the story of Rose and Ollie O'Reilly in *Good Behaviour*.

The year the war ended Molly started as a boarder at the French School in Bray, outside Dublin. Life in this prim, suburban establishment was a shock after her free, if neglected, childhood. 'It was the custom for friends to link arms on their way to a distant classroom, playing field or Chapel. I would deliberately lag behind the clatter of twin footsteps, using the gap to mask my loneliness. Unliked and unlinked, my place was always at the back of the crocodile. I might never have become a writer had it not been for the isolation in which I suffered as an unpopular schoolgirl. My unpopularity, that went to the edge of dislike, drove me into myself . . . I certainly learned the meaning of the black word "alone".'

She was frequently alone as a child, but this was a different, shaming aloneness. It focused her unchosenness. Although she makes a joke of being 'unlinked and unliked' she felt that everyone actually hated her, and that she was going to be miserable for the rest of her life. Her horrified surprise at the lack of love she experienced at school possibly shows that Ballyrankin was not quite as bleak as she declared it to be. It is true that she had met very few children outside her family. She developed prodigious social skills later on but she had none at that stage, and she had really no notion of how to make friends. She was always slightly haunted by the agonising memory of her leperdom at school. It contributed to her overvaluation of social success.

French was spoken at all times. Molly said they learned an awful 'Irish' French but she acquired a lasting admiration for the language, which she read all her life, and which eventually led her to Proust, her most loved author. To assuage her loneliness she turned to composition and writing became her great escape. This was the gift the school inadvertently gave her.

Molly was in her last days at the French School when Ballyrankin was burned. The insurgents came on a summer night. Her mother told her that the air smelt of clover and smoke. At first Nesta thought they had come to assassinate her English husband and she pleaded for his life. They were ordered into the study while furniture was piled up in the hall and petrol poured over it. Then they were taken outside by armed men. Walter defended his property so vigorously that one of the raiders said to him, 'Please steady yourself, Captain, or we will have to shoot you.' He replied, 'I would rather be shot in Ireland than live in England', an answer that was much quoted afterwards. A dry east wind fanned the flames and the house burned fast. Armchairs were politely brought for them to absorb the shock sitting down, but they preferred to lean against the newly made haycocks as they watched their home blaze.

The bravado, the courage, the politeness made no difference. A beautiful eighteenth-century house went up in flames. With it went a tangible world and also an intangible world that was perhaps more important because it carried the past into the present. People were deeply dependent on the past.

The history of objects, the aunts and grandfathers to whom they had formerly belonged, were spoken about and were as real as the desk, painting or footstool itself. Previous lives and deaths pervaded the fabric of the rooms. 'Every death thickens the atmosphere' as Elizabeth Bowen said of Bowen's Court. The Anglo-Irish needed this atmosphere to breathe. The shock of their suddenly torched homes was something their courage (fostered on the hunting-field and in English wars) equipped them to deal with, but the loss of their particular rarefied atmosphere slowly broke their confidence and eroded their way of life. The burnings should not have been so rude a shock but they were unprepared to pick up the signs. They lived in a half-mythical place and they deluded themselves about the nature of Ireland. Their empathy with the landscape made them feel part of it, and because they mostly got on well with the people around them, and with those who worked for them, they thought they were loved. They were loved up to a certain point, but the Ireland they chose to ignore, the lost country (untainted by anything English) nurtured in people's hearts and carried in code by music, song, and poetry, was always there. It was usually submerged but from time to time it erupted and overturned all other loyalties.

They did not think of themselves as English. They were rooted in the land of Ireland. They called themselves Irish and very few of them reflected on the uneasy nature of this Irishness. It was only by sticking to their blinkers that they could keep going. Molly said of her poet mother: 'She would have dismissed Yeats as just another Irish patriot. She couldn't think that the English had ever done anything wrong.'

A friend, Iris Orpen, wrote an account of the incident for

her literary group in England just one month after it happened. Although never mentioned in the family, it is apparent from this document that the Unionist nature of the household was implicated in the targeting of Ballyrankin. She says an indictment was read to the Skrines by the Sinn Feiners citing the fact that Walter had passed a resolution in favour of the Union at the County Assize and accusing his wife of writing in foreign newspapers vilifying Ireland. Her quotation from an article (with which she is in total agreement) written for *Blackwood's Magazine* by Nesta after the 1916 rebellion is illuminating:

'The truth is that the people of Ireland have acquired a profound contempt for the British Government which has so thoroughly deserved their contempt, which condones crime and disorder, refuses protection to the loyal and law-abiding subjects of the king, and releases criminals from prison and ostentatiously allies itself with their leaders. Is it too late to ask England now to show her strength in which these rebels do not believe, to do justice and punish the wrong-doers who have openly boasted that she is afraid to punish them, to give us law and order and save our beloved Ireland even now at this last hour?'

The Skrines were typically paradoxical in that they completely endorsed England politically, while in their soul they did not want to be English, even though Walter was English. Later on that fearful night of 7 July 1921 (just two days before the Treaty was signed ending the war) they left their smouldering home and walked three miles, a couple of forlorn, stalwart figures dressed in their nightclothes, towards the town of Bunclody, then called by its English name of Newtownbarry.

Afterwards they bought the house next door and joined its lands to their own. Thus the farm was extended, and so was their portion of the beautiful fast-flowing River Slaney, where kingfishers' wings glistened and where the boys caught salmon and trout. They could have used the compensation money to rebuild their house, but Walter, in keeping with the eye for land and love of stock and farming which he had demonstrated in his ranching days, chose this other arrangement instead. New Ballyrankin, as they called it, did not have the presence or proportions of the old house. It was Victorian, with rather fussy architecture. Although it stood in a similar position between the mountains and the river, it lacked the felicitous outlook of the first house, being built low down on a wooded site. Its greatest attraction was a charming sheltered stable yard where the horses' heads looked over their doors at moss roses growing along cut-stone walls.

None of the children had been at the house on the night of the fire. Ever since 1916 they had feared a raid and the younger boys had built a fort in the woods at the end of the avenue. Susan had adopted the habit of bringing the bread knife to bed with her. She said she would come downstairs waving her weapon and declaring in a firm voice: 'Now, now, stop all this nonsense.' She never got the opportunity to practise her deterrent.

Later Molly said of her parents, who were so absorbed in each other, 'the death of their house meant little to them'. This was not strictly true, but it certainly did not mean what it meant to her, who had identified with the hidden life of the house, and loved it with the passionate, youthful force of her imagination. The loss remained with her, and became part of the luminous, sometimes elegiac way she wrote about places and houses and objects that seem much more solid than oneself but are not. When she came home to Ballyrankin after the catastrophe, she grieved over a fallen fluted column, 'a stretch of limestone arm', which she saw protruding from the ruins, and all her life she continued to visit these ruins.

CHAPTER 2

After the fire the family were taken in by their cousins the Turnleys, at Drumnasole in Antrim. The calm, secluded house was built in the mid-eighteenth century on a lough at the end of a very long avenue. It was an ideal place to recover. Despite their courage, the Skrines were shaken. Molly described herself as being 'very, very shocked'. So she was not expecting to have the time of her life at Drumnasole, but that is what happened. 'I loved it there. Our cousins were so free and romantic. They had a boat, and they sailed, they had gramophones and they danced after dinner. I had an absolutely marvellous time with them.' Following the pain of losing her home, and her unpopularity at school, it was euphoric stuff. Her mother disapproved of the way she responded to this exciting life, observing her powdering her nose and flirting with her handsome cousin Archie as he taught her to dance the tango. Looking back, Molly saw this as the moment when the flawed childhood love she had had for her mother failed. 'I don't think I was the same kind of adult as I was a child. One changes every so often – at least if you are an uncertain character as I am. I am sure I wasn't the same person my mother knew me to be as a child, or would have wanted me to be as an adult.' When she speaks of her 'uncertain character', she is perceiving a particular sort of volatility in herself that sometimes caused her to turn her back on something important, as though it had never existed.

At this point in her life she was wholly bent on fun. As a child, she had never had enough of it, only whiffs which had intoxicated her, as when she ran around the garden with her lantern in the dark. She was readily intoxicated. A certain excitability was a Skrine characteristic. Molly got excited in an attractive, witty, joyous way that was infectious. She could also be silly in a manner which upset her mother. (Elizabeth Bowen spoke of her admired headmistress's constant fight against silliness in her pupils. Molly's state of mind was far from Elizabeth's at the same age.) She rushed to embrace 'silliness' in all sorts of ways. She adored the novels of Mr Dornford Yates whose heroines travelled in silver Rolls-Royces and tantalised their owners with a flash of crêpe de Chine underwear as they were helped out of them. She spent hours before the mirror tilting her hat to its most becoming angle. She was keen on 'rags', slightly risqué jokes and undoubtedly would have had an invitation in her eyes which was deeply disturbing to her mother. She put on a 'silly baby me' act which she said went down very well with the men, as long as your horse-talk and hound-talk was sensible.

She wanted to be like her cousins – 'romantic and free'. This was nearly impossible at home with disapproving Aunts' grittiness and acute consciousness of her faults and affectations. Girls didn't go away or get jobs. They stayed in the family until they were married. Except when she was out hunting, she felt trapped. The winter after they returned to new Ballyrankin from Drumnasole, Molly developed a mysterious illness which was perhaps partly psychosomatic. TB was suspected, so she was put to bed for several months. Once again she turned to her imagination as a means of escape. She passed the time (which she was never one to waste) by writing a romantic novel, very much influenced by Dornford Yates. 'It was really dreadful, but I suppose it was all the things I wanted to be, and all the things I wanted to happen, a terribly attractive girl and smashing young men riding like mad to hounds – the lot.'

This book, produced in the rather strange circumstances of her illness, has a fevered quality like the work of an over-excited child. (She said it was the only time she ever found writing easy.) It is mostly fantasy, and an outburst of silliness, but it has moments of perception which hint at the real writer she was to become.

She had discovered the publishers Mills & Boon in a copy of the *Times Literary Supplement*, which her mother subscribed to, and later, feeling the pinch of her meagre dress allowance as her social life blossomed, she submitted it and received for it the princely sum of seventy pounds. The editors at Mills & Boon must have been quite lenient in those days because the title, *The Knight of Cheerful Countenance*, is disjointed from the subject, and is there simply because she liked the Tennysonian ring of it, and she occasionally used high falutin' words with little notion of their meaning.

When returning from hunting one evening she saw the name M. J. Farrell over a pub doorway and she took it as a pseudonym. Secrecy was important to her as she thought no one would dance with her in the horsey society in which she moved if it was known she was a writer.

Hunting grew. She had been attending the meets with her father for some time, but now hunting became for her not only a great adventure in itself; hunting was romantic, elegant, savage, and the ultimate escape from the frustrations of home into the glorious life. She responded to the music and discipline of fox-hunting. It was very much a social occasion; it was 'a bit of life'. If you weren't hunting or weren't any good at it, you didn't meet people. 'You didn't have any background.' 'Hunting mattered more than anything else.' In its pauses from the chase, hunting afforded conversation with whoever was riding alongside. It meant you could encounter people in a very free yet ritualised way.

She had long been acquainted with Daphne Hall-Dare, but it was through hunting that their relationship deepened and, with some breaks, lasted for the rest of their lives. Daphne was extremely sporting; she fished, shot and, unlike Molly who was really only interested in the riding part of hunting, she was an expert on hound work. She had sleepy eyes, a hoarse voice and beautiful olive skin. She was a quite wicked and fantastically amusing gossip. She was also kind and sane, she did not shoot for the stars like Molly. Of course, she didn't have to. She came from the grandest establishment in the neighbourhood, Newtownbarry House, where aestheticism in any of its forms was not advocated. Her parents were easy-going, their house overflowed with richness, grapes grew in the conservatory, the scent of gardenias pervaded the draw-ing-rooms where fires blazed in huge Victorian fireplaces. Outside, velvet lawns stretched for miles, flanked by tended shrubs, herbaceous beds and carpets of seasonal bulbs. Molly was stunned by the tiny cyclamens of autumn, shining under the trees.

There were luncheon picnics in the boathouse by the river where the Hardy fishing rods were kept. Molly drank cocktails and flirted outrageously, finding she had a rare talent for it. Daphne's father responded and tried to kiss her behind the boathouse. She was adroit at dodging these kisses, or, if cornered, she gave in with sweetness and a cer-tain enjoyment. Daphne and she talked to each other in a secret nonsense language, and were witty at others' expense. It did not do to be fat, slow, a bad horseman, a clumsy dancer, a vulgar dresser or a know-all. They were a dangerous elite, fuelling one another. Silliness ruled completely for a time; it was an outburst, an indulgence. They communicated also through their dogs. Little dogs had a special position in that formal world. One spoke nonsense and baby talk to them. They responded in kind, and sometimes uttered insults and truths in disguise like the Fools in Shakespeare. Horses were a more serious matter. They were the elders. They carried one safely over fences, or not. They could drop one. They were adored, but one did not talk nonsense to them, or about them. There was a rather beautiful, almost academic lan-guage connected with them. It did not do to say the wrong thing about a horse.

The Skrine parents discouraged too much fraternising with Daphne, although they did not forbid it outright.

They were not social, but they were very aware of the correct code. Their reluctance to accept hospitality from the Hall-Dares had to do with being unable to afford to repay it in the same lavish style in which it was offered, as much as their disinclination for it. Therefore, communication between the two households was limited to clearly defined, mostly sporting, liaisons. Mrs Skrine felt that almost any form of luxury bordered on vulgarity, and the ambience at Newtownbarry was likely to encourage the worst traits in her daughter's character. The intense friendship between Molly and Daphne upset the balance of the carefully cultivated remoteness of the connection for the Skrines. The Hall-Dares couldn't have cared less, and were delighted to receive Molly whenever she appeared. The place was within riding or cycling distance, and Molly frequently disobeyed her parents and visited. She was irresistibly tempted by the prospect of intimate talks with Daphne while they sat in the branch of a tree, or in one of the flower-scented drawing-rooms hunting fleas in the coats of the small dogs installed on their laps. Molly was haunted by her recent unhappiness at school – 'after that, to be liked and accepted as funny and good company brought true glories into my life'. The food was another terrific draw. She described it as 'delicious, dated food', from which one imagines it to be plentifully Edwardian, composed of roasts, game, cream cakes and elaborate puddings. In a way her mother's prediction was right. Newtownbarry fostered her penchant for 'richness'. This meant freedom (including freedom from money worries), warmth, deliciousness, jokey conversation, and was in contrast to Skrine seriousness, 'the heavy sigh for the expense', and 'being at the mercy of the cook'. Her mother's disinterest in food, comfort and social life fuelled her lust for these things, and Newtonbarry was where she first became familiar with them. Her upbringing had made her suspicious of Protestant prayers and passionate about food. Her parents' dread was that she might find herself unchaperoned in a room with a young man, and they felt that this was a possibility in such an easy-going household. The fact that it was more dangerous to be alone with 'dear old Burr', Daphne's father, never occurred to them.

Much of the Newtownbarry life is reflected in *Young Entry* (published in 1928 by Elkin Mathews & Marrot), which is inscribed 'To D.'. This was no 'flapper friendship', as she said of her two heroines. There was 'sudden affinity and deep interest' in it. Daphne, no less than herself, was an observer. They stored up people's absurdities to tell one another, and their consciousness of how their society worked. At twenty-two, Molly wrote: 'Oliver Lingfield was a most endearingly unpleasant person. He took, as though conferring a favour of the highest order; he gave, seldom. When he did, it was always remembered. Men valued his friendship; women generally wanted his love; or, at any rate, his approbation – his liking. All over Ireland, he could put up, at an hour's notice, at the houses where everyone would like to stay – if they could.' Charming, cool bachelors of this ilk, coasting on their sporting prowess, were a feature of Anglo-Irish society. Molly always found them difficult. She saw their self-contained attitude as emotional selfishness. It discomfited her, and made her nervous about her own tendency to be intimate and spill the beans too readily.

She had no anxiety about spilling them to Daphne, however. She had at last found someone to tell about her trials at home, and to joke about it with her. The laughter took the loneliness out of her predicament. All her life she would make her desperation into stories for her friends, infused with wit and sparkle in the way she told them. It was her way of letting go of things. It started with Daphne, who was very interested and amused by the saga of Ballyrankin. The character of Peter in *Young Entry* has a good deal of Daphne in her. Although she is a little too wise and idealised, Peter resembles Daphne in looks, has her steadiness and the same dashing way of lighting her cigarette with a hot coal balanced between the fire tongs. Prudence, the Molly persona, is less close to the original, although in common with her creator she is 'uncertain of her true reflection in the mirror of her powder box'. She did endow her with some of her own weaknesses which she clearly sees as flaws: a certain possessiveness in friendship, a tendency to lie if cornered about particular feelings, moodiness, suddenly getting sick, and, above all, the dark side of her personal rebellion. 'Cousin Gus – she hated because she feared her. The influence of a strong personality that has ruled you absolutely, for almost as long as you can remember, is marked and abiding.' Prudence still, as she had in her tenth year, lied and schemed with varying success to hide her misdeeds. In Molly's eyes, disobedience was the adventure it had always been, but it was also a struggle which she sometimes found wearisome and bitter. She hated her own fear of rows. It was not the thrilling hunting fear you felt as you rode your horse into a fence.

Although Daphne and she were knowing, they were also childish. They did in fact, like Peter and Prudence, fish for freshwater pearls and keep them in boxes on their dressing tables. They wolfed down bunches of grapes, and made play with their cigarettes as they talked endlessly, like schoolgirls. In some ways, to be childish was to be grown up in their society. People Molly was attracted to played with passion and belief. They were brilliant at gossip and picnics, and at spiriting fun out of the air. They worked at play and played at work. Molly, in common with most of the Skrines, was a real worker by nature. She worked at her writing. This was one of the reasons she hid it.

There were other reasons as well, the chief one being that 'the chaps dreaded a clever girl'. She now had two books published and she had no wish to be classed as intellectual or arty. Intellectuals were frowsty, unattractive and uninteresting in her view. She was not untypical of her era in this opinion. Masters of Hounds were the heroes (the pop stars) of that milieu. Bright and natural as nuts, they looked over your head at the wider horizon to where hounds were running. They wore elegant uniforms, tight boots, and britches and waisted coats stretched over their fit bodies. They were sexy, and they often knew it, and took advantage of it. They were very obviously brave and decisive. They jumped the fences in front. They were in a sense unavailable, because with them the hounds came first. Everyone knew that. In summer, or at hunt balls, they were temporarily obtainable.

Mrs Skrine did not launch her girls or pay for ball dresses. Reluctantly, she sent them off to their evenings chauffeured, supposedly chaperoned by one of the stable boys, and dressed in the wrong clothes. Molly said Susan's social life was eclipsed for ever by being despatched to her first important party wearing 'a sort of tennis-dress'. This must have been galling for Sue, who was very stylish, and a reader of *Vogue* even in old age. Molly was determined not to fall into this trap. She had discovered she could write and earn money and she used her writing money to dress in a way she considered dashing and 'right'. She did not turn her writing into an alternative world as some might have done in her circumstances; she wrote to buy the dresses, train tickets and riding boots she needed to move in society, and the same society was also her subject and inspiration. Parties and hunts were the set pieces in her novels, and how one fared at them was desperately important. She took it for granted that her readers found them as riveting as she did. Tennis parties (she was never much good at tennis) were second string, and so were tea parties, except for teas after hunting when one was serenely tired, grateful for being still alive. Parties were all-important, in fiction and in life.

Occasionally Molly travelled to parties in England. These were terrifying. To most of the English cousins the Irish were the poor relations. The Skrines perfectly fitted this image when they visited the Somerset mansions belonging to their father's numerous siblings. The certainty and complacency of the English chatelaines, the beautiful, superior young men, the confident rose-like girls who felt no need to sing for their supper, were unsettling to Molly, though the perfection of the houses and the grandeur of the decor she loved and responded to. She remembered being detained by a bossy Aunt after the rest of the young left the luncheon table, and being made to memorise the names of her forbears depicted in the portraits round the walls. She seethed, stung by the inferiority complex of the provincial. These houses were like Stoke Charity, the house she would describe many years later in *Good Behaviour* – 'settings for privilege'. They were complete to the final details. The money had not run out before it reached a top storey or a far-flung wing, destined to remain forever unfinished and serving as grandly proportioned lumber rooms, as was often the case in the homes of the extravagant, horse-mad Anglo-Irish. However, tables were turned on the cousins when they came to Ireland, and had to prove themselves out hunting. When they failed, some of the awe surrounding them was dispersed, and Daphne and Molly could refer to them as 'hopeless Saxons'. Sometimes they performed brilliantly, or even became heroes of the hour with their superior attitude, humanised by the eccentricity and wildness of Irish hunting, as compared to the more orderly English variety.

To Molly 'nightclub' was a magic word. She dreamed of the 400 and the Café de Paris but never went near them until much later. For her generation in Ireland, the Shelbourne Hotel on Dublin's St Stephen's Green was the place to go. It personified glamour and was also a home away from home. To this day its two Egyptian slave girls still hold lamps aloft outside the front door. Elizabeth Bowen wrote a book about it and Molly gave her first cocktail party there after the publication of *The Knight of Cheerful Countenance*. She felt free and safe and modern when she was at the Shelbourne. Charm, rakishness and conversation ruled there. It was a melting pot of Irish life, and the first port of call for people up from the country.

She said you could leave your dog with the head porter when you went shopping. Dressed in a long grey frock coat, he welcomed you warmly when you came through the massive swing doors. He took your suitcase from your hand, and called one of his army of small bellhops to stow it away. He kept messages and gave you information about friends. Molly said he once greeted her with the news that Major Watt, one of her most charming older admirers, had had a big win at the races, and he was in Tysons (the Dublin equivalent of Hermès) buying presents for his lady friends, and she had better hurry down there immediately.

The invention of the motor car was a source of excitement. Her father wrote limericks about the young men driving up in their motors to take Molly out. Unfortunately, none of these verses have survived. Cars also brought a new dimension to flirting. Some of the cars were two-seaters, so it was impossible not to be alone with one's escort. In the backs of others, it was necessary in cold weather, especially during the hunt-ball season, to be wrapped in rugs beneath which limbs touched, and one could hold hands secretly. Molly took advantage of this aspect. She spoke of the immensity and luxury of the chinchilla rug in the Newtonbarry car. She learned to drive her father's motor though was not permitted out unless accompanied by the garden boy or stable boy, ostensibly to 'swing the car' for her, and also to act as chaperone which did cramp her style when driving home on summer evenings when the air smelt of woodbine and meadowsweet.

Looking back she said, 'We girls, some silly, all jobless, belonged to a curious social world where men were few.' The result of the Great War was felt in the drawing-rooms and on the tennis courts. Almost a whole generation of men had been wiped out. The ones who survived had a choice. Molly said, 'How I envied the really rich girls, so pursued by the scarce young men.' It was a time when English hunting ladies took charge of many of the best Irish houses. Molly's attitude to them was ambivalent. She coveted the chicness and simple dress sense of these confident girls, who were of course beautiful as well as rich, and who usually came from the ranks of the English cousins. She admired them sometimes wholeheartedly, sometimes with a tinge of envy and dislike. She wrote about them brilliantly, particularly when they tended to arrogance and complacency, but she was also conscious of their splendid, generous and invigorating attributes. Cynthia in *The Rising Tide* is her masterpiece in this genre. They are the opposites of her gardening spinsters whose qualities and meannesses she also recorded so succinctly. Although she often loved these maiden ladies and wrote about them warmly, she was bent on not being one herself. She was so enmeshed in scrambling out of Ballyrankin, and dazzled by the social process itself, that she did not think much about marriage. Because the flower of Anglo-Irish youth had fallen in the war it might be presumed that the other Irishmen (particularly the Protestant ones), the hunting doctors, lawyers and businessmen, would take their place. These prosperous young men could have rescued many houses and many 'daughters at home'. It seldom happened. In *Good Behaviour* and *Loving and Giving*, the warmth and generosity of the solicitor, Mr Kiely, and Robert the grocer, is totally rejected by Aroon and Nicandra. Their attitude is a reflection of their milieu and time, when a 'merciless division of the classes' prevailed. It blighted many lives, like a frost.

Sue was affected in this way. She rode side-saddle, and her elegantly cinched waist in her habit attracted an admirer while she was out hunting. He was a neighbour, and an excellent horseman who later came to help her father with schooling. Their romance blossomed to the point where he proposed. Even though he was, as Molly said, 'in a social strata only slightly beneath our own', he was banished and Sue was heartbroken. For once, Molly was entirely on her side. She always remembered the pain in the dining room as Sue wept during lunch, and her father poured out a glass of sherry and pushed it across the polished table towards her. Sherry was not enough. Sue never completely recovered from the blow, and, as far as is known, she never fell in love again. She was not a rebel as Molly was. Sue accepted her parents' decision, and did not reproach them for it. She went to Oxford and became a socialist. She was better at getting on with the English Aunts than Molly was, and she particularly loved her cousin Phyllis. Phyllis's mother almost adopted Susan. When she got TB, she sent her to Switzerland to be cured, and later paid her university fees. Her socialism was paradoxical and contradictory and very much of its time. In India, she supported Gandhi and also the British Raj. Like many of the educated women of her generation, she was an advocate of the welfare state, and worked to bring it about. Although her politics carried her in the opposite direction, she was affectionate towards her parents on her visits home, and accepted the class structure. She loved literature and longed to write but she did not have the gift.

Susan's experience had quite a bearing on Molly who did not rate Sue's subsequent achievements and always saw them as substitutes for a proper life. She felt her sister had been forced into becóming a bluestocking, and a spinster, and that her existence had no fun or hunting, and was devoid of sex and glamour. The family drama confirmed her in her own pursuit of these things, and encouraged her rebellion. It is hard to grasp what hunting meant to Molly in the controversial atmosphere surrounding it today. Though it was the conventional passion of her world, she had a deeply personal response to it. Hunting inspired her. It freed her from repression and boredom. It gave her all that she felt was lacking in her home environment, and amended the weariness of heart which constant fighting for air brought upon her. Martin Ross described hunting as 'tasting the wine of life'. Molly herself spoke of it as 'a certain fever which is a lust and madness of the body as well as of the mind'. Primarily it was, during its sublime moments, completely exciting, holding out to a young self-absorbed creature self-forgetfulness. It appealed to her in many ways. Most superficially, the elegant uniform suited her, the black coat, bowler hat with a veil, and the slender boots. Even in old age, she mentioned with pleasure bouquets of violets found on the hall tables of the grandest houses, waiting to be threaded into one's buttonhole with a shred of flax. The mastering of fear and subsequent freedom from it was something which appealed to her nature. She found fright interesting, and a subject not much referred to by previous writers about fox-hunting. She is particularly sympathetic towards children in this respect, and writes about their predicament with understanding and humour. Parents felt 'a cowardly child was like a hidden sore' and were inclined to take a spartan attitude. Her own pony bolted with her for what she said seemed like an eternity, galloping down an unmade road of rough stones, framed by glittering thorn hedges. There was frost, and a fall could have been a killer. She never forgot her terror, or her father's look of quelling disapproval when she finally returned to his side. She had committed the sin of not being able to hold her horse. It seems inconceivable that sensitive children could ever take to the sport after such experiences, but the mysterious magic usually prevailed, and caught fire in them as it did with her.

She, a breaker of rules, loved the rules of hunting because they were like an ancient shell enclosing the wildness. The passion was contained in ceremony and song. A huntsman speaks to the hounds in chant and short cadences blown on the horn. The ritualised phrases and notes of music hang in the air like birdsong. Molly records the evocative names of hounds: 'Accurate, Wistful, Acrobat, Sampler, Danger, Racer, Daffodil, Diligent'. The primitive poetry grabbed her. Her love of winter was connected with hunting. All her life she preferred bare trees. The sound of the 'gone away' echoing off the Irish landscape took her to what was for her the heart of life. For some people, hunting was more fulfilling than a love affair could ever be. In his novel *Helena* Evelyn Waugh distils the essence of its haunting, grounding sexual power when he describes the eponymous Helena on her last English hunt before she leaves with her difficult Roman: 'The smell of the hunt, compact of horse-sweat and warm harness, new leaf and old leaf trodden together; the call of the horn; the horselife under her, between her thighs, at her fingers' ends ...'

Just as a gangster film has a car chase, all M. J. Farrell

novels have a hunt. In Ireland, unlike England, hunting was a bond between the classes. Superiority melted under mutual respect for horsemanship and the dangerous, transcendent quality of the experience. 'Fox-hunting, with its difficult science, its ritual, its hardness, is the one thing that stands alone in life for those who love it. The one thing that can't be halved or shared, and if the spice of it lives in you, never can you lack forgetfulness of all else in life beside it.' Pretensions fell away and empathy and wit floated to the surface and were (briefly) more important than anything else. Molly adored the soaringness of the run. She was ambivalent about the kill. In *Puppetstown*, she describes a fox going to ground in a quarry: 'A retreat and a harbour it was for the thief of the world of most impregnable safety.' Like many hunting people she is on the side of 'the thief of the world'. She wants him to escape, as he often does. She loves his wildness and bravery and skilfulness. At the same time, she loves these things in the hounds, and sees the fox as their legitimate prey. Her identification with both the hunter and the hunted was part of the complexity of her character. From a tiny child, she had been used to solitary wandering in the natural world. She was formed by its ferocity and its peacefulness. Her acceptance of nature included an acceptance of its cruelty. Hunting had deep roots, and the ethical point that the hounds were loosed by man for sport and no longer for food, was not thought about by her, or by anyone in her culture. To them, hunting was necessary and in some ways still as sacred as it had been in the ancient world.

Riding home at dusk along 'the careful mesh' of small roads

with the hounds flowing like a gentle sea in front, they felt in a state of grace. Molly saw a gleaming world from the back of her horse, and she has left us many glimpses of this visionary landscape in her M. J. Farrell novels as bright in their way as the countryside viewed through the windows of Dutch paintings. At ninety-one, haunted by her sense of life's ebbing, she wrote in her diary: 'Keep me always aware of such things as the romantic glitter of a pack of fox-hounds.'

Molly fell in love at twenty-two. It was, of course, a hunting romance. But it was scandalous, as the man was married, older and a Master of Hounds. The scandal heightened her natural sense of naughtiness, sometimes paradoxically, making her leap like a fish at the fly of respectability. Usually, the opposite was the case, and throughout life she was nearly always on the side of lovers. When she spoke about the affair, she made it sound like a thrilling, piratical adventure experienced by someone else. She was not very specific about her feelings. One took it as read that this man took her virginity, that they had been happy, that her respect for passion and belief in sex was influenced by their liaison. I feel he may have seduced her in a grove of Portuguese laurel, a poisonous dark green shrub with a bitter-sweet perfume, often planted as hedges behind stable yards, or in places where gardens become wild at the edges and turn back into woods. Again and again in her writing when she wishes to signal sexual love she recalls the scent 'heady in a cold religious country' of Portuguese laurel. Events took a dramatic turn when her lover's wife wrote to Mrs Skrine, who informed Molly that she had burned the letter without reading it. Molly felt this was an extraordinary act of loyalty on her mother's part, and later when she complained about her, as she sometimes did, she was inclined to mention it appreciatively. Of course, it could have been a matter of the family closing ranks in a crisis, or of Nesta shutting her eyes to her daughter's wildness. She was a Victorian. The 1920s brought in a freer attitude to sex influenced by war and Freud, and jazz dance music. Contraception was primitive and the province of the sophisticated. Pregnancy out of wedlock was dangerous and kept hidden in all sections of society – young maidservants gave birth alone in their attic bedrooms. Molly told the story of a dead baby (unluckier than Moses) found floating down the River Slaney in a Switzer's dress box addressed to Miss M. Skrine. No one had noticed that the girl was pregnant. Seeing her own name on the makeshift coffin, Molly knew how near she had come to sharing that fate. The incident haunted her imagination.

Artists in faraway places like Paris made love, but M. J. Farrell characters hunted instead and afterwards flirted gently over porcelain cups of China tea. Hot bathwater was a big issue. There was never enough to go round. They would leave the water in for the next person, and pass each other in the corridor, conscious of the nakedness beneath their woollen dressing gowns. Molly was acutely aware of the highly charged celibacy of her young characters – *Taking Chances*, her third novel (published in 1929), shows a change of perspective. It is obvious that her notion of romance has altered, and she is writing out of what Henry James called 'the clear voyance of passion'. Although she has not entirely shifted the influence of Dornford Yates, her attitude to love is very much more sophisticated than it had been before. Molly always insisted that the subtext of her work was extremely autobiographical, coloured by events and by her inner emotional state at various times. Some of her books have this subtext more strongly than others, particularly *Taking Chances*, *Mad Puppetstown*, *Full House* and *Loving and Giving*. Mary, the heroine of *Taking Chances*, sees herself as 'one hell of a rake'. There is rueful self-knowledge, humour and detachment from her own naughtiness in this remark. She does not set out to do damage, but she has the ruthlessness of the enchanter. She arrives from England to be the bridesmaid and before it has begun she wrecks the marriage of the beautiful, unimaginative Maeve. Ravishing, witty and understanding, Mary is the villain of the piece, and it is impossible not to like her. Eventually she runs away with Rowley, the man she loves. There is no sense of a happy ending. We take leave of them in the elite Yeatsian 'country of the young'. They are pure as only passion can make them, temporarily beyond all moral, social or economic boundaries. They believe they have no choice, and the pain they cause is not their fault.

Jer, the authorial voice of the novel and the only sensitive character in it, suffers as he observes Rowley betraying Maeve, the sister he loves, with Mary, whom he also loves, although he, too, accepts the inevitable: 'No, it is hopeless to vex oneself by sorting the good from the evil with charming people of no principle. Because having no motive, they act from impulse and never fear results, either for themselves or anyone else.' Molly instinctively endorses her pair of tough, glamorous lovers, but far off in the background lurk the ethics of her Skrine upbringing. This dilemma was always with her, troubling her in life, and enriching her writing with an ironic bitter-sweetness that collided with her knowledge of the heart, and of such matters as the loneliness of being loved by the wrong man. She evokes every nuance of the flirting game, 'the evasive tricks of intimacy', culminating in Mary's soaring flight down the stairs in her silver dress on the way to meet her lover. The older generation are reminded of what they thought they had forgotten, particularly Violet, one of the best in Molly's line of venomous Aunts. Romance is undercut by her comedy of manners, 'the indefeatable manners', that kept the lid on the cauldron.

There was a rough edge to romantic passion in the continuous anxiety about unwanted pregnancy and primitive attempts at abortion involving gin, Epsom salts and going out hunting when one shouldn't. Women carried this cross alone, and protected their men from it. Men bore a burden too. Many girls suffered also from feeling alive only in the total approval of the beloved. Rowley is overwhelmed and bored by Maeve's total giving to him. He is drawn to Mary because of her elusiveness; as she is generous with her 'enthralling body', she holds something intangible back. Fresh from her own experience of being 'one hell of a rake', Molly empathises with Mary, but gave her fictional heroine the ruthlessness she did not have. She felt pain piercingly, like Maeve felt it, both for herself and for others. Her sophistication was in her head, and in her artist's eye. She was much more primitive when it came to her own emotions. She longed for love and was dependent on it to feel worthwhile even though she was always more attracted to people like her naughty heroine, and repelled by the virtuous, unimaginative Maeves of this world.

Molly never seems to have expected her man to leave his wife for her, and it is unlikely that he would have considered doing so. Though a natural flirt and passionate by nature, she was never marriage-breaker material. Later, she would struggle with her 'inclination to feel things too much', but this first love affair, like her first book, appears to have been easy. She spoke of it gratefully and, when it ended, she seems to have been able to muster an uncharacteristic insouciance. She turned to hunting, always the great painkiller, and to writing. She said it had an impact on her social life, and that at hunt balls the dowagers of Wexford and Carlow began to look up as she danced past. By then it was also beginning to be more widely known that she wrote. Molly was certainly in autobiographical mode when she observed: 'We are, even the strongest of us, largely what others think we are.' The idea that she might be 'mal vu' disturbed her. Even more seriously, her friendship with Daphne was affected. Daphne laughed about her own young men. Molly, who mocked many things, never did. She had an almost D. H. Lawrence respect for sex. Due to Molly's sudden and uncharacteristic discretion, their relationship suffered a change and a setback. Perhaps coincidentally, Daphne became very close to her cousin Evelyn Boothe at this time. Molly and Evelyn always disliked each other. Evelyn was a wit and a star, a brilliant botanist and gardener, a fisherman and a sewer of exquisite quilts. Daphne and Molly never dropped their friendship, but it waned from its soulmate status – a position it recovered in old age, significantly after Evelyn's death.

The effect of her reckless behaviour, combined with the publication of *Taking Chances*, on her reputation might have been devastating for Molly with her overdeveloped sense of guilt, and the close links between her fragile equilibrium and her social success. The fact that it proved not to be disastrous was due to her constant guardian angels, 'the rakish, charming people who understand'. Out hunting, she formed a friendship with an older admirer, Willie Perry, which literally transformed her life.

CHAPTER 3

There is a piece of land in Tipperary where a house called
Woodrooffe once stood. To get there you opened a heavy
iron gate painted white, and proceeded down an avenue for a
long time, through limestone pastures on which horses grazed.

The avenue sloped into and out of the saucer of ground
where the house was situated, turned a corner by the stables
and curved past a lake through farmed fields and boggy fields
into a wooded area, ending at the back entrance gate, which
always stood open and led to the Cahir–Clonmel road.

The grey cut-stone house was square with a pillared
porch, flanked by two single-storey wings, one opening into
the stable yard, also of cut-stone, so that the horses almost
seemed to sleep indoors. This was appropriate as the horse
was Woodrooffe's lifeblood, and horsemanship was an art form
practised by the people there with the total seriousness and
insouciance of true artists in any sphere.

Within this austere house, life flowed freely. It was a
rakish, generous, sophisticated establishment where people

found happiness, and often a refuge from perverse or difficult circumstances. The wounded were drawn to it as a cure for loneliness, and the strong because it was a hub of the world and a smart place to be: a household that visitors became part of, and remained forever grateful to, because it extended understanding. Some houses belong solely to their owners. Others do not; there is mutual giving between the guest and the host.

Molly met Willie Perry, the paterfamilias of Woodrooffe, in 1928 and they were charmed by each other. Hunting is conducive to flowerings of friendship because of its frequent pauses which encourage conversation. The element of danger is purifying and up-scuttles pretensions so people speak as they really are, and often a deep and true form of intimacy can ensue. Molly's tendency to flirt with older men sometimes got her into trouble, but it also gave her many delightful friendships and, in the case of Willie Perry, it brought her a kind of salvation because he invited her to stay at Woodrooffe. She recognised it at once as her real home. Life at Ballyrankin had made her into a writer through the well-known path of alienation. She told herself she wrote only to supplement her dress allowance. She did not want to be an artist. She wanted life and love and amusing talk. All Skrines bore the burden of melancholy. They each battled it in their individual ways, but the prevailing ethos was Protestant and courageous, with a disposition towards an edgy perfectionism, in the way all things were done. Molly wished to fight melancholy with social and domestic delights, human intimacy and glamour.

Aunt Lou, her head swathed in voile veils, putting the finishing touches to the cook's irretrievably distasteful soup, would call after Molly as she left the house for a hunt dance: 'Don't accept presents of scent, my darling, and don't talk to any strange men.'

At Woodrooffe one could receive presents of scent and one could be funny about one's fears. It was possible to be drunk, unwell or in love with someone else's husband or wife. Mrs Skrine considered it a fast house and forbade her daughter to go, causing Molly to lie and arrange decoys in the shape of mock visits elsewhere.

Molly was determined to stop being a Skrine. She did not succeed in this, of course, but in the years when she almost lived at Woodrooffe she gave it quite a sabbatical. She discovered what it was like to live in an ambience where people had faith in her, as opposed to her existence at home which was frequently pervaded by a chill of disapproval. At home she provoked dust-ups and plotted escapes. Godfrey, her youngest brother, lay up for scheming. He would push a bicycle, with her saddle tied to the handlebars, beneath the bedroom at dawn. She jumped from the window and pedalled off towards some hunt where a prohibited young man brought a horse for her. When she entered the door of Woodrooffe she was able to set guilt aside for a time at least. She was a cuckoo in the nest no longer, and embarking on what was possibly the happiest time of her life. Woodrooffe was home in this way to many others besides herself. Its commune aspect suited her. It was a smart commune where the butler boned one's hunting boots. It was not an idle place. People worked, but at leisure.

A widow woman tells her children stories about her life, especially if she is a writer. My sister Virginia and I frequently asked Molly for repetitions of these stories so they became like a hybrid of soap opera and historical, shaping myths in the family. Many of them referred to Woodrooffe. We knew of her first arrival there, having been collected by Willie from Clonmel station in a car with a 'spare wheel fastened like a brooch to the back and a generous step outside the door on which people sat drinking cherry brandy at race meetings'. Her nervousness evaporated almost from the moment she walked into the hall, where a fire smouldered in the grate and terriers dashed from the worn sofa to bark around her narrow suede lace-ups. She was proud of those new shoes – bought out of an advance from *Taking Chances* – and their elegance boosted her confidence. A wave of understanding and welcome gradually engulfed her. Small, well-schooled hunters were led to the meets for her to ride. Parties were approved of, and people appreciated her jokes, and queued up to invite her to dance the Charleston (a step at which she excelled from long practice with a dining-room chair at Ballyrankin). More importantly, she discovered that friendship flowered in this environment and could be cultivated without fear of rebuffal. The friendships she made there lasted, and had a sort of glow on them – they did not suffer from the overintensity and needling of some of her relationships. Eighteenth-century rooms afforded the safety-netted luxury of space and privacy in the midst of a crowd. People could be in company, or closeted with a friend on a distant sofa or window sill. The window seats were sought after in winter because the sun warmed one's back when the tall rooms were only heated by huge spitting logs sulking beneath the marble nymphs and shells of the chimney pieces. In the stable yard, one could converse leaning against the soft, sweet-smelling shoulder of a favourite horse, or spend hours with Jimmy Cullen, the stud groom, helping him clean harness in his wood-panelled saddle room. He was Woodrooffe's calmest guru, a dark, beautiful man with the short upper lip Molly admires in several of her characters.

Woodrooffe was not without its sharp edge, and that too suited her. Molly would have been suspicious of any world that did not bear such a stigmata, a reminder of pain, indirectly, frivolously manifested in some social brittleness. A 'honeyed spite' has been and always would be part of her vision. The wit of the 'good put-down' was applauded in Anglo-Irish society. Despite their daily perusal of the scriptures the Skrines were no slouches at it, and Molly played this game with a deadly aim. Her struggle with the two sides of her nature, the one which snatched up the stiletto of the 'good put-down', and its opposite, which radiated a total sympathy, gave her endless trouble in life. These opposing forces are very clear in her literary style and are partly responsible for its exhilarating, dangerous salt-air quality.

Woodrooffe floated in a universe ruled by the sporting calendar, moneyed marriages and social connections. The forms of society were respected amidst a compassionate understanding that life was often other than such forms declared it to be. Discretion was the framework of people's private lives. Coming to Woodrooffe from Ballyrankin when Molly did meant being propelled forward into the modern world by the defiant vitality of the twenties.

The mid-section of the house had been burned by irregulars during the civil war. Rebuilding was completed in 1928, just before Molly's arrival. Willie had been a major in the British Army, and that may have been the reason the place was attacked. In the context of unspoken politics and eerie politeness, shattering deeds occurred. The shadow and shame of the evictions was on the antecedents of some landlords, although this did not apply to Willie.

There was mutual affection and respect between the Perrys and their Catholic neighbours. It seems almost inconceivable that these feelings would survive the burning of a home. Yet it quite often happened, and in her novel *The Last September* Elizabeth Bowen chronicles such a case in all its deceptive simplicity and specific Irishness.

They loved lords and ladies at Woodrooffe, as they did all over Anglo-Ireland, but it was also one of the most classless of Ascendancy houses. In Tipperary, horses ruled across castes and divisions, and as V. S. Pritchett has observed, 'The horse has always been the heroic solvent of Irish evils.'

Whispered jokes and flirtation linked Molly and Willie Perry. This would seem to be unpromising ground for a friendship with his wife. The contrary proved to be the case. Dolly Perry became the lasting heroine of Molly's life, which was always prone to the inspiration of changing icons. She had the weary, attractive face of a worldly saint, and was quite unsurprisable, patient and slightly sardonic in manner. She was thin, and dressed in tweed skirts and narrow, ribbed jerseys, often covered with a cross-over apron. Visitors seldom met her on the doorstep. They would search for her, and talk to her as she worked in some way. Like the Aunts at Ballyrankin, she was responsible for the domestic running of the house. Unlike them, she never sought to correct people morally. Work was her remedy for all troubles. She worked quietly and skilfully, often to the point of tiredness, but without strain. Surrounded by a passionate household, she remained calm, dispensing her wisdom only when it was asked for. Molly, brought up to 'Antrim' ideals and guilt at falling short of them, referred to goodness as 'prosyness', but she could appreciate it in the person of Dolly because it came without disapproval. She found happiness with her, talking to her for hours in her sewing room, where she mended linen and darned clothes, and also smocked and embroidered and sewed jewel-like patchworks in silk brocades, some of which exist today, still bright and held together with her invisible, strong stitching.

'My mother never went into the kitchen,' Molly said. It was a refrain that accompanied her descriptions of the disgusting nursery food of her childhood: '... oranges only at Christmas ... rabbit stew and custard puddings, riddled with holes'. Although it was a source of amusing copy she regarded this lack of interest in feeding people as irresponsible and one of Mrs Skrine's failures in love. Dolly went into her kitchen a great deal, and also to the vegetable garden, the flower borders and the larders where butter was churned, eggs preserved in waterglass, and strawberries bottled, causing them to turn beige and taste entirely different from their original incarnation. Molly accompanied her, and learned much of the lore of being a housewife. She was passionately interested in this subject and she had a habit of saying, 'Being a housewife is far more creative than writing, but it doesn't pay so well.' She regarded housekeeping as a pleasure, and a duty, and considered those who were uninterested in such matters as lacking and slovenly. It was certainly her chief remedy for depression, and rescued her on many occasions.

Woodrooffe's kitchen was presided over by a cook called Murphy. She was addressed by her surname only, without the prefix of 'Mrs' usually afforded to cooks. Molly told us, 'On her day off Murphy retired to her room to shave, drink a bottle of sherry and play her violin.' This may have been a surreal exaggeration but I do remember her as a Hogarthian figure, with hair on her face, and many voluminous dirty skirts. I once watched her pick a pot off the floor and drink the broth from it, sucking it through a crust of fat which cracked and broke up like ice. She was an extreme person, primitive in a way that was wonderful but not quite acceptable in any society. She overreacted growlingly and asthmatically to the teasing of the stable boys who ate in a dark room near the kitchen, and she told fortunes with tea leaves poured onto the tablecloth. Dolly was fond of her. She cooked with her often, and every morning she stood calmly by the kitchen table, covered in objects and foodstuffs, and discussed the menus with Murphy, who leaned against the bar of the greasy range, with her cigarette turning to a hoop of ash between her lips. The only white snowy thing was Murphy's little dog, snoring on a sacking bench on the corner. Cats had their heads in numerous bowls, and when chased, scuttled from the table upsetting bags of stores. The magnificent flagstones on the floor were murky and unscrubbed. Dolly managed to coax excellent food out of this cavernous chaos. It was carried to the dining room on silver dishes by a rackety, witty butler, who – like Murphy herself and everyone else at Woodrooffe – was supremely interested in horses. He whispered betting advice into the ears of visitors as he ministered to them at the table. The pantry – his domain – was, in contrast to Murphy's, neat and smelt rather deliciously of stale coffee grounds and pink silver powder.

Molly complained about the gloom and depression of the Skrines, but she respected and understood Dolly's sadness, which was mostly unspoken. Her eldest son had emigrated to America, and she seemed to have lost all rapport with, and even interest in him. Willie was a strange and volatile husband; Sivie and John, her two other children, had swapped sexes. Both were beautiful and charming and somewhat ruthless in the treatment of their bisexual suitors, many of whom confided their troubles in Dolly. The worry of the impecuniousness underlying Woodrooffe's lavish style and generosity fell upon her. She ran an open house, uncertainly financed by horse-coping, gambles, fluctuating harvests and handouts from various people (some very rich) who flocked under her roof.

If Willie was Woodrooffe's pervading force, Dolly was its invisible presence. One met her on the back stairs, a comforting wooden tunnel illuminated only by an oblong piece of window through which a slit of sunlight sometimes danced about one's ankles. She chose to slip around the house, unnoticed. She could not have prevented Willie from selling up over her had if he had so wished, but that was never a possibility. Her position was strong in a subtle way. Her qualities were needed, used and unwasted.

Molly adored Willie. She wooed and placated him. Her artist's eye and ear homed in on the human parade around them, and she brought him delectable morsels of dialogue and drama and gossip. Many of those titbits ended up in books, but she found them for Willie and would have been shocked to think of herself as collecting copy. Her writing was filtered through social life, and people, and they came first in her estimation. There is no doubt she did quite a lot of acting in her relationship with Willie, and almost none in her friendship with Dolly. She did not love the friends she acted for less than the others. She acted all her life. She called it 'singing for one's supper'. She looked on it as a positive thing. She never wished for peace, but her relationship with Dolly, carried on in long conversations while they shelled peas or did some other task together, was peaceful and she always spoke of it lovingly. The thought of Dolly calmed her in turbulent times. She admired her perhaps more than any other person, was inspired by Dolly's attitude to life, her acceptance and patience, although in theory she did not rate either of these qualities highly. 'Acceptance – what a frightful word,' she said to me once, in the midst of a struggle.

The artistic imaginative world was not openly acknowledged or respected at Woodrooffe, but it was lived in a kind of way. It was much nearer to the surface than it was at Ballyrankin even though there Mrs Skrine was a poet. This was something very private which did not feed into the atmosphere around her, or seem to reach Molly, who was also writing and keeping it dark.

There was a direct link at Woodrooffe to one of the arts – the theatre. This came through John Perry whose profession it was. He was the youngest of the three children. He loved Dolly, and was very estranged from his father. He often came home to stay, bringing with him friends from the London stage. Molly had a natural empathy with theatre people, which blossomed through John who introduced her to many of the leading actors of the day, including Peggy Ashcroft and John Gielgud.

John possessed a most lively and malicious wit, which would not have been out of place at the court of Louis XVI. His voice had a nasal sound and kind of built-in echo. There was much laughter in it, sometimes warm, sometimes bitter. Molly borrowed it for a character in *Devoted Ladies* – Sylvester who 'spoke in a voice of persuasive interest, and no one was better aware than himself of its poultice-like power of drawing confidences'. He was tall and very elegant, with an angular face. If one visited him in London he offered Chambéry as an aperitif. Its taste is reminiscent of him, dry and exotic, yet rooted in the earth and the country.

He and Molly were destined to become 'chums' in the theatrical sense of the word, and they remained so for ever, despite many rows and upheavals. They both loved domesticity and talking. He was a most sympathetic listener, and his conversation was an enthralling mixture of jokes, shards of gossip and serious notes. Their meeting was very significant to both of them. Up until then, her close friends were rooted in a particular society. John was only a visitor to his own background he had left it for another life. He brought his homosexual world into Molly's orbit and it had a profound effect on her psyche and her work. In almost every way, except sexually, she responded to it. She was drawn to the style and secrets, the sharpness and the flamboyant honed use of language. The sensitive, confiding aspects of campness suited her, as did the fact that it was full of submerged trouble, and had a dark underside which matched the sense of sin in which she herself had been raised.

Her relationship with John had its shadow side. The Skrine in her was shocked by his capacity for betrayal and her generosity outraged by his economies and money-mindedness. Yet theirs was an enduring friendship. In old age they were extremely mutually dependent. The telephone echoed with complaints – 'My dear it is so humiliating to be linked to the loo by the cook' – and laughter still. He sent her short notes, often composed of a single line: 'Darling, the only sound that comes from beneath my bedroom door now is the steady crunch of sleeping pills.'

Such a joke was unimaginable in the early days of their acquaintanceship. The friends who followed him from London were dazzled by the sight of his long legs in riding boots, and the fact that he could easefully reconnect with a fierce, natural world that some of them had met previously only in Shakespeare. It was easy to fall in love with Johnnie. Many did. He was a seducer of the successful, but he did not value the artist in people. (This was too complex and pain-fraught an area for him.) He loved hedonism, and he loved *comme il faut*-ness. He was involved with some of the most talented persons of his era, but his influence was often not creative.

Once when John Gielgud was talking to Virginia and me, remembering his friendship with John Perry and Molly, he said that neither of them wished to discuss 'the big things in life'. To him, born into a family of artists, this was extraordinary; to us, brought up in Anglo-Ireland, it was unsurprising. In general, it was considered pompous and boring and a bit uncivilised to speak wholeheartedly of one's deepest feelings. Molly alluded to such matters only in snippets. John pretended, when it suited him, that they did not exist at all. 'If you mentioned love,' John Gielgud told us, 'he walked straight out of the room. It was not very helpful.'

Not long before he died, John Perry confided in my sister (his godchild) that he had been beaten by his father, and bitterly hurt emotionally on account of his homosexuality at school. This was, doubtless, part of the refusal of his own feelings which dogged his life.

In love he seemed to stamp on people's tenderest emotions, and in friendship to understand and sustain them. Fatherhood (out of the question for him) might have been the only relationship which he would have taken entirely seriously. He was kind and considerate to the young and cultivated his friends' children. His hobby was economising, and he would lecture one about money, but he was also a most generous boulevardier and took us to premieres, the Ritz bar and Chez Victor, a charming French bistro across from the Globe theatre where he worked. Once, when I had no job, he paid me to speak French to him. He lived at the time in a flat high up in a glass building near the Tate Gallery. Here we floated on sofas above the lights of London and the reflecting river, drinking Chambéry and gossiping for hours, frequently about Woodrooffe which he had left for ever by then.

He was brilliant without a sense of vocation. He did not appear to take work or love seriously. In fact, he had a way of mocking and undermining seriousness that was destructive for himself and for others. He adopted a particular role, a sort of cat among the pigeons, an aristocrat among the artists. He spent most of his time with people of great talent. It is difficult to know if he was disappointed with himself about work. Molly said that, as her collaborator on the play *Spring Meeting*, he was inclined to claim more credit than he deserved, as she did all the writing. His contribution was critical and discursive. 'Of course,' she said, 'Binkie would have done anything to please Johnnie at that time.' Binkie Beaumont was head of the production company H. M. Tennent. He was John's lover, and also his business partner. He gave *Spring Meeting* a West End production with a brilliant cast and John Gielgud directing.

Peter Brooke in his autobiography describes Binkie as 'a subtly concealed dictator' who 'wanted the theatre to be a place of style and beauty'. He had a look of Proust, a purring sort of voice, a feline grace and hooded eyes. His skin was a pleasing olive colour. He was a collector of paintings, roses and stone lions. This imaginative connoisseurship tended to a restrained mellow baroqueness in the arrangement of his houses and gardens.

Molly respected his powerfulness. She loved his exoticism and sympathised with his pain, which he would confide in her when drunk after their friendship matured. She felt John mistreated him and got indignant about it. He was a hero to her. John was not one of her icons; she would not have admitted it, but she was much closer to John. Binkie understood the creative process and fostered it. He was drawn to the very talented, the beautiful and the successful. The stars were attracted to him because he was one of their kind. He understood the masque of glamour and the darkness and vulnerability that it concealed. He was confessor to the famous. They told him of their sexual despair, their alcoholism and secret debts. They knew their secrets were safe with him because he loved the masque and cherished the preciousness and rarity of talent. He was cool and withdrawn when it came to ordinary life. He had none of John's interest in children.

Molly urged me, 'Talk to Binkie', 'Go for a walk with Binkie'. She felt that it was important to expose us children to such people so that some of their starriness might rub off on us. I remember one walk at Woodrooffe with him. I have no memory of our conversation, which I expect was stilted on both sides. I was struck by his lovely flamboyant clothes, elegantly cut in soft fabrics which seemed extraordinary to a wartime Irish child dressed in scratchy tweed dungarees. Binkie exuded a waft of discreet, delicious perfume. We stepped across mud and peered through the reeds at a swan nesting on the lake. She hissed, flattening out her neck, lengthening it towards us, like a white snake. Suddenly the male glided into view. There was a splash as he changed from his graceful float to an ungainly foothold in the mud. Immediately we knew he was rushing us, his wings extended to deal us blows. Binkie took my hand and began to run. His Basque beret blew off. We did not retrieve it. We could hear the wind-like energy of the swan behind us. I fell, and Binkie stopped to put me back on my feet, and we sped on. I can still remember the sensation of running much faster than I really was capable of. The defensive husband gave up the chase eventually. Molly was slightly less keen for a while after this incident to send us out on country walks with town people, no matter how sophisticated or famous they might be.

She had the idea, widespread in the twenties and thir-ties, that sophistication was highly desirable and might be acquired by association. Likewise, she felt that beauty was contagious and had its lore which could be learned, as in Colette's *Gigi*.

There are many photographs of Molly in the Woodrooffe albums. We see her in a lace ball gown, leaning back on a sofa with her friend Tighe La Terriere. She is pictured on horseback, reading in a window sill, striding along at the races, her tiny waist cinched by a belted overcoat. She often laughs, and her dark, wide-set eyes shine with mischief and intelligence. One can sense from these photos that she loved dancing. Her gift for friendship, her sex appeal and elegance reach out from more than sixty years ago. All her life she looked marvellous and original, but she didn't believe in her looks, and thought of herself at best as a *jolie laide*; she laboured always at ugliness limitation. It was not vanity, it was duty. Her Aunts spoke in their Victorian way of someone being 'sweetly pretty', but there was a hard core to it. Good looks could lead to a 'good marriage'. They were literally money in the bank, and independence. The opposite of this was the blighted destiny of the 'daughter at home', Molly's idea of enslavement and misery. Paradoxically, it is interesting to note that some of her gardening spinsters who were frequently irked by those who ruled the roost around them were often the happiest, and most whole in themselves, of her people. For Molly personally, being attractive was essential, the passport to adventure and above all to romance, the supreme undertaking of her and her contemporaries' lives.

She endorses Olivia in *Full House* for her beautiful floating white irises. Her exquisite appearance too – 'her little nose and fine line of jaw and cheekbones' almost, but not quite, justifies her crass self-indulging behaviour. Olivia's is the classic beauty of the time, especially her retroussé nose. Molly loathed her long Skrine nose, as did all her siblings, even those much less socially inclined than herself.

Woodrooffe's enchantress, Sivie, did not resemble Olivia, or have the retroussé nose either. She was stocky in build, with slender legs that looked good in hunting boots. She smoked a cigarette out of the corner of her mouth so that the smoke drifted past her beautiful, protuberant, pale blue eyes, causing them sometimes to redden and water. Her hair, parted at the side, fell in a yellow wing against one cheekbone. Her skin was very pale and seemed powdered even when it was not. She had the solemn humour of a clown. She had a habit of getting hooked on a snatch of a song, or a certain phrase like 'Life is hard and death is certain', and she would repeat it *ad lib* for a time, and then forget about it. She rode superbly, and won many point-to-point races, and eventually she hunted the Tipperary hounds.

She would walk the course before a race, pale and focused, a long winter coat covering her thin racing silks, accompanied by a gentleman friend, neither of them speaking except to volunteer some brief remark about the business in hand. Riding was her vocation, and she practised it with a sort of genius. She drew crowds to the point-to-point meetings as an opera star or prima ballerina does to a theatre. It was a brilliant career which demanded deep resources of training, courage and skill. She was an amateur jockey, and would not have dreamed of receiving wages for her profession. For her glamour, she sometimes did accept payment. Her nonchalance amazed Molly, who valued love above everything else. Men, women and children were charmed by Sivie. She enjoyed the ambience, while being pretty emotionally detached. Although she did not bother with it much, she was used to having this power and when she fell apart in her latter years, as such stylists are prone to do, she was quite lost without it.

Once when sitting next to her at the lunch table enjoying a raspberry tart, I asked her why she never took pudding. 'I got sick of it when I lived with poor rich Masters,' she replied. I questioned her about Masters, and she began to hum – a sure sign that one should not pursue the subject. I raised it again, going home in the car with my mother. She explained Sivie had been married for one year to a wealthy, kind, much older husband from Wales. 'Willie sold her to him when she was sixteen. Because she had been brought up at Woodrooffe on excellent but plain soda bread, she spent a year wolfing down meringues, soufflés and eclairs and riding Mr Masters's splendid hunters. After a year, she fled back to Woodrooffe, and never touched a sweet dish again.' The story behind this was not discussed. It was an age when people were allowed to keep their secrets.

Molly was fascinated by Sivie's lesbianism. 'In all the years I knew her she never made a pass at me, not even when she was tiddly,' she told us. This remark was meant to demonstrate Sivie's innate wisdom in knowing that she would never respond to such a move, and also to show her own fortitude, for though she was truly undrawn to this type of love sexually, she had a strong belief in the power of seduction. She was impressed by seducers, and attributed to them almost mystical powers. Sivie's seductiveness was natural, and only slightly manipulative. Her ability to be herself was the foundation of her attraction. Love to her was unpossessive, always about friendship, and occasionally also about money; the means to blood horses, or to being a crew member on a yacht at Cowes. Love itself did not greatly interest her, although sometimes the passionate feelings of others caught up with her. I remember Molly's sympathy immediately flowing towards her when she opened a letter from John Perry informing her of the death in London of Sivie's friend Jean Cochran. Molly characteristically abandoned her own plans for the day, put us children in the car and drove from Belleville to Woodrooffe to be with her. Sivie clung to Molly when she met us in the hall and looked into her eyes. 'Jean is dead,' she said despairingly. She had already moved on to another lover (probably for financial reasons). Her face was even whiter than usual, and full of suffering and remorse.

She was really free until she stopped being a star, and began to crumble in her sixties. In many respects, she actually was a boy. The majority of her friends were men; some became her lovers and many adored her hopelessly. Molly described passing Sivie's open door one morning, and being called in, to see her, pale in black silk pyjamas, regarding a man who knelt weeping at the foot of the bed. 'Look at this fellow, Moll, isn't he a damn fool?' Molly was struck by her composure, half scornful, half compassionate. 'Come away with me, little Sivie,' he wailed repeatedly. It was his wedding day. Between them, they consoled him and got him to the church on time, where he embarked on a happy marriage which lasted fifty years. Ever afterwards, like many people in Tipperary, he kept a photograph of Sivie among his family snaps. She gazes out from these period portraits with Garbo-esque indifference, her blondness, wide cheekbones and the mocking yet kindly sense of distance she cultivated in evidence, dressed in the smart coats and skirts she never wore except on the occasions when she attended the races as a spectator. Even Lenaire, the society photographers, could not disguise with their flattering, veiling filters, her originality.

A note of chic androgyny came into Molly's novel *Devoted Ladies* through her closeness to John and Sivie, and through meeting their friends. She was fascinated and, typically, both approved and disapproved. The relationship between Jane and Jessica is destructive, it is not viewed in a whole way, but it is witty and insightful. She is more at ease with Sylvester. He 'picked up his knitting, he was making himself a pair of mauve mittens against the rigours of the coming fishing season'. One can sense how she relished writing this sentence with its brilliant image of kaleidoscoping worlds, and because she knew it would shock some of her readers. In life she sympathised with homosexuality in men far more than she did in women, unless they were real friends, like Sivie. In a real friend she accepted everything.

Both John and Sivie's way of life depended on physical strength and glamour. These two stylists ended up quite sad and broken, their insouciance smashed. Neither cultivated resources that might have been useful in old age. He became emaciated, depressed and hollow. She drank more and more, and the agony of giving up riding was long drawn-out. Eventually, bad falls, arthritis and fear (hitherto unknown to her) forced her to stop. Her body could no longer accept what she demanded of it, and her spirit quailed instead of soaring before the banks with their wide ditches and the stone walls.

Although she could always call up the hounds with the music of her horn-blowing, even the puff for that began to take too much out of her, and her eyes were sad above the pursed-up lips which made the beautiful sound.

Her hair lost its sheen and became like rained-on straw. She spoke less and less. Her capacity for friendship dimmed almost to the point of disappearance. Yet the glow of what she had been still warmed those who had known her before her collapse. Molly, who could be astringent when people became boringly drunk, never lost patience with Sivie, and always blamed others, and not her, for her final troubles. Her friends were lifelong devotees, as were most of the lovers who had loved her more than she had loved them.

In the year before she died, Molly acquired from John Perry's estate a portrait of Willie painted by Roger Furze, who had designed the set of *Spring Meeting*. It shows a fine-featured old man in a brown tweed jacket, glancing downwards with the translucent eyelids of age behind which life gutters with a mysterious beauty. The picture is truncated at the waist because he had developed gangrene, and suffered the calamity of having both legs amputated. On her increasingly wavering journey from the drawing-room to her bedroom, she would stop in front of the painting. 'Darling Willie,' she often said, with deep affection. 'I was his little friend.' She had arrived at Woodrooffe in this role, and she never forgot it, even when she was now older than he had lived to be, and her life had been transformed in so many other ways from going there.

Willie's funniness and charm captivated her. His diffi-cult, cruel side lent an exhilarating whiff of danger to the friendship. It was like being the favourite of a king. In fact, such people were like tiny kings on their own patches. Their anger had to be placated and deflected by holding up before them life's pleasanter and more amusing prospects. They had to be comforted for things that were not mentioned; the grief of their often unshouldered responsibility and power; their inability to take time from sporting activities to render their establishments solvent; the unwinnable battle against weeds and brambles and other 'buzzing tormentors of the leisured life'.

Molly had Willie's ear, and she could ask favours on behalf of others, make him laugh and distract him. They whispered together. She adored being at his side at the races. She was a born wooer and she really enjoyed it. She was free to be at full gallop with an older man, her affection appreciated, and not considered intemperate. She had wished for a similar relationship with her father, but his intense intimacy with his wife had prevented it. Feeling excluded by other people's love is a recurring theme in her books. It frequently befalls her children and a character who longs for more love than is possible from another – as Eliza does in *Full House* – is seen deeply sympathetically, but occasionally made to appear ridiculous and overdemanding. Molly's attitude in this regard towards herself and others was ambivalent.

John was fascinated by Willie, but he kept well away from him. He asked Molly for stories about him. She was his messenger from what was to him a minefield, and to her a sanctuary of intimacy and fun. He tried to persuade her to admit that she had had an affair with his father. She always denied this. Eliza, a giving, almost self-accepting character closely connected to

Molly in her later Woodrooffe years, 'has been loved, but not so often as was thought'.

The ambiguous dance of flirtation was an art form in that era, and Molly practised it to perfection. Flirtation and charm pervaded the relationship between Molly and Willie, giving to it a talkative, unconsummated intimacy, specious in that it evaded passion, but delivering instead a trusted and shared world full of twinkling promise and warmth. Molly benefited from such gazebos. They were to her one of the things that made life worth living, and she frequently evokes them in her writing. These moments often occur in bars. She and Willie had the habit of calling to MacCarthy's Bar in Fethard after hunting. Free of the 'big house', they sat in the dark stone-floored room before a turf fire. There was something magic about a drink and a cigarette in these circumstances. They opened the gates of an inner landscape often ceremoniously shut by other forms of social intercourse. Alcohol helped, but Molly was a modest drinker; a few sips of Jameson caused her to relax and sparkle. Although the talk could be confessional, there was much repartee. They encouraged wickedness in one another. She entertained him with disloyal, embroidered tales about Ballyrankin, which he called 'the Bogs'. She told stories to Willie, but with no sense of desperation or stress. Even though flattery was involved, there was a true mutual cherishing between them.

Years later, she took me into this pub to meet Mrs MacCarthy and her husband. They spoke of Willie with laughter and nostalgia, evoking him through a haze of half-remembered stories. I felt, as I wrestled with a straw and ginger pop, they were linked by a relationship of lost happiness.

The character of Sir Richard in *Spring Meeting* draws on Willie, but he is a broader comedy version. Willie was complex – his portrait shows an expression of suffering, gentleness and loneliness at odds with his reputation as a subtle horse-coper, bitter wit and boss of Woodrooffe. It is most likely that the loneliness apparent in this picture is one of the things that united Molly and him. She had an unerring understanding of loneliness and a deep knowledge of it. She writes about it often in the persons of her dispossessed governesses, sometimes scoffing at them with the other side of her nature. Several of the people to whom she was closest in the very social milieu she favoured had this submerged element, almost of the wild, in them. She recognised it, and it magnetised her.

Willie was one of her bedrock people. She quoted him as though he was still there long after his death, and he lived on in her psyche until she herself died.

The confidences in the dark in MacCarthy's pub with their currents of gallantry and jokes, were usually warm and occasionally barbed. No friendship was safe from barbs, which lent a piquancy, but were dangerous when tinted with depression. Willie gave Molly 'jackdaw glances' and his jokes became barbed when she fell in love with Bobbie Keane. It was inevitable that their intimacy would alter and suffer loss. Despite this, the friendship survived.

Later, when Virginia and I went with Molly to visit friends in Tipperary, she would point out to us the ribboning green ditches she had leapt out hunting, splendid horses grazing in the never broken limestone fields, and the Norman tower houses she loved, with their sprigs of scented wallflowers growing out of the stones. The landscape is not greatly changed today, but Woodrooffe with its stark, sheltering shape and its humming life has vanished. It was demolished after it was sold in the late fifties. There is a ruined churchyard beside what was once the back entrance. Dolly, Willie and Sivie are buried there, but it is impossible to find their graves under the towering thicket of trees and brambles.

CHAPTER 4

When she was involved in the effervescence of life, Molly seemed to have assimilated the tragedy of her husband's untimely death. She appeared to be reconciled and healed. In fact, it was an unstable acceptance which she frequently lost and despaired of. Her references to her dilemma in her notebooks have the bleakness of acute grief about them, even years after the event. In 1984, when she was eighty, she wrote, 'To me, it was more than death ... a terrible value of the past was born for me.'

Her time with Bobbie at Belleville was her Garden of Eden, and the loss, sudden as a knife blow, became the shaping wound of her life. Of course her marriage was a Garden of Eden with shadows which afterwards she was reluctant to acknowledge. Belleville had the atmosphere of a safe house. It faced south, and the sun shone into the rooms through tall windows. It was built in 1820 on a gentle hill, protected by an L-shaped screen of woods behind which the Monastery of Mount Melleray stood. It was modest and countrified, not a grand mansion, but everything about the fabric of the house had the comforting elegance and robustness – 'the dignity with so little heaviness' – of late-Georgian architecture. This quality was apparent in numerous ways, in the small arched chamber linking the chain of reception rooms, in the thin glazing bars of the windows and the slightly uneven rocklike front steps on which people often sat.

Although Woodrooffe had been her real home, and remained so, the time came to progress. The sense of place running through her work – almost its backbone – was rooted in her own nature. Belleville, with its generous, sunlit proportions, was the home she dreamed of both before she went there and after she lost it. Later, as children in other houses, we were made aware of objects coming from there which had a fragrance like petals fallen from a midsummer flower. Her grand coffee ice cream laced with cognac and scattered with roasted almonds was always served in a cut-glass bowl. She said, 'I decided to marry Bobbie when I caught sight of that dish with a rich trifle in it the first time I dined at Belleville.' Her domesticity was so ingrained that there is a shred of truth in this joke.

He was six years younger than her, she seduced him in a sense, and in so doing she herself fell entirely in love with him. He was gentle and humorous, tall, with a dark skin that loved the sun, and long green eyes. He was sympathetic, easy to confide in, and apparently very relaxed, except for one thing. He suffered from a stammer. This seems to have been an affliction besetting children of his era. King George VI stammered, as did Elizabeth Bowen. There was a theory that it was caused by forcing left-handed children to use their right hand. Molly, who believed that love solved everything, claimed she had cured Bobbie. In fact his stammer did improve after they met. Eliza in *Full House* has affinities with Molly at this time. She also set out to heal with her love and she is the visiting angel, a role Molly often played very creatively in life. Having cured, Eliza leaves, and Molly – because of her complex emotional make-up and an innate sense of undeservingness, and because Bobbie was younger – carried a small, incipient residue of guilt at not having done the same.

For four years, Bobbie and she conducted a love affair at Woodrooffe, and on holidays abroad in the discreet and rather thrilling style of the time – 'in those days, it wasn't done, but of course it was done'. They were married in October 1939. Their wedding picture shows them on a London street, smiling, their fingers interlaced. Molly is wearing a fur coat with a spray of orchids pinned to the lapel. Her play *Spring Meeting* had been produced to great acclaim the year before; it was Molly's dowry. This triumph – and being mentioned in the same breath as Noel Coward in James Agate's review in the *Sunday Times* – was much more than financial in a peculiar way: the success had released her to marry Bobbie. She came as the giver, not the taker, and that was very significant to her. She could plot and contrive and take when she felt she had to in lean times, but this was very hard for her, and turned her into a much tougher person than she wanted to be, or indeed was, and was sometimes carried to lengths of perversity. It drove her into the protective shell of sharpness which benefited her literary style, but was often destructive in her personal life. She was on the crest of a wave, artistically and emotionally, when she got married.

She was inclined to pronounce the word 'success' in a breathless voice, as though it was a sort of alchemy, but in her notebook she made a real attempt to describe what happened to her through *Spring Meeting*: 'praise sets me free ... my secret vanity all I have lessened saying "it is so unimportant" when I have failed, still it doesn't quite belong to me. How did I do it? I worked so bluntly and clumsily and hard as a child at its geography, and it has become this.' What was this? She called it something to walk into a room on. The impish mood of the provincial making good in the city – 'I thought Bond Street was looking rather dirty this morning. I think I'll buy a broom and give it a good sweep.' The serious business of being funny – 'My jokes, I suppose there was a flash when I saw them first. A breath of air and then pawed over terribly unfunny ... to sit and hear lots of people laughing at them, it gives you back a lovely feeling of strength.'

Success, which came and went from her several times during her career, seemed to make her innocent and trustful, and give her a sense of herself in which the dark notes and guilt were quiescent. She lost the feeling of stealing Bobbie away. Her third eye functioned better than ever before or since. In her notebooks of that period she was self-critical in an uncharacteristically calm way. Because she was a star, she could see that being one was fairly unimportant. When her light waned, the old craving returned.

Bobbie was a good husband for an artist. He grew up in the hunting world, but he was equally at home with actors and writers. He was able to heal Molly's labyrinthine tendency to compartmentalise her existence because he was proud of her writing, and comprehended the pain of the creative process. His intuitive kindness supported and strengthened her when she was vertiginously stretched between living her life and writing about it. 'Writing takes something out of my comfort and makes my resistance very thin.' Stepping off the high wire of a morning's work put her in a strange exhausted state. Bobbie understood what she went through. She describes him literally rescuing her from this one afternoon at the sea: 'I felt stupendously disinclined for effort spent and in dread of further expense. Bobbie was so sweet. My God, how sweet he is. He came back in the boat to get me and made me play like a determined child.' He was a countryman, a horseman, a person who sat back on the sofa relishing conversation, and flirting gently, a mechanic who liked to spend a day – his arms stained in oil – mending an engine, a connoisseur sifting through piles of junk in an antique shop until his eye fell on something beautiful, a swimmer sunbathing on the rocks with his eyes shut. When Molly woke early, trembling with nervous plans, she reached out 'to touch him with the ends of all my fingers to see if strength and quiet will flow out of him to me'. Typically of his era, hunting and leisure activities occupied much of his time. The working part of his life was low key, consisting of managing his farm and working part-time as a director of the small bacon-curing factory which his father had founded primarily to augment employment in Cappoquin.

In 1939, *Spring Meeting* transferred to Broadway with some changes of cast, notably that of Gladys Cooper in place of Zena Dare. It brought Bobbie and Molly to America on honeymoon. They sailed from Cobh, the lonely emigrants' port, then still referred to as Queenstown. Their liner was delayed, so they spent the night in a bad inn. As usual before an adventure, Molly was excited, but nervy. She jotted down shreds of dialogue in her notebook:

'My God, what a joint!'
'I have a suspicion that those sheets have only been ironed since the last visitor!'
'How is your bed?'
'Like a rock and too short.'
'Don't let's touch anything we can't help.'
'No, goodnight.'
'Goodnight, I adore you.'
'We had better have breakfast. What could we eat?'
'I don't see anything but a dirty plate full of rosary beads.'

Once on board the *President Roosevelt*, they sent for two ices to be brought to the stateroom. The waiter warned that there were storms expected and they might be better off with ginger ale. 'We will have them anyway,' Molly said, although she was a bad sailor. They were like children loosed in a grown-up fairground, relishing the sofas upholstered in pale brocade, the cocktails, the dance band, being wrapped in rugs by a deck steward 'with Spanish eyes, and a divinely bullying manner'.

This floating limbo of thirties glamour had the distant menace of war over it. Molly describes the families of rich Jewish refugees from Czechoslovakia and Germany. She dimly understood that they were not ordinary passengers, but people fleeing before a dragon. 'A few of them look stricken, not all. Gay, ugly old women, jewels on their hands and crossed scarves under their coats. Ruling their families, little jokes, a word of severity, a word of indulgence. Old, small men learning English, with copybooks and grammars.' Her imagination is caught by the submerged tragedy of these people. She gradually enters into their predicament, evoking them as she does her characters by the objects about them, and the mood that is inside them. 'When it is dark, they form into little secret groups, circles of excitement and eager low talk. They drink red wine in the sea-dark, thin-necked bottles, sweet, rich wine, none of your dry cocktails from the bar. The old women's shoulders go up and their thin ringed hands fly into the dark air, and their scarves go over their heads as they stoop, whispering together, of God knows what – their tragedy, the featherbeds they left behind, their daughter's miscarriage, or what?'

The first night on Broadway was a grand occasion. New York beauties turned up with their powdered faces, and orchids in their hair. They seemed too tired to laugh. The actresses in the audience were more responsive, Judith Anderson wearing a red evening coat and unset hair, exuding kindness; Bea Lillie (less kind), Tallulah Bankhead's hoarse laugh ringing out at a crack no one else had seen. *Spring Meeting* was not a real success on Broadway, but it ran for three months. Writers longed for recognition in America, and the generous remuneration this brought in. Molly, with her talent for dialogue, hoped to go on to write for films. Later (possibly as a result of this production of *Spring Meeting*) she was asked to do a movie script of Enid Bagnold's *National Velvet* but it was turned down by the studio. Until *Good Behaviour* she really never succeeded professionally in America. Social life was a different matter. She reflected the attitude of her generation towards America. They looked on it as a place full of hope. It was before the hard sell took over and the country still had an innocent image. Hers was a very Manhattan vision, vibrating with wisecracks, dance tunes and ice rattling in Tiffany cocktail shakers. Hers was an F. Scott Fitzgerald America of the rich 'committed to hedonism' in a casual, stylish way that had echoes in her own world.

Molly responded to New York's knowingness and sophistication manifested in the witty, unjaded style of language which in that pre-television age was like someone juggling with fresh-minted coins. She discovered Damon Runyon, and recognised him as a master. Bobbie bought the complete stories, and placed the gangsters with their poetic talk on his bedside shelf at home beside Yeats and the Romantics. He would read them to Molly.

After she returned to the Blackwater Valley she could still hear the language of New York spoken by her friend Adele Cavendish and her mother, Mrs Astaire. She had a special affection for her American friends, and the ones to whom she was closest were Adele, and later on Phyllis Mitchell. Molly and Bobbie both loved Adele, known to everyone as Dellie. Her small face – resembling that of 'a delicately beautiful monkey' – has been painted by Kokoschka. She referred to herself as a hoofer. When they met her, she had just become the chatelaine of Lismore Castle, and she was bringing panache and irreverence to the job and the county. She retired from the stage after she married Lord Charles Cavendish in 1938. Before that, she had always danced and sung, even as a child. She and her brother, Fred, had performed in vaudeville, chaperoned by their serene disciplinarian mother. They grew up to become stars of Broadway musicals, which transferred to London. Fred Astaire, with his casual grace masking a faultless technique, later became the sublime master of all film dancers. He has said that, in the theatre, Dellie had been better than him, and he had always followed her.

She and Molly were a similar bird-like shape, and Dellie often gave Molly her clothes, including a suit made by Chanel, which demonstrated the cut and structure for which she was renowned. It had a military look, softened and gently flared with silver buttons and a trim of red, green and blue braids. Molly kept it for years, and wore it at Virginia's christening, with its matching braided cap and eye veil, which only came out on rare occasions. Dellie and Molly were alike in temperament as well as physique, both originals, quick-witted, prone to changes of mood, and in a dark fit, to saying the unforgivable. They would relieve their feelings with a shower of foul language. Dellie did this on purpose to '*épater les bourgeois*', especially during a lull at her dining table. Molly applauded Dellie's daring. She was daring herself, but she was imbued with her society's rules. Adele neither knew nor cared about the rules. She came from another world, married into the highest echelons of the British aristocracy and regarded Anglo-Ireland as quite pretentious and ripe for send-up. Molly records an incident when Dellie, surrounded by rather strait-laced company, was inspired to embark on one of her sophisticated fantasies. 'I lay there in my bed with nothing to do, and thought I'd like to meet a very chic middle-aged man – the type of Ribbentrop – and he should have a really happy home life, only I'd give him just that extra thing he couldn't expect from his wife after twenty-five years. He'd have a *garçonnière* in Paris, and we would travel there separately, and meet . . . and we would have lots of fucks and I'd like him to have hair going grey, and all the money in the world, and he would have to – you know – take the little woman round to Cartier's.'

On another occasion, she remarked to astonished hunting ladies: 'I've seen such cute looking tweed pinafores. Let's all get one run up, and then we must go nutting. We'll go through the woods in our pinafores, and we will just be girls looking for things.' There is an oblique sadness apparent in this mocking. Dellie suffered from the loss of practising her art. Sometimes she felt depressed and trapped in her high, beautiful house above the river, and longed to be back in the theatre. Molly understood this, she was intoxicated by her recent discovery of it. Paradoxically, Dellie was also in love with Lismore Castle. It is a romantic citadel, perched on a cliff. If you approach it from the east, or the north, you feel you might be dreaming, it is such an unexpected sight in the Irish landscape, yet it is subconsciously familiar because it is the quintessential fairy-tale castle. Much changed and added to over the years, its present form was shaped by the bachelor duke, son of Georgiana and a cousin of Lady Caroline Lamb, another original whom he brought to his home in 1812 to recover from her love affair with Byron. This was evidently before his improvements, because she disputed with him about the relative dampness of the place and one evening, to prove her point, she opened the door to a frog. As it hopped slowly inside, she followed behind with a candelabra, saying, 'Pray walk in, sir. I have no doubt you are the lawful possessor, and my cousin only an interloper.'

A sheltered courtyard lies beyond the ancient gatehouse, where for a short time in winter the softness of a huge mimosa tree brings the South of France to this universe of limestone walls. The interior was Gothicised by Pugin, and the rooms high above the river and the trees give one a disembodied, floating sensation. Adele's husband devised an ironic standard which used to fly from the highest tower, depicting the snake, banished for ever from Ireland by St Patrick, twisting and golden on an emerald-green background. The series of demesne walls, based on what were once fortifications, create a secret universe removed from its surroundings. In his brilliant book *The Village of Longing*, George O'Brien describes growing up in Lismore, architecturally dominated by this exotic building, with people endlessly speculating about what went on there, and wondering if Fred Astaire might be in residence.

In some ways, Dellie's story was the classic one of the dancer (the twenties equivalent of a fairy princess) and the grandee. Her husband Charlie was very adorable, sensitive, elegant and funny, but he was tragically afflicted by alcoholism. Among others, he is rumoured to be the model for Sebastian Flyte in Evelyn Waugh's *Brideshead Revisited*. Molly and Bobbie said that during Prohibition he carried a hollow walking cane which he kept topped up with iced champagne, and they believed that it was the prohibition which drove him over the edge into drunkenness.

His worsening condition was very sad for Dellie. She, who

was herself full of vitality and given to health-giving draughts of sorrel soup, had to watch him becoming ever weaker. During their marriage they had three stillborn babies who lie in the graveyard of Lismore Cathedral.

Dellie announced to Molly, 'I'm a secret drinker. I can't bear for the servants to know. I just whisk into the dining room and take a glass of whisky, and it does make me feel wonderful. I feel just like Charlie feels, but I know when I've had enough. I've had enough when I've had one glass.' Her understanding, her dancer's self-discipline, could do nothing for Charlie, nothing to halt his tragic journey. I remember his last visit to our house. Chauffeur-driven, he was too ill to get out of the car, and leant against the leather upholstery, dressed in a beautiful blue overcoat. Molly sat next to him and held his hand, while my father and I installed ourselves opposite on small fold-up chairs, like those in a taxicab. The poignancy of the scene escaped me, I was so excited by those little snap-up seats. Charlie had made other visits that day, to his friend Paddy Walsh, who owned the hardware store and undertaking business in Cappoquin, and to the Lord Abbot of Mount Melleray. He died that night, and was borne to the church on the shoulders of his Lismore employees in a shining coffin of oxidised silver steel made up in Paddy's workshop, and designed by himself.

Bobbie liked to quote a little verse: 'A smile perhaps? A kiss perhaps? And then perhaps a rendezvous?' He would recite it as we set off in the trap, after the car – for lack of petrol, due to rationing – had been put away to sleep in a shed perched on hefty logs with its wheels removed. The Anglo-Irish were invincible visitors of one another's places. To allow war to stop this practice would have been considered a victory for the enemy. Fun was a much used word carrying not frivolous but almost moral connotations of courage and character. Molly reflected a pretty general view when she wrote ironically in *The Rising Tide*: 'A civil war was going on in Ireland, much to the inconvenience of social life.' Two young soldiers in *Mad Puppetstown* are killed because their hostess expected them to attend a tennis party and travel back to the barracks at dusk through remote country. The boys themselves would not have dreamed of refusing such an undesirable invitation. During the Second World War, ambush was no longer a problem, but petrol rationing was. One old lady used to cycle at least seven miles to lunch at Belleville, her fox terrier riding in the basket on her handlebars. She descended slowly from her bicycle with her long skirts and her jet earrings swinging, and walked graciously into my parents' embrace on the doorstep. Mostly people put their hunters, and sometimes even retired racehorses, between the shafts. Not all of them took to it – a few animals bolted down the hill from the house. We, however, had a noble angel called Dick-John. He was a big bay, and he carefully drew the jaunting car which we climbed into off the library steps. It had a rug box in the middle where I went. Molly and Bobbie sat on opposite sides back to back (turning their heads frequently to talk.) Rugs were an important part of the procedure. There were heavy checked ones so closely woven they were quite rain repellent in themselves, but a tarpaulin also travelled with us in case of a deluge, and a cashmere shawl, the colour of a baby chicken, zipped inside a soft leather cushion. Molly had been given this luxury item by Adele for a wedding present, and she relied on it for comfort in times of crisis to her dying day. 'Where is my little yellow rug?'

We often visited Clodagh Anson in her small Regency house near Lismore. It stood on a bend of the River Owenashad, a feeder stream of the Blackwater, which sometimes flooded dramatically, cascading from the mountains across the garden and into the house, where the quilted aquamarine drawing-room curtains had to be hastily knotted above the water. Clodagh was characteristically brave and resourceful during these events, and very amusing about them afterwards. She was sensitive, funny and extremely original. Giraffe-like, tall, her small face perched on a long neck, she talked quickly in a light, low voice, which was capable of reaching high notes when she sang Cole Porter tunes, or hymns in the cathedral choir. As a boy, John Perry had proposed to her and later retracted, not that she had had the slightest intention of accepting him. He confided in her about his homosexuality, and, despite her youth, she completely understood. All her life people told her their secrets. Nothing shocked her, although she was an outstandingly good person herself.

Clodagh and Bobbie grew up together and when he married Molly an intimacy developed between the three of them. Like Molly, Clodagh loved intimacy and had a gift for it. She said her confidence was at a low ebb at that time, and they helped her. She had recently recovered from a harrowing bladder operation. Her parents were separated, and both bullied her. She lived with her father, Pop, who was wheelchair-bound from a stroke, and irascible. She bore it by dining out on stories of the dreadful way he behaved, while treating him with the greatest kindness. She said she never read anything until she met Molly. As well as encouraging her to read, Molly and Bobbie did their best to get her to overcome her nervousness about sex, and accept one of her suitors. She never did marry, though this was due less to sexual shyness than to some fundamental damage inflicted by her experience of her parents' unhappy marriage. She was always very sympathetic to lovers. Friendship was her destiny rather than marriage. Being single was a disadvantage in those days that had to be transcended, but she made a success of it. Her house was a honey-pot to people.

Dressed in mist coloured tweeds, she would stand on her doorstep, holding the railing as though she was on a ship, and watch us descend from the sidecar, helped by her elderly groom, who led the horse away to the yard. She was inclined to usher one immediately to the latest improvement in the garden, where she worked prodigiously. She loved blue flowers, and grew agapanthus banked up along the sides of a stream, and pools of blue windflowers in her rough grass. She had two drawing-rooms, one with Pop in it. Molly and Bobbie would take it in turns to visit him as though entering the lions' den. If the name of someone he disliked came up during the conversation, one could hear him shouting in the distance, 'Brute, beast, ought to be shot'. In the other drawing-room, Clodagh served China tea, butterfly cakes and thin-cut bread with country butter. Later she would make up strong Martinis. I did not drink these, of course, but I did partake of the mood of loving bonhomie and wit they produced in my elders, and it gave me an affection for the juniper perfume of gin. Clodagh swam as much as possible. Dressed in black togs and a white bathing cap, her tall form stretched into a perfect arc, she would dive off the rocks behind the pier in Ardmore. She taught many of her friends' children (including us) to swim, and later to drive a car. She had far more patience in those matters than one's own parents would have shown. Cards were part of the air that Clodagh breathed. She was quite competitive about them, as she was about fast driving and shrimping. She was very secretive about some of the shrimp runs she fished at neap tides. She only revealed their whereabouts to Patrick Cockburn, her godson, after her retirement to St Mary's Convent, in Youghal, struggling, marooned in her armchair, to remember the landmarks for distant rock fissures, usually covered by the sea except at new or full moon.

She was snobbish and savoured the fact that she was related to several dukes, but she was also classless, perhaps in the way that Princess Diana was, in that she linked up with human beings from all walks of life because she had an instinct for, and was drawn to, the essence and not the surfaces of people. Time flew in her company. Her intimacy had a sensitive, humorous light touch about it. Her shyness, like Molly's sharpness, was pushed aside by the depth and strength of her compassion when it was tapped. She was completely forgiving and she had need of this forgiveness once or twice during her long friendship with Molly, particularly when *Good Behaviour* was published and many people assumed she was the prototype for the ungainly spinster Aroon.

*

Immediately after I was born in March 1940, Molly began to work on *Two Days in Aragon*. She felt that the lying-in had been a big expense for Bobbie, and she must make some money. She always responded tenderly and intuitively to children once they began to talk, but her attitude towards babies was complicated. When I, the longed-for child, arrived, instead of surrendering to total love, as one might have expected from someone of her nature, she became overwhelmed with anxiety about my wellbeing, and the relinquishing of my care to a nanny was probably completely wrong for her. She did the same when Virginia was born. It was, however, the custom of the class and time in which she existed. Motherhood was not meant to disrupt one's previous life in the slightest. Exhaustion, Molly's bane, was unacceptable. Stamina was demanded to keep up the structured leisure of those days; not one less rose must be put in vases, dinner parties had to be given and attended, gardens dug and the minimum of hunting days skipped. Tiredness was a secret shame which must never impinge on one's brightness as a social being. She did not feed me herself, and felt quite nervous whenever she entered the nanny's kingdom of the nursery. She sent to London for the softest shawls, and white lawn dresses. She worried desperately about whether the nanny was managing rightly, depending on her expertise and jealously mistrusting her at the same time.

When war was declared, it was feared that Ireland would be sympathetic to Germany even to the point of becoming the antechamber of an invasion. This compounded Molly's anxieties and caused her to send me with the nanny to her Turnley cousins in Antrim, where she thought we would be protected by British soldiers, and where she herself had felt safe after Ballyrankin was burned. The poet Louis MacNeice, around the same time, despatched his baby in the opposite direction, thinking he would be safer in the south.

Molly, who had momentarily handed a complete victory to her rival, the nanny, received weekly letters reporting my progress and requesting supplies of brown sugar. She records ringing her grocer, Mr Russell, trying to persuade him to send a stone of demerara to keep for her baby by putting on 'my sexy, please do voice'. Our return in the autumn of 1940 was followed by a great frost in the New Year. 'In the frost, the lavatory is the coldest place – the books feel very cold in your hands, more surprisingly than the seat's cold. I am glad I stored up the dahlias so snugly. It is nice to think of their fleshy roots dry in a box of rabbit sand, not rotting black in the ground. The dogs hate going out for their evening run . . . they look very well and sweet, flying round like black cats. These nights you have to stuff a woolly into the corner between neck and pillow . . . Sally's hair frizzles up, and I keep wondering if Nanny really has her warm enough, but I suppose she does . . . '

She could lift her dahlias from the cold earth, gather up Sue and her puppies, but it was harder for her to get her hands on her baby, and this was part of the shadow of depression which sometimes assailed her in the midst of happiness. When she was old, she wore the thinning, lacy shawls she had bought for me wrapped around her throat if she suffered from a cold, and in her kitchen she never had a new measuring jug, but always used the battered enamel one that had portioned out our milk in the nursery, as though she was trying to hold on to something which had eluded her.

The first nanny was English. She had once worked in a

maharajah's household, where she said 'one baby lay on a cradle of pure gold and one on a dividend'. As war shortages set in, she made Molly feel small, telling her about her previous position at a grand house in Kildare. 'There is a year's supply of coal in the yard, lots and lots of candles. Then she has got any quantity of rice, as the General is very fond of rice, and farola, golden syrup, everything, tea ... Oh, they aren't short of tea at Rathmore.'

She was dismissed after a shocking drama when she lost control of the pram, letting me hurtle, unpiloted, to the bottom of the avenue, and subsequently tried to cover up the incident. Later Molly felt that this misadventure was responsible for my nervousness. The next nanny was Irish and she was there for Virginia's birth. I remember her affectionately. She stayed with us until I was seven, and Virginia two. She was a little bleak in manner, and, unlike the English nanny, she was not interested in making her charges look pretty. Molly complained about this, but really liked it because it gave her the cue to come and fluff up her girls' curls, and put us into starched, smocked frocks. At the time it was considered important to have well turned-out babies. A witty cousin of Bobbie's once attributed the failure of an entire family to the fact that their neglectful mother clothed them in what she described as 'cut-up pillow cases covered in crumbs'.

Having smartened me up, Molly then carried me off to the drawing-room. As I grew older, being with Molly in the drawing-room greatly attracted me. The word 'drawing-room' has almost disappeared. Most people have never heard of it. I myself would barely remember it if I had not started out in this graceful, hospitable room where a lot of life went on. Molly's intense response to houses and rooms and objects in rooms is evident in her writing, and, of all the rooms which she herself created, the drawing-room at Belleville, which she and Bobbie planned together, was undoubtedly her favourite. It was decorated in peaceful shades of pale grey, rust and dark blue. The damasked stuffs were plain except for one chintz printed in an inky Chinese cypher. Although there were elegant, robust pieces of eighteenth-century furniture, the room had a thirties flavour, like her clothes. It was sort of glamorous, with plump cushions and a cocktail shaker in the corner.

Molly bit the stems of flowers and fixed them in huge bouquets which fanned against the gable walls. In the evening the smell of these seasonal blooms poured into the air, the astringent scent of daffodils, azaleas, 'like a fog of honey and pepper', the sweetness of lilac and the sharpened aromatic smell of autumn plants, particularly the phlox with its subtle powdery scent. The stems of the floating branches were anchored in their boat-like vases by rolls of chicken wire, weighted with stones and lumps of lead. She swore when the flowers swivelled, stripped off the leaves and wildly wielded her secateurs. When she was finished, she would smoke a cigarette sitting in an armchair gazing anxiously across at her creation. She was sometimes pleased, but often dissatisfied. Flowers were a source of cut-throat competition. Molly said 'we vied with each other in the forcing of bulbs'. The chatelaines were frequently scornful about one another's endeavours. She, who was sharp herself when it came to stiff gladioli, unscented 'new' roses, and too much mauve, had a deep passion for flowers. They released a kind of pure love in her – connected with place and her feeling for places. Wanda, a gleaming purple primrose which blossoms in February, was an icon to her. Whenever she moved home, she would cultivate a little piece of ground for it at once. It is emblematic of her spirit, being vivid, delicate and tough. Among her fictional characters, her grand and bossy mothers, jealous for their power, often experience their few self-forgetful moments when contemplating their beds of rare irises or nerine lilies. In *Time After Time* Jasper Swift is 'bent, like a reed in a cold breeze', and his negativity is only revoked when he is in his garden, or carrying in the flowers he has managed to rescue from its engulfing wilderness. Most gardeners share in this vein of secret passion, but it seems to take a particular extreme form among the Anglo-Irish ones, as though making the land which does not quite accept them bloom affords them a sense of communion they long for, and are usually deprived of.

Many visitors came to this room, relatives, neighbours, with their silk stocks and narrow-waisted coats, mud-bes-mattered after hunting, writers, actors, monks from Mount Melleray Abbey, ladies dressed in the beautiful speckled tweeds of those days, and prone to Chanel No. 5 perfume. A Garda superintendent called regularly on his bicycle, and kept Molly and Bobbie up to date on the progress of the war. He was said to be in touch with secret intelligence. Mr and Mrs Paddy Walsh were a remarkable couple who visited. Paddy, the provider of Charlie Cavendish's silver coffin, had long been associated with the Keane family. His leather dressing case and collar box were gifts from Bobbie's father, the Colonel. He was one of those people who were deeply import-ant in the Anglo-Irish life of that time, because they were like a junction leading out of its narrowness into the other country. Woodrooffe was full of such persons, and Molly, with her instinct for freedom, was often drawn to them. They existed at Ballyrankin in the workforce (to whom the little Skrines, like most children, were devoted), but they did not exist socially because it was virtually a Unionist household. The Keanes had half their roots in a different Ireland. They were descended from the O'Cathain clan, although they had also prudently contracted moneyed, English marriages. They remained Catholic until the Act of Union (1798), when they pragmatically converted, and put a Union Jack into the paw of the cat on their family crest. Bobbie's background was more liberal than Molly's even though the sporting life still came first. His view, combined with the plays of Seán O'Casey, shifted her perspective, and influenced the Ireland she wrote about in *Two Days in Aragon*.

Paddy Walsh hunted the same horses that drew the hearse for his funerals, and he worried about how they would behave if they met the hounds on the way to an obsequy. He was able to get things done. He could provide help of all sorts: a coffin, a high-class hammer or oat-bin, a taxi ride. His shop smelt deliciously of rope and grain and sawdust. As well as this practical assistance, he dispensed a kind of reassurance and love to people. He had no children, and he rather adopted the Anglo-Irish community, and treated them like his children, looking after them and attempting to keep them from making mistakes. He was shrewd. Everyone relied on him. After his death, his wife said of him 'for all his gaiety, he was one of the best judges of character I have ever met'.

They were both full of heart. They lived near the grocer, and brought sweets. Mrs Paddy, dressed in black with cream blouses of silk and lace, wore a hat. They were naturals, brimming with talk and gossip and fun. They were also very prayerful. Molly relied on their prayers. They took to her extremely. Mrs Paddy quoted her husband as saying '... there is nobody like Mrs Bobbie. She is a hundred percent.' Paddy was a kind of king. He was a king to his wife. She never recovered from his loss. She was frequently near to tears afterwards, but good company and funny with it. Molly was very close to her, and kept some of her letters. She signed her letters 'Martha', but they always called each other 'Mrs Bobbie' and 'Mrs Paddy'. Later on they understood the devastation of each other's widowhood. Mrs Paddy also ended up living in Ardmore, in a tiny tin house which later belonged to Fergal Keane, the journalist. Her compassion eventually became too much for her, her depression thickened and she finally succumbed to it.

Molly often sewed as she conversed, deftly and speedily embroidering daisies onto blue linen, or darning sheets and clothes. She sat with me and Sue in a big chair, chatting or reading aloud. When friends came to play cards, she spread on a table a blue damask cloth, tasselled at the corners, with pockets for holding chips and money concealed in its drapes. She never took to bridge, but she loved poker because of its elements of secrets and danger. Nobody has ever recorded the cruel jungle that the drawing-room could become more painfully and hilariously than Molly. She herself was a little too quick and brilliant with words. There is a strange remark in her notebook: 'How do you defend someone who is being really well sent-up?' More than anything, she enjoyed a real talk with a friend over a drink. All her life it was her idea of an unfailing oasis. Sometimes a remark would pop out and shatter the loving, benign atmosphere she had created, enhanced by firelight, embroidered cushions and cocktails. Molly would usually be sewing at such moments, her eyes fixed not on her companion, but on her needle, as it darted among the leaves and flowers of her embroidery. It is to her credit that most of her friendships survived these occasional abysses. A few succumbed and made her defiant and miserable. Adele, prone to similar debacles, said people without animosity had no vitality in them. Molly liked this idea, but was unable to endorse it entirely. She was shackled by her guilt and kindness.

It was not a musical household. The piano in the arched antechamber between the drawing-room and the dining room was mostly silent. Mícheál Mac Liammóir was one of the few people who sat at it. As he played, the light fell on his spotted cravat and his sensitive, painted face. 'Mícheál wears more makeup off the stage than on,' John Gielgud wrote to Molly when he was appearing in a play with him. I found him pleasingly exotic. I grew up loving the tone of actors' voices, and the way they would tune and change them. Mícheál's creativity was boundless. He and Molly talked about cooking a great deal. He was like a wizard in the kitchen, charming everybody, seducing with his voice. The huge blue eyes of Bridget, the cook, floated with tenderness towards him because he treated her like a queen, she, who had been knocked about by life, and had to keep her beloved illegitimate daughter in fosterage. He constructed with Molly a paella full of lobster claws, prawns and blue mussel shells emerging from a mountain of yellow rice, dyed by saffron brought from Spain, and stored for years with other weakening spices in biscuit tins.

Later on, Elizabeth Bowen visited. Sometimes, a little tired after the journey, she would lie down flat in front of the fire, smoking elegantly – not guiltily as people do now. She had a unique look: her fair skin picked up red marks easily, they faded and she carried them off with grace, like her stammer. She wore heavy baroque costume jewellery. Her earrings sometimes fell off, and she held them in her hands as she talked. She said once, when she was in the midst of a story at a house in Paris, one of her earrings rolled across the floor, and the Duke of Windsor retrieved it and handed it back to her when she was finished. She had a soft spot for him ever afterwards. Her face was just post-medieval, like the virgins in Flemish paintings, with a wide, pale forehead. She drew her hair back, as a great beauty would do. She was beautiful, but not according to any principles of her own day, so she supported herself with style, and was always quite dressed up. Hers was the protective fashion of a woman alone. Although she was always called Mrs Cameron, her marriage seemed a little misty and in the background. She told Molly once that when you are young you think of marriage as a train you simply *have* to catch. You run and run until you have caught it, and then you sit back and look out of the window, and realise you are bored. This, of course, was not the full story. Although the great love of her life was someone other than him, after Alan Cameron's death she often had tears in her eyes. She frequently mentioned missing him, especially when she came downstairs, still absorbed from writing, and she found herself saying, 'Let's go for a walk', and he was not there to answer. Once we all knelt in front of the drawing-room fire, roasting chestnuts; Bobbie lifted them out of the embers with fire tongs onto the black floor of the twinkling brass fender. The room was hardly lit except for the firelight. We were surrounded by aromatic chestnut smoke, and Elizabeth's amused, slightly breathless voice, speaking of *David Copperfield* (a book she revered). She said it had the best first chapter she knew. She quoted the tremendous opening: 'I was born with a caul ... ' and the words seemed to echo in the darkness.

Well water ran out at Belleville in the middle of summer, and had to be carried in milk churns by donkey cart from a surer well. Molly listened nervously for the creak of the pump as it failed to propel water from a dwindling supply to the upstairs bathrooms. She felt panic-stricken and oppressed by the heaviness of the river valley, and yearned for freshness. Briefly her home became uncongenial to her, and she welcomed the retreat to Ardmore in July and August. She was inclined to hide from the sun in an age of picnics and lying down on rugs. In the azalea grove of the sun walk at Belleville, Bobbie would be naked beside her, while she sheltered under hats, scarves, umbrellas, long-sleeved blue shirts and floppy linen trousers. Autumn and winter suited her better, and she loved the bare shapes of trees as they became 'less gold and more bone'. With winter, an abundance of freezing water arrived from the mountains, crashing powerfully along the streams and into the rough stone fountain where the horses drank in the yard. It made the summer drought seem unimaginable. I remember weather as being more classical in those days, with a real summer and a proper winter, when the terrain was chilled and frosted with the sounds of ringing hooves, iced twigs breaking, and sometimes a fox barking at night. Hunting kept people on the move through the cold landscape, riders and hounds, countrymen with handfuls of undulating ferrets, and cruel wire rabbit snares. Shooters brought in shining-feathered bouquets of limp creatures. I would look round the larder door, and feel saddened and intrigued by the sight of them, strung from hooks on the ceiling. Molly plucked them strongly and deftly, so that the feathers and down puffed into clouds onto the kitchen table. She instructed Bridget to cook them for a very short time in a very hot oven. They arrived in the dining room, reposing on toast in a chafing dish with a domed lid, sometimes accompanied by a small sauce boat of gravy with port in it. The tiny thighs of snipe were pierced with their long, long beaks, and they bled into the toast when cut. Pheasant was served with fried breadcrumbs, cabbage and thyme-flavoured sautéed potatoes. This food was tremendously respected. The reaction to it was both primitive and complex, reflecting the central place of the hunt in that world. The flavour, fresh from the woods and bogs, was delectable. I tasted slivers of these creatures' tender breasts held out to me on my parents' forks.

The Skrine men were expert fishermen and shots. Molly, always longing to be close to her brothers, grew up applauding their skill and admiring the trout, salmon and game birds they laid on slate shelves in the larder at Ballyrankin. This was about the only praise which Charlie, in particular, allowed himself to accept. His perfect horsemanship was a matter of course, and must not be mentioned. He disapproved of flattery, and suspected Molly of it. He sent birds to Belleville by post, or bus. Fish came by train, sewn into flat reed baskets. Molly delighted in these gifts. But at the same time her identification with wild things was deep. The vacillation of empathy between the hunter and the hunted, so apparent in her books, was perhaps the chief paradox besetting her own nature. The pull of conflicting elements is her natural habitat. It is evident in her leanings towards glamour and austerity, courage and nervousness, the call of the wilderness, and the aspect of her that liked to see 'rushes well trimmed, and gravel raked carefully, and money saved through thought and denial'.

Conflict was at its most acute in the struggle between her passionate desire to live life, and to write about it. The latter was a mostly submerged longing which she usually ascribed to the need to make money. Sometimes the anguish surfaces: 'If only people and life did not matter quite so much to me. I would write better, and give my writing the passion I give to my living. Not always, but often, I live passionately, inspired about food and doing flowers, and being amusing, and all the fire that ought to eat me up over my writing goes into those things.' It is moving to me that in this statement she nods towards the fact that she is unfair to her writing. She did not often admit that she had a gift. It was a burden she carried that kept her alienated (she who feared to be left out) upstairs in her bedroom, struggling to earn a crust in the most grinding manner possible. Her writing called her with the spoilsport tone of a strict governess. She complained frequently about the suffering, and was mostly silent about any happiness or satisfaction involved. She hid her love of writing from herself until the process began to unravel in old age, when it became obvious that she was grief-stricken. Unquestionably she was in a hard place. When the stuff of your life is also the clay of your creation as totally as hers was, the cutting-off point and the refocusing is anguish. 'In writing, you have to achieve this awful separation from living, and still write about life.' Marguerite Yourcenar puts it another way. 'Books are not life, only its ashes.' In retrospect the latter added: 'Books are also a good way of learning to feel more acutely. Writing is a way of going to the depth of being.' Molly tried to ignore this difficult truth in the surface of her mind, but she seldom evaded it in her work, and that is why her writing, like her living, is passionate and has the power to transcend its small social world and conversational mode and reach out to all its readers.

Molly wrote and slept in a pale green room at the top of the house. The thirties twin beds – 'the best from Heals' – were upholstered in brocade and pressed together. Two windows faced south, so that on a fine morning if one rose a little late, warm sunshine bathed the bed. On clear days, the view across the valley glistened with glimpses of the river like bits of ribbon threaded into the landscape. Much of her life evolved in this room. Her love affair with Bobbie, their talks and quarrels and reading aloud. She wrote in her bedroom and corresponded with friends involved in a war from which they were both eerily shielded. She lay against her pillows, her thoughts flying, plotting what to write, what to plant, what to eat. She watched dogs and children playing and making tents out of pale silk eiderdowns. Here she experienced worry and bliss, and sometimes calm. In 1949 after her life had changed, she added a postscript to her journal: 'I wish so much I had written down more of my absolute happiness.' The entangled roots of her sense of loss made her give to love attributes which it cannot have, except in the brief romantic timescale of a marriage such as hers. She could not quite believe her own words: 'I was putting on my shoes outside my door, with the sound of Bobbie dressing in his dressing-room, and suddenly all the start of the day rush dropped from me, and love flooded through me, and patience.'

CHAPTER 5

Molly said 'Bobbie and I really meant it when we said it took us more than a year to recover from marriage.' She wanted to feel that marriage was miraculous, that it put an end to loneliness and anger and depression. Guilt assailed her when these things surfaced and she held herself responsible as though there was something she was not doing which could put matters right.

In her novels matrimony is usually seen as a blessed state (with its advantages far outweighing its disadvantages). Not all her female protagonists were married but most of them longed to be. This attitude is surprising in such a precise observer and it was partly formed by the environment of her growing up where the 'good match', 'the house' and 'the garden' were so revered that the efforts made about them bore fruit. Molly was inspired by marriages that had acquired a splendid mellowness through what the protagonists, especially the wives, put into them. Particularly she was influenced by her parents' marriage which she saw as a dream of love and a charmed circle which she had felt perpetually outside of.

Metamorphosed from being an outsider to an insider she discovered that happiness was a testing thing. Although she loved Bobbie and was thrilled by her transformation, through the magic carpet of Woodrooffe (she often said 'I owe Dolly everything') from the constrictions of Ballyrankin to the generous expansiveness of life at Belleville, she was troubled by some of its unanticipated complexities.

For much of the time a war was going on outside her marriage, and people's lives were being shaken to the roots or broken while she was determinedly cherishing a small paradise. This sheltered place existed only because of Bobbie's stammer which prevented him from active service. Molly felt blessed at finding herself in a sort of Arcadia, but it was threatened by many anxieties, not least by Bobbie's ambivalent, internalised thoughts about not being involved.

Despite the tensions, the happiness and fun was real. Molly describes idyllic trips to the sea in her journal. Escaping to the sea was very important to both of them as it was to most Anglo-Irish people. They were drawn to Ardmore and many chose to be buried there, perhaps because it was somewhere they had felt free, away from the shadow of the 'big house'. Bobbie had been going to Ardmore since childhood. The Keanes owned a house there, as did several other families in the Blackwater Valley. He introduced Molly to Ardmore and she fell under its spell immediately: ' . . . we lay in a corner of the low cliffs gazing upwards into a horseshoe shape of sky, sea pinks tufted against the blue, across the narrow bay the fields of the opposite headland maintained their pattern as far as the sky. A small town was built low under the headland, pink houses and white cottages and queer stiff little Georgian houses and inland beyond the town, the mountains faint and airy, and wild … A mist came down across the bay and paths of a curious radiance lay on the water. The mountains that had been so faint rose out of the mist and were suddenly bluer than the sea-water and the different fields had such a warm and separate brightness.' This description, luminous with new love, conveys a feeling for Ardmore which stayed with her until she died.

They often went there with Clodagh and Sivie (both serious swimmers and prawners), setting out in the late morning, after she had finished writing. They, like Bobbie, were conscious of her vertiginous state of mind at such moments. Molly mentions Sivie with her hair 'like a yellow helmet' and her body 'like a stout Viking' encouraging her from the top of a bluff. 'It's nice up here Molly, all flowers and grass. Will we carry up the lunch?' After a stinging dip in the cold sea, she was shaken out of her gutted, anxious feeling and was able to rejoice in the lunch she had ordered – a lobster in its shell, smoked salmon, lettuce, eggs, little baby beets and an open apple tart with lemon and almonds.

Ardmore is at the centre of a panoply of bays and beaches each like a different world, among them Whiting Bay with its endless stretch of sand and flat rocks where prawns and shrimps migrate at neap tides; Shell Rock at the Curragh with its unceasing supply of cowries and other delicately tinted small shells fetched by the waves from unknown deeps and thrown onto the shingle there and not elsewhere; Goat Island (Llangar), surrounded by its clean swimming beach, which disappears at high water, and its deep-tunnelling caves, some of which served the purpose of eighteenth-century French smugglers of cognac, lace and muskets.

Molly, Bobbie and their friends, sophisticated grown-ups, played here, shelling, prawning, swimming, as intently as children. A certain state of mind came back to them through the natural world in which they found themselves: anxiety, pain, the war itself, vanished into a Zen-like happiness.

She cites an evening when the scent of woodsmoke and sea joined in the air and made her feel calm. They departed reluctantly, taking in last gulps of salty air: 'Going away from the sea your brain keeps its clearness for a little while as you drive inland.'

At home, the atmosphere was sultry with the heaviness of a river valley in summer. It affected her body and her mood. A little sick during the early stages of pregnancy with me, she sat down to breakfast and had a row with Bobbie about sausages. Since they were made at the Cappoquin Bacon Factory, she felt he was responsible for their flavour.

'Are those sausages the same as last week?'

'Exactly.'

'You know they're not.'

'It is exactly the same mixture. It is just the way they are cooked.'

'I wish she would cook them more.'

'She can't. She says the more she cooks them the paler they get.'

'Oh what rot, I think it is the sausages' fault.'

'Nothing is ever quite right, is it.'

She has underlined his last remark in her notebook. She sensed the danger of her edgy perfectionism that was also the vehicle of the marauding Skrine melancholy, which, when it lacks one outlet, will find another. This quarrel with Bobbie frightened her and made her cry. Peggy Ashcroft, who was visiting them, walked in on the scene. She laughed, of course, when she discovered the subject of the row, but she rushed to comfort Molly. 'Peg came down and embraced me. She understands all about tears of every sort.'

Anyone who saw Peggy acting in Shakespeare will recognise the truth of this remark. The friendship between them was a deep one. They seemed to share affinities of the psyche; a very passionate, compassionate response to life, combined with a certain ferocity and vulnerability. It is not surprising that Peggy, years later, reacted favourably to *Good Behaviour* and was not shocked by its darkness as Billy Collins, Molly's then publisher, was.

Like many people of strong character, Molly had no idea of the power of her moods, how they created the weather among the people around her. When very distressed she reacted with tears or with anger. Her tears were heartbreaking, wrung out of Skrine grit and a determination not to cry. Her tears came from a deep part of her. They brought her relief, and they evoked in the bystander a longing to console her, as they did with Peggy. Her anger was harder to deal with. It had a glitter about it that was alienating. Sometimes it took her a long while to shake it off and it took her victim time to recover from the panache and totality of it.

In her Belleville notebook, she records in some detail two quarrels she had with Bobbie, the one just mentioned and another when she responds with anger. She analyses succinctly her feelings of sadness in the first instance, and of pure rage in the second. Sausages, the reason for the first dispute, are succeeded by an equally absurd *raison d'être* in the next one – 'fiendish rabbits'. Caught between her violent emotions and her detached artist's eye, she brilliantly evokes the scene:

'Yesterday morning I got up swaying, a bit sickly, like one does, looked out of my window. I did not look across to Dromana or up to the sky, I looked down to my lawn and garden and saw what I knew I would see, only worse. I saw those fiendish rabbits had been scratching caverns everywhere and the hillocks they cast up looked enormous in the first morning mist. "Oh that Spillane," I cried out, "he won't try about the rabbits. He won't do a thing."

'"What do you want him to do?" Bobbie asked from his bed.

'"I want him to do what I said, set traps and stop the holes in the wire."

'"You're very difficult, aren't you."

'"I'm not difficult, indeed, I'm not difficult, but he's hopeless. You know he is."

'"What exactly do you want him to do? Say exactly what you want and he'll do it. Just tell him."

'Something snapped, all reason and patience. I threw my comb violently into the open drawer where it fell with a sharp rattle. "Tell him yourself" I screamed and gave two curses and whisked into the bathroom. I felt deliriously free for a moment, freed from love, alone and angry and independent. Of course I was in tears in a moment. But only angry tears. I paid no attention to them at all. I didn't go back near Bobbie. I thought he was waiting for me to come and say I was sorry. I heard him getting up, dressing very violently and quickly and going downstairs. Then I was frightened, I thought now he will sack Spillane and never forgive me and it will always be there. Then I heard him speaking to Spillane about rabbits and wire. They walked under my window discussing it.'

So this drama resolved itself. Rabbits might seem a minor inconvenience but a lawn full of burrows was a disgrace in her world. It was slovenly and something she would have noticed at someone else's house. She threatened to sack Spillane but she never did. As a child, she had felt closer to the servants than to her parents. In adulthood, she had to have a special rapport with the people who worked for her. It was necessary for there to be a kind of mutual attraction or the relationship became tricky, even disastrous. That alchemy was lacking with Spillane but was present in the case of Murray, his assistant. She considered both of them idle, being herself imbued with super-industriousness. Skrines were prone to referring to others as idlers but Molly minded this much less in Murray because she liked him. She enjoyed his imaginative, convoluted excuses and evasions. 'When he tells you how he has put a nut in the mowing machine you feel as if he has built a ship.' Her friendliness conflicted with her desire to be the mistress. Giving orders was awkward for her so she gave them in a sometimes imperious, awful way. Her sharpness and determination to get things done was tempered by empathy and consciousness of shared weakness. She was unsuited emotionally to commanding while at the same time being a ruthlessly determined perfectionist.

By the time I was conscious of it, she seemed to have got quite good at having rows, but her Belleville journal is full of misgivings on the subject. 'My heart glowed with relief at not having to scold ... Oh this awful mental cowardice about having rows. I lay in bed shuddering.'

Being a new broom in an old regime was stressful. Although obliged to go along with any changes on the surface, the servants had the advantage of her; they knew the whole story and its subterranean hazards. They were watching her performance with ironic interest as established plants were rooted out of borders and her favourites put in.

People were also being rooted out. It was not possible for Molly to run a Woodrooffe-type commune. She knew herself well enough to realise she could not share a household with her in-laws.

Alice, Bobbie's mother, had moved to Belleville after her husband's death in a shooting accident at Fort William, their previous house near Lismore. Harry Keane, enchanting, good-looking and beloved, died 'tragically', a euphemism for suicide in Ireland. Nobody knew for sure. He was said to have tripped over a fence while carrying a loaded weapon, an unlikely scenario for a shooting man. There were rumours that he had fallen in love, or that he was in financial trouble. Bobbie's stammer worsened from the date he was brought back from Shrewsbury School to attend his father's inquest. The people of Cappoquin erected a memorial plaque to Harry just outside the village, in part of the demesne wall which sprouts charming filigree daisies every summer.

As a child and his relation, I remember benefiting from the general warmth in which he was held. After this tragedy Alice might not have felt like leaving Belleville, but she was a very English person and returning to London was not an alien step, except that she went back to a town on the edge of the Blitz.

Her daughters Frida and Diana also lived at Belleville. They both married soon after Bobbie and Molly did, and subsequently their husbands went to war. Frida was the oldest child and a sort of Irish version of Lady Diana Cooper. People stood on upturned boxes at race meetings to see her go by. She was willowy and her features were perfectly proportioned with broad cheekbones, wide-set eyes and an ingenuous, kindly smile. In the thirties, society beauties were treated like film stars. Frida was modest and none of it seemed to go to her head. Men yearned for her and married other people as second best. Although the background music to her life was proposals of marriage, she refused all of them until she married Hugh Delmege in 1939. She was amused, amusing and restful company.

Molly and she had an entirely opposite way of going about things. Molly believed that life was all about making an effort. Frida almost never made an effort of any kind. She waited for everything, from cups of tea to men, to float towards her and they always did. Molly was certainly a bit envious of Frida, of her general popularity, her unlaboured-for beauty and the ease with which she negotiated society. She was irritated by Frida's tendency to bury anything painful or unpleasant and drift away from it as though it did not exist. Molly homed in on this fault among others in a terrier-like manner and was sometimes pretty sharp about her sister-in-law. Frida must often have found Molly quite hard to take, but she never showed this side of her feelings to me. She practised family true blueness and Molly endeavoured to do the same, but it was much harder for a firework like her to keep this up than it was for someone of Frida's temperament. She was an elegant, solitary swan floating on a lake while Molly resembled an assertive robin busily engaged in every aspect of survival.

Diana Keane, the third born, had red hair, green eyes and the broad, pale brow of an Irish queen. In looks she was a throwback to the Celtic side of the family. Molly felt she was overshadowed by Frida's success and was sympathetic towards her. Nevertheless she left Belleville when Molly arrived. She married a Scottish pilot, Donald Macdonald, and found herself in wartime RAF quarters, pregnant and struggling with domesticity, having never before cooked or lived in a house without servants.

War was cutting off the future and infiltrating lives with sudden change. In England a German landing was expected. Writing to Molly about the new play she was working on, John Perry said, 'If there is no invasion we might do it in autumn.' This play, *Ducks and Drakes*, was produced in 1942. H. M. Tennent put it on with much the same good production team as before, but without John Perry. He had joined the RAF and was training at Eastbury Park, Middlesex.

In her Belleville notebook, Molly expresses a secret resentment at John's lack of input into *Spring Meeting*, combined though it was with his full billing as co-author. She felt he was freeloading off her toil. At the same time, she realised that his knowledge of stagecraft and of making a play was very valuable, as was his influence and position in the theatre world, and his closeness to Binkie Beaumont. She was also glad to have put money and prestige his way for his mother's sake, because she knew how much Dolly worried about John and loved him. Whether it was through lack of John's expertise, bad timing – Ireland in any form had become unpopular in England due to its refusal to lend its ports to Churchill – or the weakness of the play itself, *Ducks and Drakes* closed after a very short run.

John must have been slightly pleased by the disaster which vindicated his role but, despite its vulnerability at this point, their friendship survived. He wrote sympathetically to her just as he himself was posted abroad. 'I am so sorry about the play which I attended on the second night. I was on duty for the first. I won't write about it now. I know a little how you must feel and believe me I am very very sorry. Some charming friends seem to think I might be glad but it isn't so at all. I would want nothing but good to you all!'

Later (from Gibraltar) he elaborated on what he felt was wrong with the play.

Feb. 14

Darling, about the play, please don't think me unkind or bitchy if I say it was really wrong in itself. I agree it was not helped by Lillian or John's over-production. But even if you had those two faults removed, you would never have had a success, that fatal uneasiness caused by your transition from serious psychological studies to purely farcical situations would always kill it. Audiences must know where they are with a play; they must know whether they are meant to laugh, and to know whether they are to be seriously interested in a character. You never let them settle down (neither did John!). I feel very awkward, or I did, about the whole thing. I would not have you think I am saying 'Oh well, you see what happens when she tries to write a play on her own.' You can write a play and will do so I feel sure, but you must simplify the whole time. You write brilliantly, but you still lack a knowledge of 'theatre'. Dodie Smith knows everything there is to know about theatre but if she had your real spark of genius she would be in a very high class. If you are going to continue writing, why don't you get hold of Maugham's plays or Noel's? I know you dislike reading other people's, but I believe it would repay you, they are both great master craftsmen. *The Vortex*, *Private Lives*, *The Circle*, *The Sacred Flame* all finely made plays, though not necessarily inspired. I will say no more of it.

John's strictures on the well-made play make interesting reading today when theatre has changed so much and the object of most modern plays seems to be to unsettle the audience rather than to let them know where they are! His tutorial tone was always part of their collaboration. She both resented and depended on it. At the start he had persuaded her that she could write a play and proved it with the smash hit *Spring Meeting*. He had guided her into the theatre world which she found utterly congenial and exciting and more important and lucrative than novel writing. *Spring Meeting* and, later, *Treasure Hunt* worked with that era of drawing-room comedy because of her ability to write dialogue and create characters, her sparkle and wit and her feeling that life was dramatic in all sorts of subtle and entertaining ways, but her sense of theatre did not expand beyond that. Her talent was always better accommodated as a novelist than a playwright. Just before *Ducks and Drakes* her novel *Two Days in Aragon* was being well received and hailed as a major step forward in her work. Because her mind was set on the theatre, she was hardly consoled by this.

After the play closed, in a letter to John Gielgud Molly made a very perceptive comment about her own work: 'I do think, John, that anything I write is terribly hard to change. Not that I mean it is so good or so witty, or so funny, but it is <u>peculiar</u> and once the balance of it is upset in any direction, all its importances go astray.'

The war had an extraordinarily beneficial effect on John Perry's character and brought out his best qualities. Brilliant to meet and to talk to, he had tried many things in the artistic field and nothing had really worked for him creatively. Everything had resulted in a slightly equivocal situation rather as he had become co-author of Spring Meeting without having actually written a word of it. This had forced him into a jester's role. In many ways he was a very good critic, occasionally an embittered one. Likewise, he had enchanted and found love, but could never help himself mocking the beloved. He was better at friendship than love, as his letters to Molly show. His affection for her was both imaginative and practical. During the war years he was frequently finding couriers to bring her silk stockings and bottles of scent. They were linked by their love of Dolly, and by their mutual passion for a good joke and domestic doings.

War wrong-footed the theatre world at first. It didn't know what to do to help. Did you bring the troops (most of whom probably preferred Bob Hope and stand-up comedy), Macbeth or Oscar Wilde? John, having joined up, looking terrific in his RAF blue, frantically learning Morse code, was suddenly at the centre of things, rather than the periphery. He came home from training at Eastbury Park and told Binkie and Dick

A meet of the hounds at Cappoquin, Co. Waterford, *circa* the twenties

Molly's mother, Agnes Nesta Skrine (Moira O'Neill), with her sisters May and Lou

Molly's sister Susan

Sivie Masters

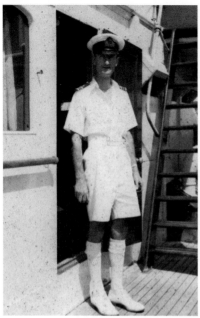

Molly's brothers Charlie (*left*), in naval uniform during the Second World War, and Godfrey (*right*) fishing

Molly's brother Walter winning a race on Martin M

Londesborough Handicap Chase (2½ miles) Sandown Park 22nd. January, 1949.

Won by "Martin M." (Major W. A. Skrine)
2nd. Sir John (A. Grantham)
3rd. Steel Arrow (R. Turnell)

Molly and her husband Bobbie out hunting in the thirties

Adele Cavendish (Adele Astaire) harvesting

Molly with John Perry, Lady Patricia Miller, Clodagh Anson, Sivie Masters and Hugh Delmege

Bobbie and his sister Frida Keane in the thirties

Molly and Bobbie on their wedding day

Photographed by the *Tatler* at the Clonmel Horse Show, 1936: 'M. J. Farrell' with Captain and Lady Katherine Dawnay.

Book jacket painted by Norah McGuinness

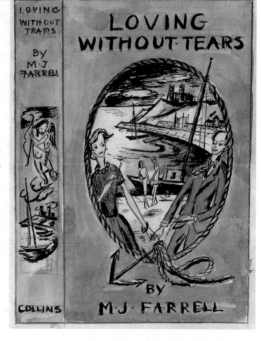

(*Right*) Molly with Virginia, and me on Bramble, in the yard at Belleville

(*Middle*) Bobbie and Molly picknicking

(*Bottom left*) Virginia and me 'helping' in the garden

(*Bottom right*) Polyphotos taken in the fiftes

Molly gardening at Belleville

Clowes about his activities rather than vice versa. His sense of realism came into its own as did his natural courage and humour. Mockery and bitterness receded. He wrote Molly a series of remarkable letters from London and Gibraltar which evoke his experience of war and the magic of his personality with its paradox of kindness and malice.

John's thoughts in his letters are honed by the underlying echoes of loneliness and death that is war. These are distant echoes, however, for in Gibraltar his aristocratic capacity for leisure, for cocktails and tennis was perfectly accommodated. It was the place where the sailors (including sometimes Godfrey and Charlie) came on leave to have fun. Godfrey describes running into John, every inch the elegant ADC, in a restaurant unexpectedly. 'I met the rare John Perry incognito with someone I only saw the back of. John was delightfully bronzed and delicately perfumed. I have his phone number and will see him the next time we get in.' Having rather enjoyed the excitement of the Blitz, even when the windows fell in shards onto the table as he sat at cards with Binkie and Dick at 142 Piccadilly, he was at first disappointed by his luxurious posting to Gibraltar, perhaps not least because it gave him time for introspection, something from which his busy boulevardier's life had always protected him.

Affectionately bent on amusing each other, Molly and John exchanged their funny, spiteful, thoughtful correspondence in relative safety, she from her Irish Arcadia, he from his Mediterranean antechamber of war.

At home Molly's relationship with 'the Bogs' improved after her marriage. Writing in 1942, Godfrey commented, 'you paid with many a savage tear and bitter struggle for your emancipation, but how well worth while it has proved'. Distance, motherhood, being the mistress of a beautiful house made her elders treat her less as an *enfant terrible* and more as a respectable married lady. She loved her brothers, and always wanted to assist them with their affairs of the heart. Charlie married Theo Thompson from Belleville in a quiet ceremony at Cappoquin church. Their marriage caused an impact at Ballyrankin. The Aunts refused to believe in it at first, and referred to Theo as 'that person who thinks she has married darling Charlie'. Molly stood up for Theo, but they were not soulmates. The softening between her and her mother, apparent in the latter's letters describing me as a baby when we were both refugees at Drumnasole, was furthered by a mutual dislike of Theo.

Aunt May, writing to Molly for her birthday in July 1941, complains of Theo keeping Daphne Hall-Dare to herself when she visited and says, 'I wish I could like her more than I do but it is no good wishing.' Molly now went to Ballyrankin in a new role as peacemaker and visiting angel. Godfrey congratulated her on her efforts. 'I thought the atmosphere of the bogs much improved by the cooling draught of your visit. Wonderful but no doubt they will be at it hammer and tongs again before long. It is such a pity that people cannot manage to get on. Happiness seems so odd. I think the Elizabethans were nearer right than us when they decided it all had to do with the state of one's guts.'

Molly's Arcadia was suddenly bombarded not literally but figuratively. The bomb actually fell on the Guards' Chapel during a service on Sunday 18 June 1944. Mrs Alice Keane, Bobbie's mother, was one of many people killed. News of her death did not reach Ireland for nearly a week. Frida immediately made plans to travel to England where Diana already was. Bobbie did not go because Molly, convinced that to be in London at the time was almost certain death, intercepted the telephone messages to him from Diana, and deceived him as to their content, leading him to believe that not more than one travel pass (Frida's) could be granted. She was facilitated by the fact that he was in Ardmore and she was at Belleville at the time. Among her papers she left the following note. 'Keep this in case anything was ever said to Sally and Virginia about Bobbie not going to England when his mother was killed. I was entirely responsible for stopping him. He never knew till later that Frida and Diana were insisting on his going. I got him to Ardmore where there was no telephone and took all their messages at Belleville and never sent them on to him. This was the form I got Sippy [Sippy Williams, their solicitor] to dictate to me to pass on his authority to Frida if necessary. Tommie [Jameson] helped me by "losing" Bobbie's passport. Everyone thought it was absolute madness going to London then. Mrs Keane had been dead for 5 days before we knew she was dead at all.'

This was written in 1949, five years after the event. Enclosed with it, scribbled on an opened-up brown envelope, was a copy of the confession she sent to Diana at the time. 'I want to tell you that I didn't give Bobbie one single message about permits, passports, collusion and going to England that you gave me for him last week on Tuesday evening. He didn't come back from Ardmore Wednesday and I didn't ring him up on purpose as I wanted to speak to Frida myself, as I thought if Bobbie talked to her he would start off at once by Thursday train to Dublin and cross to London as soon as he could. I rang Bobbie Thursday and told him Frida was determined to go and collusion would only grant one permit and to send her on the legal form she wanted. He doesn't know any more than that now.'

This mad act of hubris was not the only time in her life that she did something similar, but it was the most serious. I believe that it was misplaced love not power which motivated her. She always had an impulse to throw herself between those she loved and any harm or danger which threatened them. The intensity of her imagination collaborated with her pessimism and played against her. She was prepared to plot and tell lies. She didn't mind how bad or devious she appeared, provided she could save the other person (as she saw it) from themselves. Arrogance, of course, came into it. She took no account of Bobbie's feelings for his mother. She herself had found Mrs Keane grand and English and boring and it was as though she almost expected him to share this view. She had no idea of the ambivalence of her position. Even when she wrote that most poignant note for Virginia and me at a time of great anguish for her (after Bobbie's death) she still felt that Frida and Diana were wrong. 'Everyone thought it was absolute madness going to London then.'

It was true many people did think as she did. Tommie Jameson and Sippy Williams collaborated with her. Being close to a war zone but not of it makes for another reality. Going to London without a compelling reason then must have been like arriving in Baghdad in 2007. However, it was psychologically more disastrous for Bobbie not to go than to do so. He was a hunting man not used to refusing danger. The situation merged with his already troubled feelings about not fighting in the war, and harmed him mentally and physically and affected their marriage.

Molly hid from the repercussions of this major event in phalanxes of other anxieties, particularly her recurrent ones about money, and, to a lesser extent, illness. 'I go to sleep as calm and as happy and blessed as if I were slipping through waves and then I am woken by a terrible unrest, a desperate feeling of domestic crisis. The flour, the meat, the chicken food, the extravagance, a feeling of trusting nobody and thinking that nothing can be right. A feeling that I am guilty of every carelessness and stupidity, that I deserve to be robbed and lose money and love and even dogs, Oh, everything.'

'Problems about cakes, about washing, affect me terribly. I'm not born mean but there is so much uncertainty about our money. Or am I born mean? I think this money despair comes from a weak lack of knowledge about how much money should do for one.'

The uncertainty about money that she describes was common in Anglo-Irish life; it was about living grandly on a modest income. Remembering this time years later, she said, 'Bobbie was wise about money. He said "It would be alright if we had just over two thousand a year and we have a bit under."' What distinguished Molly and Bobbie's situation was her ability to spirit money out of the air with her writing. The financial necessity worked as a spur and a block. Sometimes it caused her desperation and panic, even illness. It was a tidal thing, when the tide was in you forgot the empty beach ever existed. Molly's reaction to times of plenty was celebratory and generous. She was quick to lend money to others in the position she had just escaped from. Her sparkle and self-confidence was instantly renewed. When the tide turned, her addiction to nervous ills was inclined to take over. She had a tremendous ability to overcome them and get on with life. She constantly questioned herself as to whether sickness was real or surmountable. She would torture herself over this, briefly closing her eyes and taking to her bed before pushing on. 'I feel worn and my eyes are very unsteady. I can't see well. They quiver. I lie very still in bed. I mustn't bounce about. I must rule my quietness or I would feel sick. I wrote a good deal. I feel I must do this. It would be terrible if I got ill and had to stop.'

About four miles from Belleville across the River Blackwater was a place where all pain dissolved. This was Tourin, the home of Joan and Tommie Jameson, and the capital city of West Waterford's Arcadia. The magnanimous, casually grand atmosphere of this house overflowed into another more informal one at Ardmore where the Jamesons had a seaside retreat, Rock House.

In these two places, Molly and Bobbie forgot their troubles in an ambience of generosity and pleasure where poker hands were dealt, cocktails drunk and rugs spread on sheltered corners of the cliffs for lying down in the sun and gossiping with one's eyes closed. A sophisticated milieu that had not lost track of simplicity, it was grounded in the natural world and in an acceptance of the intricacies of the human heart. Similar to Woodrooffe in spirit it was a more cosmopolitan and wealthier version, with Canalettos hanging on the drawing-room walls. Sivie was also an habitué of Tourin and Rock House, as were Clodagh and Adele, both of whose portraits Joan painted.

Tourin is a neo-classical structure built in the early nine-teenth century. Beautiful in a robust, optimistic way, it has none of the romantically waning, *Grand Meaulnes*-ish quality of many Irish estates. Surrounded by tall trees and fragrant shrubberies, it was sustained by a kitchen garden which filled the dining room with seasonal treats: asparagus, sea kale, purple sprouting broccoli, loganberries, figs, peaches, sweet peas and lily of the valley. The hall, large enough to turn a coach and four in, had an elegant cantilevered staircase rising from it. On the landing where the stairway separates into two parts, there is a neo-classical statue of a half-naked goddess reposing on one elbow. She personifies the restful, sensuous grace of the place.

I remember myself, as a rather melancholy child, only having to hear the names Joan and Tommie to feel cheered up. Children were loved and indulged by them, and expected to be witty and natural. In the adult version of Tourin, love affairs flourished and friendship was cultivated and cherished. Rather a lot of gambling and drinking went on. The generosity and extravagance of the hospitality was barely dented by the war. Tommie arranged the flowers and the menus. He loved growing things and was an excellent shot and fisherman. Tall and athletic, he had played cricket for the MCC. His family had founded the Jameson whiskey distillery. He was a man's man who adored women and understood their feelings. He had quite a French attitude to sex, discussing it with humour and without vulgarity. He gave people much happiness, and of course some unhappiness occasionally, perhaps to his wife. Joan was the extraordinary person at the centre of his life. She was calm and tough enough to keep his love. She was very skilled at dealing with his infidelity. She was elegant and wise, very funny and understanding, and spoiling of those she loved, especially children. She had wonderful taste in a sophisticated thirties style. She was an ardent antiquer, gambler and collector of shells on Ardmore beaches. She adored her sons, Shane and Julian, both remarkable characters. If she had not been so social and had given more time to her work, she would probably be famous today as one of Ireland's best artists. She exhibited regularly in Dublin and London. She painted mostly at Ardmore in the summer. Molly described her in an introduction to the catalogue of a retrospective exhibition of her work in 1989. 'Despite her gift and understanding, Joan was in some ways an unwilling painter. Reluctantly arriving at her studio, nearly hidden by fuchsia and hydrangea, she would sigh a little, and grow a little pale as she sorted out her paint-brushes, and looked almost with dislike at the canvas on the easel. Before starting to paint, she was nearly ready to welcome any interruption whether from her adored children or her rather frightening giant Dachshund, Hansy. "Hansy, come in. Hansy do you want to go out? What does Hansy want?" But once she conquered such impediments to concentration, her strength was indefatigable. She painted cautiously. Her brush seemed to be pushing its way as it followed her eye into the canvas.'

The studio was behind the rose garden at Rock House, overlooking the sea and the Holy Well. It was the other Ardmore, so different from her own, that she frequently painted, the people she could see walking across the strand and streaming into chapel from her window, the fishermen, the nuns, the women in shawls and their children. Her archetypal, noble figures seem to be hypnotised by the sea. Her landscapes are exoticised, filtered through a gently Cubist lens. The shapes of boats and small fields, the sea distance, nuns' veils in the wind fascinated her. She depicted this rural Catholic cosmos as though seeking to fathom its mystery. Her own world overlapped with it; her fishermen often have Tommie's long legs, and an elegant woman with a handbag and a yellow blouse wanders among boats drawn up from the tide in one picture. She left a portrait of her son Shane clasping his toy yacht, from which his childish beauty and integrity and her love for him shine forth.

Joan had to have a new mink coat when the current one became even slightly worn. She was the only person I ever met who had a lady's maid. She had to be in Monte Carlo at a certain time of year. In the catalogue's introduction, Molly tells a story of Tommie leaving Joan alone for a few days in Cannes with strict orders to keep away from the card tables during his absence. 'His instructions immediately ignored, she was back at the Casino losing a small fortune. Undismayed, she returned on the following night to recoup all her losses and win a lot more. As a surprise for Tommie she pinned all the notes like a counterpane across their bed.'

Many of Joan's friends were artists. She introduced Molly and Bobbie to Norah McGuinness who painted them together. This charming portrait is painted in soft gouache colours with a diagonal slightly tipped composition so that the figures almost seem to be floating in a boat of plants and greenery. In fact their boat is a rug placed on the ground in the paved garden outside Joan's studio at Rock House. Molly sits beneath her parasol and Bobbie lies in the foreground with a book open beside him. Despite their romantic summery appearance, one can see some unhappiness in this painting. Bobbie's expression is a little strained. And Molly's hands grip her knees beneath her fashionable floppy slacks. It was 1946, the war had ended and they had recently had a new baby.

Although delighted with the baby, Virginia, the pregnancy had not been a happy experience for Molly. Mostly because during the course of it she had become convinced that Bobbie had fallen in love with someone else. She had reacted with deep agony and generous offers. She probably sought Joan's advice but would have been quite unable to take it. She was consumed with guilt and self-doubt. She was older than Bobbie, she had seduced him. She felt it was not quite fair. She felt that she owed him his freedom, and typically offered it to him. He refused, saying he would never want to leave her. Because of the pattern her distress habitually took, it must sometimes have been hard for him to stick to this resolve; as the anxiety spiralled and sharpened inside her, she would have been hard to live with. Longing to be loving, she would have been grittily brave, razor sharp and hurt to the quick. She told me years later that she often considered turning this experience into a book but was prevented by the fact that it would have been painful to people she did not want to hurt.

She did write about it very obliquely in *Loving and Giving*. Among her papers there was a scrap of an idea for a novel. 'Bobbie went away with his beautiful lady. I remarried a divine, angelic bore who did everything for me and loved the girls, and I was really nasty to him.' It is impossible to know how serious this affair actually was or how much it gathered strength in Molly's powerful and pessimistic imagination.

Frida maintained she was overwrought due to her pregnancy and greatly exaggerated the whole thing. I would guess Bobbie was indeed in love but was equally (or more so) consumed with his war troubles, his mother's funeral, friends not returning, others coming back, perhaps not changed in themselves, but having experienced the test of battle which he had not. Some, like his brother-in-law Walter Skrine, returned shatteringly wounded.

The war ended on 8 May 1945, and the baby was due in August. Early that summer Molly wore pink linen smocks which suited her, and sat on the garden seat making mayonnaise. Her mixing bowl with yolks in it was perched on ice cubes inside a larger one. She poured in the oil sparingly and carefully, and stirred it with her favourite small thinly worn wooden spoon. I peered into the bowl watching for the yellow rose made by the tracks of the whirring spoon when the mixture thickened. Life was risk-laden and guilt-ridden. If she began making mayonnaise it was in the gift of the gods if she succeeded and somehow her own fault if it failed to emulsify. Things were not cause and effect in the quotidian way. For a perfectionist it made life endlessly exciting in its triumph, devastating in its feeling of deserved disaster. It was an exhilarating hard way to live with its plateaus of rest in the savouring of things well done.

Lizzie brought elevenses and Bobbie, if he was at home, joined us. He no longer drank stout at this hour but sipped out of his tall pint glass hot water with a pinch of bread soda in it, as he had begun to suffer from indigestion. For the sake of the coming baby Molly drank milk, which she hated. She grimaced as she drained the glass. I missed sipping the froth from the surface of my father's Guinness as I had done in the past. Those glasses of hot water appeared at the end of every meal, and I was aware of Molly's bright, anxious glances directed at them and at him.

Her fear compounded his problems. Although he approved of Ireland and the Free State, there was in him and in most Anglo-Irish people a sense of duty towards England. It was as though England was an elder brother whom one did not love particularly, but one must not let down in times of trouble. To the rest of the country, England was a recent enemy. The new state was raw from the past. To some, neutrality was a generous act. There were even a few who, at the start, advocated supporting Germany. De Valera signed a Book of Condolence at the Embassy after Hitler's death, not because he was for him but as a demonstration of Ireland's neutrality. Perhaps if he had fought, Bobbie would have been affected drastically for opposite reasons. Someone of his gentle temperament could have returned a complete pacifist, as others did. He distracted himself with hunting and poker and jokes but his worries turned inward and gave him an ulcer.

Virginia was born at the Portobello Nursing Home in Dublin, as I had been. Molly adored her gynaecologist, Ninian Falkiner. He and his family had become friends, as most of her doctors did. Virginia came home to Belleville on a perfect late summer day. I waited in a mood of Christmas-like euphoria, wearing my favourite blue and white striped sundress and bonnet. I wandered around my familiar haunts, the cool tents made by the rhododendrons, the scorching slopes of the lawn, and the edge of the wood with its brown stream and grove of Portuguese laurels. Everything was transformed and illuminated. Lizzie, polishing champagne glasses in her pantry, gave me a warm smile and called after me as I passed, 'Your baby sister is coming home today.' An only child for five and a half years, I felt a sense of pomp and status through this new relationship.

They did not arrive until evening. I peered into the basket at the round-headed, sleeping baby. She was transported to the nursery by the monthly nurse led by Nanny. Molly was still wearing the pink linen top. She put her arms around my father's and my waists and we followed the basket, walking slowly abreast up the wide, shallow steps of the front stairs. They both made a great fuss of me for fear I would be jealous of the new arrival. They produced for my room a beautiful inky blue lamp with a yellow and pink rose and lily of the valley painted on it. They had found it, as they had found many treasures, in Miss Burke's Antique Shop in Youghal, and had it changed from an oil lamp to an electric one. It is still in my possession. I was delighted to have a new sister.

During the war years, Molly wrote a play entitled *Guardian Angel* which later became the novel *Loving Without Tears*. It was produced in 1944 at the Gate Theatre in Dublin by Hilton Edwards and Micheál Mac Liammóir, with Micheál playing one of the main roles. At this time, the diarist of the *Irish Times*, Quidnunc, went to meet Molly and Bobbie at the Shelbourne Hotel, and wrote the following description in his column: 'I saw a lady come down the stairs with a gentleman slightly resembling the Duke of Windsor, wearing a grey flannel suit. The three of us circled one another warily, waiting for recognition. I would have gone forward only that I thought M. J. Farrell was a spinster of about 70, connected vaguely in my mind with Somerville & Ross and bustles. There was no reason for this, but everybody gets vaguely connected in his mind. The lady was young, she wore a very expensive russet-brown suit, a diamond and sapphire dragon on her lapel and a diamond and sapphire ring, both a tasty size. I found it was M. J. Farrell and her husband Mr Robert Keane. M. J. Farrell is Mrs Molly Keane – Miss Molly Skryne as she started off. As M. J. Farrell she has written the comedy *Spring Meeting* which ran for months in London shortly before the war with Arthur Sinclair as an Irish Crichton. And now as M. J. Farrell, she has written *Guardian Angel* which opens tomorrow night at the Gate Theatre. This is her first time with the Gate company and she is thrilled with Hilton Edwards as a producer. She has eyes the same colour as the brown bits of tigers, and when she is excited they glow like anything. All round this is a tiger-like lady, a small elegant tiger, neat and well-behaved. But suddenly she makes a small comment on something or somebody and the air is filled with the whistle of claws. Do not think she is malicious, she is too interested in what people do to dislike them, or to be nasty about them.'

The play was well received in Dublin and, in the autumn of 1946, Molly and Bobbie travelled to London to discuss its possible production by H. M. Tennent. While they were staying with Binkie, Bobbie suffered a duodenal haemorrhage and was rushed to hospital. He was operated on and after about a month was pronounced fit to go home. Molly arrived to bring him by taxi to Lord North Street. She was conducted into a side room to wait. The matron arrived, sat opposite her, and said, 'Mrs Keane, you must be very brave, your husband is dead.' He had died of a clot to the heart. At that time, it was not common knowledge, although it was beginning to be known, that after an operation patients must be got up as soon as possible. This had not happened to him. Molly went into total shock and amnesia. Bobbie was buried in London and she had no idea where. She did not go to his funeral. She spent that day with June de Trafford, Joan's cousin, and they went to a Bond Street shop and bought a smart shade for the blue lamp she and Bobbie had given to me. He was thirty-six years old and they had been married for just eight years.

At June's house, her young son Dermot whom Molly loved, came and sat with her on the sofa. He was a Catholic and after a time he said, 'Molly I am going out to pray for you and for Bobbie.' She always remembered Dermot saying this and quoted it on the few occasions she talked to me about this time. Even fifty years later she could not speak of it without being in tears. Dermot told me that he had visited Bobbie with his mother on the evening before his death and they were the last friends to see him alive.

There was an interlude when I didn't know Bobbie had died. Molly was still in London and she wished to tell me herself. I remember it as a time of strange happiness. I suppose he was near me. There were equinox winds blowing and I rode my green tricycle among swirling beech leaves. Later I went to stay with my cousins Vivien and Charles Keane. Although I liked playing with them, I missed the feeling of happiness and safety that seemed to stem from being under the trees at Belleville in the wind.

Lady Eleanor Keane, my great-aunt and my cousins' grand-mother, visited at one point. A very direct lady, she said to me, 'What about your father?' 'He is not well,' I said. 'No, he is not at all well,' she replied solemnly. I don't know whether it is retrospective thinking but I afterwards felt I had experienced a slight frisson during this conversation. Eventually one morning Molly arrived in Bobbie's Ford Prefect, chauffeured by John Rea, the Cappoquin blacksmith who sometimes drove us, and took me to Tourin. We walked in the garden outside the house. She said, 'God loved Daddy so much' – 'that he made him better,' I interrupted hopelessly. 'No, darling, he took him to Heaven.' It was not a shock because I already knew at some level just below consciousness that he was dead, but it was desperately sad. We both wept as we walked hand in hand under the towering Tourin trees shedding their leaves around us. I have no recollection of it, but she said I told her, 'Mummie you will have to marry again. You will never manage without a man.'

Tommie and Joan sheltered us in our grief and poured their warmth over us. Tommie had travelled to London to fetch Molly home. That morning when she and I came in from the garden we walked up the stairs, past the white goddess who always, even now, intrigued me. We went into Joan's bedroom where she was with Mabel, her lady's maid. Mabel was a real Londoner with a cockney accent that I loved listening to. She was a rock of sense and often very funny. She and Joan embraced me full of compassion and I was comforted by the fact that they were the same as they always were. Joan took out her jewelled musical box and put it on the dressing table. She asked me if I would like to hear it and when I said yes, she wound it up with its gold key. We all stood still and listened as the song of a nightingale rose out of the little box into the room.

CHAPTER 6

Writing in the small notebooks she used for lists and engagements, Molly, sometimes in short snatches, endeavoured to record what had happened to her. 'In happiness I was enclosed as closely as a nut in a nutshell – Bobbie was half the shell now the shell has been split off me and the naked kernel is open to the world. It must defend itself, strive for itself – give that it may get. Love others that it may have love enough to keep living.' She struggled with her broken feelings of being stunned and almost dead herself. She describes a young woman with a glowing complexion, wearing a becoming curly lambskin jacket wheeling her baby in a pram. She catches sight of this lively looking person reflected in a shop window and realises it is herself. She knows she is coming back to life and leaving Bobbie in his grave and she finds the pain of it unbearable. Her notebooks are sprinkled with small prayers – 'Dear God, help me to get the eiderdowns recovered.' She tries to keep her feet on the path of salvation. 'I'm going to say my prayers if it kills me and write a word if it kills me, for these are the things that prevent me from lapsing into absolute despair. May God keep me clear enough and sane enough to help Bobbie's children.'

In the New Year of 1947, she and I went to Villars in Switzerland to join her friends Mecha and Robin Cazalet and their daughter Gillian. While she was there Tommie Jameson wrote her a letter trying to extract her from grief:

Tourin 31.XII.1946

Mollie [sic] dear,

What a terrible and boring time you had waiting at the airport. We were so upset for you but glad you had Robin and I know he would be a help in any adversity. We have not even heard yet that you did get off but presume that you are now in Switzerland. I do hope you enjoy yourself – I know how difficult it will be, but you will have to put your lovely life with Bobbie in a very sacred compartment and start a new life.

We can never forget you and Bobbie, the loss to us is only second to yours; you don't really know how much we enjoyed our visits to Belleville and yours to Tourin. I hope we will hear from you soon. Do write me just a line. Don't tell me about the awful time you had at the airport, I want to hear that you are able to enjoy some of the minor pleasures of life.

His words went unheeded. The silver mountains and white world sparkling under the sun were too much for both of us. We were stunned and too weakened to respond – I found the delicious foaming cups of chocolate slightly sickening and I felt frightened all the time, especially when a tall bear (a man in a bearskin) put his arm around me for a photograph – Molly was frequently in tears. We were still lost and unable to enjoy or be distracted by such an exotic experience. At home, Molly wrote to Norah McGuinness and requested her not to send on the picture she had just finished of herself and Bobbie. She had a feeling that getting one's portrait done was a portent of death and that they should never have sat for this painting. For quite a time she banned all photographs of Bobbie. This was not as extreme as it would be today for then photographs were kept shut up in albums and had not yet become an intrinsic part of daily life. When summer came she turned away from foxgloves when she passed them on the roadside. The previous year she had been in love with them and picked them for her flower vases even though she had heard that it was unlucky to bring them indoors. She never allowed a foxglove inside her house again.

As well as a broken heart, there were practicalities and finances to be considered. Molly felt very poor with no strength to write her way out of it. A solution appeared through the state of British politics at the time. The election of a Labour government created a new form of refugee. The Conservative hunting English flooded into Ireland to escape Attlee's taxes, a possibly revolutionary regime and food rationing. They needed cream and beef and Georgian houses to rent or buy. Bill Scott arrived to hunt the West Waterford hounds. Molly sub-let Belleville to him and he and his wife Pamela became her friends. She herself moved into a wing of Cappoquin House, the home of Bobbie's cousin, Richard Keane, and his wife Olivia. Their children Vivien and Charles were slightly younger than me and we were close friends. During the war Richard had been dropped by parachute into Yugoslavia and was in charge of allocating supplies to the partisans. He had a very good brain and when peace came he was torn between working as a journalist in London and coming back to run his Irish estates. For many years he did both – making a profit on his farm when many others were going broke. Olivia was remarkable, beautiful and strong-minded with the original taste and colour sense of an artist. She adored houses and gardens and they were her art form.

Molly arrived at Ardavoo (as the wing of Cappoquin House was called) with a reduced household consisting of Bridget to cook, and Mary Ormond, a new maid. Mary was small, young and comely and she had grown up on the farm owned by the monks and managed by her father at the gate of Belleville. We children quickly fell in love with her but her presence was tinged with sadness for Molly. She had intended to take Sheila, her housemaid, with her. Of all the people working at Belleville, she was closest to Sheila. Both domestic perfectionists, they did things in a similar manner. They trusted one another and were real friends. Soon after Bobbie died, Sheila developed TB and together with most of her family perished from the plague which swept Ireland in the forties and fifties before the advent of antibiotics. Fostered by untested milk, coughing and poor housing, it devastated families, especially those living in cramped accommodation in the villages and towns. In privileged households such as ours boiled milk was *de rigueur* for children and because one was supposed to develop antibodies to one's usual milk source, when we went to parties in other Anglo-Irish houses we carried with us in a shoebag our own bottle of milk together with our dancing pumps decorated with small bronze rosettes and fastened with crossed-over elastic.

Molly described Sheila poignantly in both the past and present tense – 'She is slight and active, square shoulders and hips like apples on wire springs. Watching her cycling up hill, late for Mass, Paddy said Sheila is the best little cyclist we have on the place – that was on a sunny morning when we were all happy. We didn't know how happy. She was a great eater and had a natural taste for good food. She would eat pâté with garlic or game or food cooked with wine which the Irish usually detest, she could cook too very well but with such nervousness that it destroyed her. She was nervous in waiting at table and would flush and bite her lip and look so pretty with her little black head and its white bow at the back.'

Sheila's death so soon after Bobbie's deepened Molly's despair – she was not in a good state when we first came to Ardavoo. She planted her purple primula in a former ash pit at the back door. She had the mud and ashes cleared out and a trailer load of soil bought to create a very steep terrain rising above a small wall. Dressed in her working trousers and old riding coat, pale with tears streaking her cheeks, Molly dug furiously on this precipice while I stood at the bottom, hopelessly conscious of her grief and my own. It was rather a dark, tree-laden place in contrast to the sunny herbaceous border at Belleville with its background of rhododendron groves buzzing with bees where I had felt happy watching her gardening in the past.

Certain people gave her a lift. One of these was Georgie

O'Brien, a brilliant carpenter whose skills the Anglo-Irish jostled among themselves for. He has passed into literature through *The Village of Longing* written by his nephew, also called George O'Brien. She fetched him in the Ford Prefect to work on the wing and his intelligence and wit and rather Chekhovian conversation brought her a glimmer of hope on the beautiful road running beside the Blackwater from Cappoquin to Lismore which she had traversed frequently with Bobbie. About this time she wrote in her notebook: 'I drove past the dog-wood and the golden willows which I had passed so often in my times of complete happiness. I had the idea that it might be possible to look back on the brilliant past with some or all of the joy and expectancy with which we looked forward when young into the unknown future. Not to look back in sad longing and retrospect but with the tension and delight I knew when I hoped, but was unsure whether, I would marry Bobbie.'

She also found consolation through Elspeth, the young Swiss governess who replaced Nanny, and above all in her relationship with Virginia. A small child knows nothing about death and has no respect for grief. Virginia, a spirited three-year-old with a mass of wild curls, was bent on discovering life and dragging Molly along with her. Without Bobbie or Nanny there they were thrown into a new, intimate relationship. Later Molly said she regretted parting with Nanny soon after my father's death for my sake. I had loved her and I resented Elspeth as a result, but in the end even I warmed to her. She was tall and gentle with an Ingrid Bergman brow and golden hair and skin. Molly had an intense desire for us to speak French – I was attracted to the language from the beginning despite a textbook called *Madame Souris* which Elspeth and I struggled through together. When Bridget was out she cooked delicious suppers. The young men who visited Molly for drinks were keen to carry a cocktail into the kitchen for her. Julian Jameson, returning from watching her stuff fish with herbs, said 'Molly you are going to dine on trout and teardrops.' She had recently arrived and was homesick for her Swiss fiancé. She was engaged but when she was with us she fell in love with Willie Sargent. It was almost impossible not to be in love with Willie. He was dark and handsome with a mischievous smile. His family were prominent in Cappoquin and owned the garage at the foot of the hill below Cappoquin House. He rode a motorbike and had a magnificent tenor voice. Sometimes he drove us places when Molly didn't feel up to it and he would sing arias from *The Student Prince*, *Rose Marie* and other light operas. Molly adored his singing and she fostered his romance with Elspeth. It cheered her up, as romance always had. She described driving through Cappoquin and catching sight of Virginia devouring a packet of biscuits in her pram which was tied to the petrol pump, while inside the garage, her elbows on the counter and her blonde hair glittering in the gloom, Elspeth was deep in conversation with Willie. Eventually she did return to marry her young dentist in Switzerland. Willie yearned for her for a long time but, of course, he did find another girlfriend. Tragically before he could marry he was killed in a motorcycle rally. The whole neighbourhood was thrown into mourning.

Always a social being, Molly immersed herself in West Waterford society. Conscious that her passion for friendship had lapsed because of her relationship with Bobbie, she sought to rekindle it, telling herself that she must now court with her 'wit and nonsense' the friends she had liked well enough. 'I burn with gratitude to them for their love because without that I am nothing.' Her diaries reveal a frenzy of engagements. She went out and invited people back to intimate and large gatherings. She is comforted by a party she gave at Ardavoo – 'I enjoyed my party very much. The room looked lovely with the lilies and stripped Laurustinus and only the flowers lighted up. The food was perfect – small and cold when it should be and not when it shouldn't be. I was very free with the drink and they all drank like mad. Gracious, what a lot the quality drink and how nice they are when drunk. The expansion is such the room can hardly hold it. I was bunched and given words of love meaning nothing by men and women. I let Sally come down and hand things and she enjoyed it so much and was full of comments and said how nice I looked, and chose Pam Jackson out for kindness.'

This commentary encapsulates her attitude to parties, her belief that if one put together particular elements harmoniously a beneficial alchemy ensued. Like Mrs Ramsay in *To the Lighthouse* she felt that a microcosm of perfection was possible. Being Irish she respected alcohol and considered it a key factor (among others) in the unblocking of a short complete moment of happiness and a mood of love. When it was over and the room was empty again, she would sit back on the sofa and relish the brief after-effect. On the rare occasions when the magic failed and a party turned stiff or sour, she became very upset, convinced it was all her fault because she had not taken enough trouble to get it right.

Sometimes she attended a lawn meet followed by a

luncheon, tea, drinks and dinner one after the other, driving herself up and down the Blackwater Valley to different locations. Her diaries record many such days, one wonders how someone prone to exhaustion stood up to it but she was still quite young, in training and desperate for distraction. Always but particularly at this point she needed the warmth of friendship contained in the ritual and almost army discipline of social life; to have fun and to be fun you had to have your wits about you. It was unthinkable to be in tears during a poker game. There was nothing like a splendid gossip and a cocktail to shift you temporarily out of grief. If she broke down, as she occasionally did, she was mostly among friends who had loved Bobbie too. Usually her courage and good behaviour carried her through until she was in her car driving home. In her diary she wrote, 'My heart is sad and my body is alone.' She was sustained by the obligation to sparkle, by her noticing artist's eye, by the recurring pattern of giving and receiving hospitality and by the necessity of getting dressed up for it.

She was fascinated by clothes. She adored her dressmakers and made several close friends among them during her life. They were her trusted allies in her social campaigns. One of the consolations of Ardavoo was that her dressmaker of the time, Mrs Fraher, lived just beside the demesne wall at the top of a hill in the village. We children were less keen on dressmakers, standing for what felt like hours with outfits not chosen by oneself (sometimes horrid hand-me-downs from older children) being pinned on one, while our elders stood back and deliberated about hems and tucks and buttons. Mrs Fraher was the exception for us because she had a talking budgerigar. It shone pale blue in her dark parlour and had an amazing vocabulary. It cheered for the Cappoquin hurling team, swore in front of the priest, quoted poetry and trilled songs in Irish. Mrs Fraher drew the cage close to her face and with love in her eyes and soft tones coaxed it to begin speaking in its tiny computer-like voice. It seldom failed her. We were all enchanted, even Molly, who clutched pictures cut from *Vogue* and whose mind was teeming with ideas about the business in hand. Mrs Fraher's *pièce de résistance* was the remodelling of a black velvet Victorian gown which had once belonged to a great-aunt. It split into two halves. Molly wore the whole thing, including the décolleté bodice which flattered her slender figure, for hunt balls or exceptionally grand dinner parties such as those given by Bendor, Duke of Westminster, who had bought Fort William – the house where Bobbie grew up – and came there for the hunting. The magnificent skirt which swelled a little over the hips and fell into a small train at the back she wore frequently with a narrow thirties linen jacket given her by Adele.

I sat on her bed in my nightgown watching her transforming herself into the princess who went out in the evening. She struggled with the soft gold pins of antique brooches, her emerald daisy with its coral petals, her amber angel or her Greek lady cameo. The clasps were bendy and intractable and inclined to miss their catches causing her to swear and grimace as she peered into the dressing-table mirror. Once ready I could sense her anticipation of I knew not what. In a cloud of Chanel No. 5 she kissed me goodnight, leaving an imprint of lipstick on my cheek and forehead. I listened to her skirt rustling like leaves as she descended the stairs.

After her departure, I was supposed to return to my own

bed. Instead I ran downstairs to the kitchen. Bridget sat on an austere wooden chair telling her rosary beads or sometimes holding a rather heavy battery radio up to her ear, spinning a knob and trying to get it to speak up. Her big blue eyes lit up at the sight of me and she put down her beads or her radio at once. I drew up another chair opposite her so that I could look into her soft peach-coloured face framed by tendrils of silvery hair escaping from the kirby grips which anchored her chignon. She knew stories of all sorts, some terrifying ones about the exploits of the Black and Tans, but she did not tell those at night knowing that with my nervous disposition I wouldn't sleep at all after them. At this time, she mostly told stories about the saints. I loved these saints and grew to rely on them as she did. St Jude, the patron of impossible causes, St Blaise who cured sore throats and St Bernadette, the little Pyrenean shepherdess to whom Our Lady appeared, creating the healing cult of Lourdes. Once Molly turned back because she had forgotten something and caught us in the act. We stared at her guilt-stricken as she stood at the kitchen door in her evening dress. We both expected a terrific row but she only said we could finish the story for once, but we must promise never to do it again.

At this time, strangely enough, her sparkle was very high. When she entered a room in one of her original outfits, friends rushed up to talk to her. People wanted her because she made them laugh. Laughter – always a precious commodity (the currency of her world) – was particularly valued then when the war was still very close and so many terrible things had happened. The worst she could imagine had happened to her. She took consolation in laughter and gave it through it. In her depiction of certain characters (such as Eustace in *Treasure Hunt* or Wobbly Massingham in *Good Behaviour*) she saw the power to be amused in a certain way as an heroic gift.

Judging by *Treasure Hunt* her wit was the least barbed it ever was. She did not set it aside entirely but she employed her stiletto rather sparingly in this play. It reflects the kindness and understanding she herself was experiencing at the time she wrote it. In it, she sought to repay with laughter as she personally knew so well how to do in the safe houses that sheltered her. This was particularly true of Tourin and, in a different way, of Dromana, which stands on the opposite bank of the River Blackwater, perched on a high cliff, from which you can see Tourin, and beyond it the Knockmealdown Mountains and Mount Melleray Abbey. It stands at such a high point that you look down on the backs of the birds in flight. The river is still tidal there and changes every day from shining mud to majestic depths of flowing water. 'Dromana' means 'Hill of the Fairies'. The immediate entrance is mysterious, cut through tall rocks and sprouting trees and ferns and mosses that grow in shadows. Suddenly, in front of the house, there is a burst of river light. It is the most historic house on the Blackwater, permitted to pass by the female line; its family connections reach back to 1215 when it was a medieval castle. The Villiers-Stuarts who live in the house now acquired it through Barbara Villiers, the mistress of Charles II. Molly modelled the house in *Two Days in Aragon* on Dromana. Unlike Aragon, it remained unscathed throughout the Troubles. It is said to be haunted. Molly was very attracted to ghosts. She changed the character of Dromana's ghosts but was inspired by them in her novel.

When Molly came to live in West Waterford, Ion Villiers-Stuart owned the house. He was first married to Elspeth, an English beauty, but he lost this eccentric, original wife when she died as the result of a fall from her bicycle during the war. His second wife, Emily, was American. Her magnolia flower looks were combined with a very determined character. She brought with her Peter-Patrick, the child of her previous marriage to Lord Hemphill, and he and Ion's son James became brothers. Two only children, tossed about in an adult world, their friendship was a blessing to them both. Emmie loved them but she was quite strict and when they became young men she still treated them like children. They got into trouble with her for the usual youthful crimes, arriving late for dinner, driving too fast, going off with the cellar key in one of their pockets. They hid from Emmie's strictness at Belleville. If they wished to absent themselves they said they would be staying overnight with Molly. Usually they were, particularly when going rally driving, an activity that had to be screened from Emmie. Years later at James's funeral, Peter-Patrick said to me, 'We were two lost boys and she took us in.' Recovering from losses of their own they helped her in her loss. She was always sympathetic to youthful rebellion except when it hit Virginia and me, when she took it hard and was extremely hurt. In the case of other children, she struck a diplomatic balance between them and their parents. She particularly loved boys, chatting with them over a drink, treating them like grown-ups and making them feel fascinating and witty. Patrick Villiers-Stuart, a younger cousin of James's, said of her, 'Always and ever I give thanks to Molly for her generosity of spirit towards me as a gauche teenager. I found myself coming alive and sparkling in her encouraging presence. She would desert her sophisticated adult friends to spend time with me to make me scintillate.' Sons perhaps would have suited her better than daughters.

Ion died suddenly in February 1948. It was heartbreaking for Emmie. As soon as Molly heard the news, she went over to Dromana for a week. When a friend lost someone they loved, she dropped everything for them, children, writing, and her domestic and social affairs. It was a pattern throughout her life. The depth of her friendship was unfathomable on such occasions. It was a sort of vocation. She gave everything she had calmly, not emotionally: love and practical support, words and silence. She knew she possessed the gift of helping in these circumstances and she offered it with confidence and love. It made her feel needed and fulfilled but she understood when to stop, when to withdraw, her natural tendency to feel rejected absent. Many people have spoken to me of how she helped them in this way. It was the sweet fruit of her own bitter experience and a sort of exorcism of it. She who had run like a wounded deer from the sight of Bobbie's body, and from his funeral, went to Ion's room to say goodbye to him. 'Ion in bed, so pale, no colour at all except in his bluish fingernails. His dignity was complete, he even looked glamorous in his best pale blue pyjamas and he had that look of deep peace men have when they are asleep after an absolutely complete jump. Emmie had put the first primrose in his pocket ... '

In *The Rising Tide*, published in 1937, a year before her marriage, Molly writes at some length about widowhood. One of the main characters, Cynthia, despairs when her young husband Desmond is killed in the 1914–18 war. Unlike Molly in almost every way, she is rich, canny and confident, an English beauty who up until then has known nothing but enjoyment and success. Her youth is crowned by a brilliant marriage full of sexual ease and real friendliness. Suddenly stricken, she is 'like a person wilfully keeping herself half-anaesthetised. The final reality of being without him was more than she could endure ... but though she denied him, trying to save herself from pain, he was still so real to her that she dared not think of him.' It is devastation in a way that is prophetic of her own state in 1946. Eventually Cynthia succumbs to drink and a series of affairs with ever more unsuitable hunting gentlemen. For Molly drink was not an option because of her weak stomach. It never agreed with her except in judicious amounts. Love affairs were a more complex matter. Despite her approval of sex, her natural tendency to spoil men and to flirt recklessly, she found herself, perhaps for the first time in her life, rather reluctantly and to her view ungenerously saying 'no'. Poignantly she writes in her diary: 'I don't want to love unless it is serious enough to hurt me.'

In the end perhaps it was the Skrine grit which saved her. Again in collaboration with John Perry, she began a new play and working with her usual self-discipline threaded it into the rest of her busy life. She produced *Treasure Hunt*, a light-hearted piece from which her personal anguish is almost entirely absent. Her characters also came to her rescue. The love she was struggling to reawaken in herself through friendship is reflected in the zany people in *Treasure Hunt*. She perceives them with an ironic compassion and warmth. There is only one person she really hates in the play – Mrs Cleghorne-Thomas, inspired by a type she often clashed with in life, a smart, moneyed, slightly crass English lady. Her special brand of malice is there but restrained. Dirk Bogarde wrote an introduction to the novel she took from the play when it was reissued by Virago in 1990. He puts it thus: 'Fun is one of Mrs Keane's greatest gifts; mixed in with the very gentlest of seasonings; malice smothered with charm. Oh! Indeed. There is malice here; but you'll hardly know it, it's like garlic in a properly cooked dish.'

Treasure Hunt put life back into her. It opens with a funeral, that of Sir Roderick Ryall, a charming old rogue who has had a wonderful time spending all the family money and in so doing has given others and himself a lot of fun. Molly's own pain does not surface in her treatment of this funeral. The sense of life is all-pervading particularly in her characters, all of whom are brilliantly themselves. It is essentially a drawing-room comedy but her light touch is not superficial, it is always combined with an unspoken knowledge of her people's inner world.

Her chief character, Aunt Anna Rose, has been widowed long ago in a quite different way from herself. Her husband, an elderly Austrian Duke, opened the door instead of the window and fell out of the train on their honeymoon. It is possible that she, a young girl in an arranged marriage to a rich old boy, may have pushed him out into the snow herself. Afterwards Anna Rose returns home and retreats into an imaginary world. She travels a great deal in the sedan chair in the drawing-room; charming, still beautiful and elegantly dressed in the Edwardian fashions of her girlhood, she veers between childlikeness and wisdom. Molly's attitude to Anna Rose is revealing of her own personality. She has a real affinity with the Mad Aunts and other eccentrics in her work. Her masque is 'I am outside them observing them' but her heart is inside them, agreeing with them.

She was very conscious of how we slip in and out of childhood and grown-upness – Irish people are prone to doing this. It is a trait that either enchants or infuriates the English as it does the paying guests in the play. Molly had grown up with her Aunt Lou and Aunt May and she understood 'their grip to the last on the pretences which supported them'. Anglo-Irish society as a whole was very polite about such things. It was bad form not to be, and this respect for fantasy went through all classes. Even the disapproving family solicitor who arrives to read 'darling Roddy's' will full of generous legacies with no funds to support them, takes out of his briefcase a few travel brochures he has collected to inspire Aunt Anna Rose on her sedan chair journeys. Everyone joins in her world ostensibly to protect her but also to protect themselves and by so doing they release in themselves sympathy, playfulness and a sense of joy that breaks down the barriers of good behaviour and brings into being a mutually beneficial imaginative reality.

The timing of *Ducks and Drakes* had been disastrous for a London audience on the edge of the Blitz, but the opposite was so with *Treasure Hunt*. English people didn't seem to mind any more about the Irish refusal of the use of their ports. Bogarde describes going to the play in 1949: 'I saw it myself, all those years ago (1949 to be exact), and have never forgotten the sheer hysteria of that audience before a cast of dotty, beguiling grotesques. The play was as full of stars as the heavens, and a British audience, exhausted, despondent, rationed, taxed and still recovering from a savage war with all its terrors and deprivations, welcomed it with roars of delight.'

Time is very important within the play itself. It is concerned with a revolutionary clash of generations. Full of fun and charm and selfishness, Consuelo and Hercules are of the old order. They belong to the people who genuinely believe that it is always cheaper to stay at the Ritz in the end. Faced now, for the first time, with economising, they put their heads together and generously offer to give up champagne and English race meetings until things come right. It is impossible for them to see that their way of life is the problem and that it will never be the same again. The second war has finally finished what the first one had begun. The sheltering hedonism of the twenties and thirties is no longer retrievable. The younger people, Consuelo's daughter Veronica and her nephew Phillip, perceive a different reality. They are a new sort of Anglo-Irish person prepared to work with the same energy with which their elders played. Phillip, back from the war, knows he must face another sort of battle to hold onto the battered eighteenth-century house and the romantic landscape he has just inherited. His dream and his necessity are to haul them out of debt and (revolutionary idea) to make them pay their way. He is sympathetic to his elders. He is of the culture. His idea of a treat is a day in the snipe bogs and a glass of champagne at the end of it. It is not natural to him to act like a schoolmaster. He loves Hercules and Consuelo for their sense of fun, but he sees the new reality as an inspiration rather than a loss. To him farming is not something that goes on in the background of a busy sporting calendar. It is one's work and purpose in life. He thinks longingly about tractors and milking machines and other thrilling expensive innovations just as his elders think about a glorious day at Ascot or ordering a basket of plover's eggs at the Berkeley.

Elizabeth Bowen described the Anglo-Irish as being 'sustained by style'. The change of style involved in the notion of paying guests was appalling to Hercules and Consuelo. It is an affront to the lavish hospitality they have always offered for free and it is also, as Molly used to say, 'about letting in the gypsies'. In attempting to control the excesses of their elders, Veronica and Phillip become the adults, as often happened with children born in the twenties and thirties. Sybille Bedford's book *Jigsaw* is the classic account of this situation. Then there is the question of the servants. The naughty old things certainly don't want to share the servants because they nanny them and enable them to live like the spoilt children they have never ceased to be. There are three of them and each has their special adoptee in the family. Mrs Guidera, the cook, adores Consuelo, and they have created many beautiful meals together, swimming in cream and brandy. Bridget is an amateur herbalist and healer and she nurses Herky's aches and pains and runs after him with his gumboots in case he gets his feet wet. Willie, the house boy, takes care of Anna Rose, putting hot-water bottles in the sedan chair and sometimes bringing her to the pictures on the back of his motorbike as both are devotees of the Jungle films. All three of them are passionate about their particular favourite and they fight with each other and against the world for their interests. They are among the last era of servants like this, united with the family and the house as much as with their own lives. They are dignified, sure of their footing, not bullied in the least; full players in the politics of the whole thing. There is reality and affection in their attitude to their bosses combined with an acceptance and enjoyment of the general madness. The relationship is very unmodern, based as it is on a deep co-dependency, but there is a mutual sense of fun and respect in it.

When Dirk Bogarde asked Anne Leon, who had played Veronica, for her impression of the show, she said, 'Oh! What a joy it was, every single performance, and what a dear little darling Molly was. So sweet, so funny, so gentle with us all, but, and it's a *big* but, she was on the ball all the time and very much in evidence. Golly! How we all loved her. *How* we laughed.'

He himself comments, '"Dear little darling Molly" is as sharp as a box of knives, and her work is here to prove it.' He is right, of course, but her sharpness is combined with pity for each of her characters' plight. Eustace Mills, the English paying guest, is a subtle, joyous person. He is one of her angels of light. He and Aunt Anna Rose almost fall in love. As an outsider he sees Veronica and Phillip's predicament more clearly than they do themselves and he is determined to help them. Bridget loves him and in a small betrayal actually lends him Herky's gumboots. His heart is enchanted by this new world he has stumbled upon while, at the same time, his shrewd head notes the pitfalls. His tendency to see life as funny is redemptive. Humour in Molly's writing has many nuances. It could be spiked and mean and it could be blessed like holy water. She felt that people such as Eustace were slightly miraculous. On a personal level, it was one of the few virtues she ever gave herself credit for. When trying to fight her way through bouts of despair and guilt she would console

herself by saying, 'Thank God for giving me the power to see things as funny.' Dirk Bogarde concludes his introduction with a trumpet blast to the reader: 'You have in your hands, at a reasonable price, the work of a Master Writer, although I am pretty sure she'd scoff at such a high falutin' description of herself. But go ahead: step into wonderland and you'll see that I am right.'

Treasure Hunt turned out to be a sort of wonderland for Molly herself. The hard labour of writing it lifted her out of grieving and rewarded her once again with the alchemy of success. Fear retreated and she was restored to her best self. On a basic level money worries vanished for a time and she was able to indulge without guilt the natural generosity which was prerequisite to her sense of wellbeing. She loved working with John Gielgud. She was inclined to put him on a pedestal – something he never wished for – but rehearsals brought reality into their relationship. He had a habit at the end of the day of indicating a scene and saying, 'We must have a funny line here.' She would sit up half the night and bring him the new dialogue next morning. He would read it over and comment in his rapid way of talking with its sublime echoes of the Terry voice, 'Is that a funny line dear? Not very funny dear.' Nevertheless they were real comrades and he often spoke of her diligence and what a pleasure it was to work with her.

Molly made a new friend in Gladys Cobb who was the wardrobe mistress in the production, assistant to the designer Tanya Moiseiwitsch. She was one of the backstage theatrical people who contribute so much to the substance of a play. Molly was delighted by Gladdie's understanding and fleshing out of her characters in the subtle way she clothed them. Herky's shabby exquisitely cut jackets, Aunt Anna Rose's romantic Edwardian tweeds, Mrs Cleghorne-Thomas's sweeping, arrogant smartness. Gladdie was shy and retiring, but like most perfectionists she was a strong character. She invited Molly to her home to meet her elderly husband, Peter, a charming old-fashioned person who for special occasions wore a Gloire de Dijon rose in his buttonhole. Her flat was beautiful, created by her artist's eye from the antique shop gleanings of many plays on tour and of Chelsea where she lived. Objets d'art and pictures and elegant original pieces of furniture gleamed against the dark colours of the walls. Molly relaxed there in interludes of ease and fun after the effort of rehearsals. She and Gladdie empathised with one another's romanticism and domesticity, and courageously concealed nervousness. They both knew what it was to struggle with an oversensitive nature and a determination to be successful in a tough world, and they were mutually somewhat damaged by it. Later on I too became close to Gladdie. I took refuge in her flat; we went to museums and theatres together and she made me my first grown-up dresses. She was a genius at sewing and when she sat down at her machine on its wrought-iron stand, this gentle person suddenly turned into a dictator, but she was always right in these matters.

Binkie gave *Treasure Hunt* a glittering cast from major to minor. Some of the best actors of the time were in it, among them Alan Webb, Marie Lohr, Irene Brown and Milo O'Shea. Sybil Thorndike was Anna Rose and Lewis Casson her husband played Eustace. They were a remarkable couple; sort of royalty of the stage, they were also communists. You would not have guessed this from meeting Sybil. A queenly person, famous for serious, classical roles, she succeeded in evoking with a light touch Anna Rose's panache and vulnerability. John Gielgud had to struggle with her queenly side. Molly said, 'he lifted her performance until the fun became airborne'. I remember the kindness of her huge aquamarine eyes edged in kohl as she bent to kiss me, still wearing her stage hat with its white bird and long gossamer veil. It was my first visit to the theatre. We went backstage where we were assailed by the exotic comforting aroma of painted boards as we stepped in the semi-darkness across lengths of lighting cable to reach the dressing rooms. Everyone we met embraced Molly after her absence. One was struck by the atmosphere of peace and friendliness and glamour in theatre people at that particular moment at the end of a performance when they are emerging from the tent of their creative edifice into the everyday world.

Molly stayed at Lord North Street for the rehearsals of *Treasure Hunt*. The last time she had been there was during the terrible days of Bobbie's illness when she had often rushed out of the house to pray in the beautiful ruin of the recently bombed eighteenth-century church on Smith Square, which is mentioned disparagingly by Dickens in *Our Mutual Friend*. Binkie and his entourage sustained her (and other Irish visitors) in good and bad times, and for many years his house was her home in London. John Perry lived next door at No. 15. Binkie's high, elegant house was dominated by a staircase supported on one side by walls hung in Impressionist paintings. The downstairs loo was papered in framed photographs of actors and actresses exotic in costume and lovingly inscribed to Binkie. The bathroom had a soft carpet which drank in one's footprints when one stepped out of a perfumed bath. It was tremendously unlike most Anglo-Irish bathrooms with their bare boards and hissing pipes. The spare room beds were covered in antique patchwork quilts worked in frail bright silks. Breakfast was brought to one's bedside, eggs and bacon and toast and Lapsang souchong tea. Later, when Virginia and I accompanied Molly to London, she would anxiously instruct us not to break the Sèvres china when we poured the delicious smoky tea into our cups. She felt that being in Binkie's exotic, civilised home was an education and a privilege for us, and she urged us to notice the paintings and the beautiful objects.

Jack Osbourne was the chauffeur in this household. He was a person of integrity, wit and brilliant common sense. His head was unturned by ferrying the stars from place to place in a Rolls Royce. He heard but never repeated what they said when they unburdened themselves to Binkie in the back seat. Molly, among others, confided in Jack himself. He understood anxiety although he did not seem to suffer from it personally and his calm was uplifting.

Elvira, the Italian cook, ruled Lord North Street. She was quite fierce and tough, and people were somewhat afraid of her. Diminutive in stature, she wore cherries as earrings in summer, and cotton dresses, once the uniform of Italian village ladies, that were like a cross between an apron and a frock. In winter, she put woollen English cardigans on top of these garments. She always had a string of corals around her neck. Her cooking was brilliant. She took advice from a stockbroker friend of John Perry, and invested her earnings advantageously. She was probably very generous to them, but she was always complaining about her relations in Italy blood-sucking her money. Her dog

Hamlet, a schnauzer, was so fierce that no one dared enter the kitchen unless Elvira was there to subdue him. She was full of self-confidence and she admired success, but was not at all in awe of the famous people she met. Binkie and she were mutually devoted. He often summoned her at the end of dinner, so that guests could thank her for her sublime food. When he was alone, she sat up to talk with him for hours. He drank steadily while she sipped a small glass of port. They respected, even admired, the grain of ruthlessness in each other. Molly sent over Josephine, who had worked for her at Belleville, to help Elvira. She was tall and warm and natural, and not at all ruthless. When she got married she was followed by Anna, who was the opposite sort of Italian to Elvira, being a soft, Madonna-like beauty of infinite gentleness. Both Josephine and Anna, who worked closely with her (the latter for many years), were extremely fond of Elvira, although they often had to mend fences on her behalf. Molly said, 'The night my husband died, Elvira looked after me like a saint and a nurse.' She never forgot this but in ordinary times she found Elvira's tough approach unsettling if she was feeling low and insecure herself. In good times, they got on very well, drawn together by cooking. They were perhaps at their closest when *Treasure Hunt* was a hit. Elvira always kept up to date on the box office receipts of every H. M. Tennent show. In a letter to Molly after her return to Ireland she wrote: 'I hear the play is absolutely full every night ... I have not had the pleasure of seeing it ... I will have to wait for a slack time.'

She goes on to say that there are no raisins available in the market and she can find only one gram of currants. She asks Molly to send her a parcel of these fruits for her Christmas

cake. Although the war had ended three years before, rationing still prevailed. Molly posted provisions to friends. Currants
were quite suitable for posting through the mail but parcels
of butter, which at one point she sent on a weekly basis to
her friend May Ainsworth, seem rather less so. Elvira's letter,
written in nearly impeccable English in an elegant flourished
script, ends with an Italian accent: 'Are you write more
play ... or just have rest for a while?'

Molly's idea of a rest was to forget writing entirely and
plunge into lavish cooking.

Binkie, in a letter written on 4 October 1949, warns her
against too much largesse: 'Well, the Apollo is really packed
out. Last week £2,450 – so you should be a very happy girl,
as well as a very clever one. All are happy and enjoying the
packed houses. So may it go on and on – but mind you build
up a fine fat "rainy day" account before you start pouring gin
down all the chums' throats.'

Of course she paid no attention. Luxuries such as little
pots of caviar brought back from Fortnum's (London was not
entirely bereft of supplies) began to appear at her dinner table,
accompanied by fairy toast laboriously prepared by herself as
she did not trust Bridget or anyone else to cut it thin enough.

John Gielgud wrote in a different vein: 'I couldn't be more
entranced at the wonderful success of the play. It was the
good luck of the cooking (omelette-like) good cooks, good
things inside, and happy timing. Thank you for all your helpfulness and sweetness at the rehearsals. I expect you heard
Queen Mary went to the night before last. When they were
presented, Sybil talked so much none of the others could get
a word in edgeways ... '

This affectionate, gossipy letter, written in a minute, slanted script, was typical of him and displays him as the true artist he was, with a simple unglossy attitude to his craft. To Molly the theatre was a sort of dream place; to him it was everyday life, and he understood its nuances without illusion. When they worked together, he always spoke about her diligence, her helpfulness. Without saying so, he recognised the artist in her, and he nurtured that side of her, and that was what she needed most to flourish. Gina Pollinger did the same thing years later when she became her literary agent.

In the year of the triumph of *Treasure Hunt* we moved out of Ardavoo and back to Belleville. Bill Scott found himself in conflict with the Irish farmers across whose lands he hunted. It was a critical time in Ireland for an Englishman in such a position. He decided to abandon the anguish and return to Britain, where, apart from high taxes on the rich, the revolution was not really materialising. He very kindly gave back the remainder of his ten-year lease of Belleville to Molly. There was a reason for this. One night, returning late from a party, she had found the middle gates on the avenue at Cappoquin House locked. She abandoned her car and in her Victorian velvet skirt and high heels climbed the gate and walked up the hill. Soon afterwards the Scotts with friends returning from dinner with Molly discovered the gates locked in the reverse direction. Bill, being a Master of Foxhounds, always carried wire-cutting equipment in his car, so he broke the lock and next day sent it back to Richard in a kind of declaration of war. At first, Molly, feeling strong at the time, quite enjoyed the drama, but it was a dangerous game with bad repercussions which went on for years. Richard requested her to leave. She agreed to do so on condition that he reimbursed her for the renovation of the wing which had been the original agreement between them. He no longer felt obliged to do this, presumably believing it was all part of the rent. He tried to freeze her out. Vivien and Charles were no longer encouraged to play with me. When I went to find them in one of our accustomed trysting places in the bamboos or the rhododendrons, they would not be there, or they would seem different. Sometimes, of course, we forgot the quarrel of our elders and behaved as normal, plunging into our secret houses in the undergrowth, but I began to meet them much less. Molly was asked not to go personally to buy vegetables from the kitchen garden (she was extremely friendly – perhaps too friendly – with Michael, the head gardener) but to send her cook instead. She must at no time appear in the courtyard. It was as though they were trying to make her invisible, something she was a particularly bad subject for.

The situation simmered on, fuelled by the past pain, tribulations and misunderstandings of everyone involved. Later the problem set up ripples that continued for decades as a family row in a small community can. Richard and Olivia and Molly would turn their heads and not speak if they happened to arrive at the same cocktail party simultaneously. Nobody invited them together to small gatherings any more. Molly's social side hated unpopularity of any sort. More than that, her heart was wounded; this was Bobbie's family and his grandfather's house rejecting her. It brought back the feeling of leperdom which she had experienced at school, combined now with widowhood, and being the poor relation of the big house in the classic Jane Austen sense. Molly was a hot person, and coldness drove her wild. In her diary, she wrote: 'How deadly cold I feel in the moonlight of Olivia's jealousy and dislike, and now impotent to stir out of Richard's crazy disfavour.' It was a case of a very emotional person in conflict with people who were much less emotional. Her sharpness and bons mots (probably most unhelpful under the circumstances) hardly dented the armour and boomeranged back to her. Molly definitely suffered – sometimes she was the independent lion, and sometimes the helpless widow. Many mutual friends were sympathetic to her in private, but few took her side openly in public. Nobody wants to get involved in family row over money. She had a certain sense of betrayal over this. She was furious with Dood and Kid Godfrey, a pair of sisters, sharp-witted domestic queens, brilliant poker players and gardeners, who sided with Richard, and stopped talking to Molly. She took what some saw as a petty revenge on them when she put them as the Crowhurst twins pretty well undisguised into *Good Behaviour*. Both were dead by then, but it was painful for their relatives and friends.

Her brother Godfrey, now a practising solicitor, prepared a case against Richard, who settled on the edge of its going to court. Moneywise, things were arranged, but in human terms they remained in prolonged and bitter disarray. Resolvement occurred almost twenty years later, after *Good Behaviour*, when Molly was once again on the crest of a wave. Both sides were in the mood to make peace. Molly felt strong enough to do so and she was greatly helped by the Keane children, Charles and his younger brother David (not even born when the trouble began). They and their wives and children gradually became enchanted with Molly and she with them.

In her declining years when Molly seldom left home, Richard frequently visited her. They would sit on the sofa side by side holding cups of Earl Grey tea and conversing animatedly. It was a sight I had never expected to see. When one looks back on such small wars, they seem trivial in the extreme, but in the cramped theatre of West Waterford's intense social scene, their pain impinged almost daily and with cruelty on someone of Molly's volatile sensibility. As Chekhov said of the Russian bourgeoisie, 'Their grievances are trivial, but their suffering is profound.'

At the time she was going through the acute stage of this upheaval Molly was consoled and sustained by the Scotts. Her relationship with them was unorthodox. She had a brief affair with Bill and a long friendship with his wife, Pam; such apparently incompatible circumstances were to some extent a pattern in her life and not so unusual in her milieu. Bill resembled a Master of Hounds in one of her books. Hunting was his *raison d'être* but he was a man of passion in other ways too. He had many affairs. He was frequently followed around by what his wife called 'a bevy of sporting gals'. He had enchantment. Pam wrote to Molly, 'They don't see he's got a purple face and a stomach, they just think he is It. And as for me, they don't see me at all, they just gallop over me.' Molly very much did see Pam, and benefited from her strength and wit and sense of reality. The affair with Bill cheered her. He was passionate, easily bored and responsive to clever wooing, just what she needed at the time. He took her to restaurants in London, and when she mentioned she was allergic to oysters, he refused them too. 'My dear, the only point in eating oysters is to have them together.' He was romantic. She laughed at him about his tendency to talk forever about the breeding of foxhounds, but she respected him for it. To her also the chase was sacred. He came to dinner with her alone before she left Ardavoo and showed her a fox bite on his hand. She was thrilled by the paradox of his wildness, his closeness to nature and his Cavalry Club smartness. The night of the fox bite he said he had brought his wound to George Healy (the much loved chemist in Cappoquin) 'who had poured on wine and oil'. He had a poetic, biblical way of talking. He gave Molly a present of a beautiful Bible, gilt-edged and bound in blue leather. It was by her bed when she died, the places marked by children's drawings and photographs that were precious to her. For years she read a passage from it every night. Like all Skrines, she had a deep-rooted inclination to pursue God and to feel pursued by Him. The fact that this bible was given her by a glamorous lover was important because it overcame her early resistance to Ballyrankin Calvinism and memories of dust-ups with her Aunts during family prayers and caused her to start reading the scriptures again.

Bill was very emotional when things went wrong. He fell into depression, drank too much and turned to Pam for help. He appealed to her also when feeling bored with a girlfriend, or tormented by hostile Irish landowners. I remember Pam on a summer evening while I played with her daughter, Maxine. She was pruning a high shrub at Belleville, and though she was tall she had to stretch up to do it. She was dressed in a 'New Look' yellow tweed suit, with a waisted jacket and a skirt almost to the ground. It was a total change of fashion and it was the first time I had seen anyone dressed like that. She had a low, plummy voice and a beautiful lipsticked mouth. Molly admired how capable she was, and how versatile. She could sort out a home-killed pig, or dress up and be the belle of the ball with an equal sense of enjoyment. She understood the social game, and was never rattled by it, as Molly could be. She loved a game of poker, or what she referred to as 'prattle, a nip and a laugh' with a friend by the fire. This appealed to Molly as did her ability to deal with adversity. Soon after their return to England she wrote:

'Bill seedy and depressed and in throes of worst financial crisis he has yet had. A shock when the hammer falls. I've sacked my best daily maid and moved the Frigidaire into the kitchen and got the gardener to distemper it primrose to help our morale, and am now feeling better again. Bill is so seedy that a quiet life with me whipping up omelettes suits him well . . . I fear we're going to get dreadfully dull, and when he is well again he will want to go gay in London and hunt madly instead of doing his own horse at home and collecting the eggs, while my big entertainment is patching his underpants and frying garlic.'

In another letter, she chides Molly about getting on with the novel of *Treasure Hunt*: 'Mol dear you must get cracking with your writing. Naughty girl, your book will only just catch Xmas selling if you work hard now, and if you leave it longer everyone will have forgotten who you are.'

Molly did not usually take to this sort of lecture, but she accepted it from Pam. In June 1950, she writes: 'How sweet of you Mol dear to say you are mad about the Mainsail domestic details. No wonder the fatal Irish charm is famous. Three subjects before the war considered the end of boredom were servants, children and operations and now look at us. And we are so interested and you at least belong to the intelligentsia ...'

Molly preserved many of Pam's funny, stalwart letters – they are fascinating in their picture of a rich lady adjusting philosophically to social change. After 1945, life would never be the same for the leisured people whose work was play. The British upper class did not come to an end (as some of them feared they would at the onset of socialist government) but they were obliged to find a new way of doing things.

We returned to Belleville in 1949 – Bobbie was dead and, despite this, Molly felt safe going back, convinced the house would take care of her. Belief in the sheltering spirit of place was very strong in the attitude of Anglo-Irish people to their houses. This was to them a reciprocal relationship of the heart, and which included something undefined, even supernatural. It is a constant theme of Molly's work, of Elizabeth Bowen's and of others'. The spirit of Belleville was welcoming, the unpretentious square eighteenth-century rooms husbanded only benign ghosts. The house creaked consolingly at night, and smelt of old polished wood. We did not live there quite as before. Molly left the huge sunlit bedroom she had shared with Bobbie and moved closer to us in the darker nursery quarters. The drawing-room was only opened up for parties. The hall became the sitting room because of its proximity to the kitchen. Pam had papered it in yellow Regency stripes. Molly indulged in two dark pink velvet chaise longues with soft wool rugs to throw over oneself if necessary. She felt prosperous enough to give run to three of her favourite occupations, interior decorating, lending money to people who needed it and giving parties.

She cultivated old and new friends. Chief among the new ones was Penelope Hamilton. When she was divorced by the man she loved, she had come to keep house for her uncle, Sir George Colthurst, at Blarney Castle (home to Ireland's most famous tourist attraction, the Blarney Stone). She was elegant and imaginative. This friendship had very good repercussions for me because Penelope had a daughter, Adrian, and she and I became close friends. Our relationship did more than anything else to lift me out of melancholy because, even at the early age of seven, Adrian was one of the funniest people in the world, and one of the most companionable. We talked endlessly and shared when we were together the real world and an imaginary world which we were always changing according to our wish. In adulthood, Adrian became very beautiful but when we met the only intimations that this would happen were her gold-coloured skin and long blue eyes. Penelope liked to dress her in frocks smocked by some nuns in Cork – very pretty in themselves, they were slightly at odds with Adrian's tallness and tomboyishness. In different ways, we had lost our fathers, and we romanticised them. Mine was a fairy prince who had ridden away for ever, and hers she seldom met except at very long intervals when he took her out to flirtatious lunches and filled her head with dreams.

Our mothers recognised that we needed each other, and made an academic arrangement for us so that we shared a governess and spent alternate terms in each other's homes. Mrs Brock owes a lot (not quite everything) to one of our governesses who knitted intricately, played the piano loudly when distressed and hid things in order to find them clairvoyantly.

Soon after returning to Belleville, Molly developed back

trouble and had to go to hospital in Dublin. It was an agonising slipped disc and none of the treatments worked until
she ended up with an osteopath called Dr Kevin O'Flanagan,
who cured her. From then on, she lived in a certain amount
of fear of her back. Every morning she lay on the floor and
faithfully did the exercises that Dr O'Flanagan had recommended. For years she returned to him if she got twinges.
He had been a famous footballer and now, in his professional
capacity, he travelled with the Irish team. Brilliant at his job,
he was kind and charming; he became one of her icons and
a friend. She nearly always had a special relationship with
doctors. They were father figures. This was especially true of
Dr Robert Wilson, who had failed to fix her back, although he
helped her with many other problems over the years. He was a
Northerner, sensible and humorous. She laid her fears before
him, and he knew which to take seriously and which to laugh
at. They talked about the world, and gossiped about people as
well as about health. It was a very creative, time-consuming
form of doctoring that would be unlikely to occur today. It
was immensely helpful to Molly who was prone to anxiety,
especially about the health of those she loved.

She stayed in Dublin for nearly two months. I was at
Blarney and Virginia was sent to some rather Protestant
friends who teased her about the pale pink rosary beads she
carried everywhere with her. This was a gift from Brother
Gerard, a Cistercian monk from Mount Melleray who had
made it himself. He, too, was a new friend. Adrian and I had
brought him into our lives. Adrian had received a present of
a statue of the Madonna, such as those one saw in shrines all
over the country. She was dressed in a dazzling blue robe and

a white veil that fell in Gothic plaster folds, and she stood on snakes and roses. We set about making a church for her out of a small laurel grove in a vaguely cruciform shape in the wood at Belleville. We scraped back the leaf mould to make paths, and made pews of moss and stones, all architecturally one-dimensional, as if we were drawing on the ground. It was a lot of work which absorbed us for weeks. One morning we looked up from our labour to see a figure approaching, dressed in working boots and thick stockings, and carrying in the skirt of his habit some massive white stones. He came every day for about a week, bringing more crystal rocks off the mountain which he built into a cave to protect our Virgin from the weather. He had heard of our activities, and felt that they should be encouraged. He became a lifelong friend of Molly's and of all of us. There was something exotic in that more religious and more religiously segregated age about the monk to the Protestant and vice versa. The attraction of Brother Gerard went much deeper than that. He was a truly loving person who had conquered his own demons, and most things in life made him laugh. The harsh aestheticism of the order when he entered (it was said on the run from the Black and Tans) had matured and not broken him. He was eloquent and adored talking. When Molly asked him how he managed in a silent order, he said, 'The first ten years were the worst.' Full of energy when we met him (he died many years later, clear-headed and just short of his hundredth birthday), he was patient and gentle. He wanted everyone in the world to be a Catholic but it didn't worry him or prevent him from loving them if they were not.

My brother-in-law, Kevin Brownlow, corresponded with

him for years and was devoted to him, even though he himself was strictly agnostic. He often worked on one of the monastery farms which was beside Belleville, and Virginia and Adrian and I drove around in his van or tractor-trailer with him. Luckily, in our case, this was before anyone had heard of abuse scandals. Today the unusual and beneficial friendship we had with him would not be possible.

Molly went on holiday in June 1950 to the South of France – Binkie and John had rented a house there. They went swimming at the glamorous Eden-Roc and the warm seas benefited her back. She came home pale honey-coloured and in very good spirits. Noel Coward was also staying with 'the boys' and she was thrilled to meet him. His nickname was 'The Master' and he was a maestro of the sort of comedy she aspired to. His powers of concentration were prodigious and he could turn out plays in a few weeks, several of which have become classics. She longed to be more like him, to write more plays that made it to production on a frequent basis, but she did not have his engine, nor was she a child of the theatre as he was. Critics sometimes compared them and this, when it happened, delighted her. On this holiday they had a delightful, flirtatious relationship. They never became close friends but they kept in touch, and whenever they met they got on well. She liked to quote his great line about death – 'Do try and remember grief is no more durable than happiness.' She mentioned his way of ' ... giving one the feeling that he enjoyed one ... only once when both were in the sea at Eden-Roc he did say "dear Veuve" (so much nicer a word than widow) "I am devoted to you but nothing can make me swim beside you to the raft while you are doing that Margate breast stroke."' It was the only stroke she knew ... She kept all his Christmas cards, in which he wrote her affectionate notes addressed to 'Darling Veuve'. His recognition of her talent was a lasting encouragement to her. He also recommended on a practical level, the dictionary of synonyms. Molly thought, because of her Skrine Calvinism, that getting words from a reference book instead of out of the labour of your head was a kind of cheating, but when Noel Coward sanctioned it she acquired a *Roget's Thesaurus* and, in desperation, sometimes used it.

France always suited her. After *Spring Meeting*, Molly and Bobbie had also been on holiday in the South of France, staying with John Gielgud at Grasse. After Molly's death, he mentioned this visit, among other memories of her, in a letter he wrote to Denise Long, who had requested information from him as she was embarking on a PhD about Molly's writing:

'Shy and modest – surprised, I think, at her own cleverness – straight-forward, witty, quietly observant, originally gifted, congenial and appreciative. What a wonderful friend, my long friendship with her right back to the early twenties never faltered, though she was only a visitor to England from time to time. But she belonged intrinsically to her Irish background, so of course her books and plays owe much of their charm to her home and early life in Tipperary when she evoked so well her childhood surroundings, the race meetings, hunt balls and family life ... She wrote with apparent ease and fluency, but I doubt if at first she had little expectations of interesting a very big public, certainly not the tremendous popularity of her work which suddenly came to her after her husband's death, so sudden and unexpected. This was a great surprise and delight to her as she grew older. Just before the war I was lucky enough to have her as my guest at a villa I had rented in the South of France, when her plays *Spring Meeting* and *Treasure Hunt*, both of which I directed, were both successful in London, and we were able to see more of one another, and wrote affectionate letters to one another.

'During her visit to Grasse she recounted a charming anecdote when the local maid who did her room suddenly looked very sad, and being asked by Molly what the matter was, announced ruefully. "Ah Madame, les années filent si vite, si vite" – a remark which I often cherish in memory of a dear and brilliant friend whom I remember so devotedly.'

He understood her as a person and as an artist as she, when she did not treat him as an icon, did him. She wrote at once to support him when he stumbled into his version of an Oscar Wilde scandal. He was on tour with *A Day by the Sea*, when he went alone to Chelsea police court to answer a summons for soliciting. He was not imprisoned as he could have been at that time before the Wolfenden Report, only fined. He returned to the play that evening, and it was not until the next day that the story broke in the newspapers, and caused an immense scandal. Binkie refused to close down the production, although he was advised to do so. Gladdie Cobb was with the company, and she said that everyone was very frightened. She described how Binkie requested Lewis Casson, the actor who entered after John, to walk onto the stage alongside him so that he would not be alone. They were expecting rotten eggs or even stones to be thrown. Gladdie said John gave a calm and beautiful performance and that at the curtain call he was received with prolonged applause, not just for his acting. A sense of British fair play came to the rescue that evening.

He wrote to Molly from the Adelphi Hotel in Liverpool on 30 October 1953:

Dearest Moll,

What a sweet letter you wrote me. I loved it – so like you. It has been utter hell, but John and Binkie and all my dear friends have supported me with such incredible loyalty and sweetness. I can never repay them except by justifying their faith in me with good work and exemplary behaviour for the future. I hope I'll never forget what I've been through for I am sure that's what it is meant to teach me and pretty bloody at that. Would so love to see you. Are you ever coming over again? Avanti, with that new play and fondest love to you.

As ever, John.

The simplicity and honesty of this letter is characteristic of him. He was my godfather but I never knew him very well. Sometimes my mother would take me to lunch with him in his house at Cowley Street. He would do his best to converse with me but I was aware that Molly was longing for me to say something original and I was consequently stiff and shy. My older impression of him is that, in an unorthodox way, he possessed purity of heart, perhaps more so than anyone I have met, and this contributed to the luminous quality of his acting. Molly wrote of his 'embracing appreciation of other people's work' and said that 'he was valiant in failure and modest after success, deprecating his part in it'. His modesty was amazing. I remember his being asked by Russell Harty in a radio interview which he considered his best performance. Instead of referring to one of his famous leading roles such as Hamlet or Richard of Bordeaux, he answered in his quick way: 'I think I'm best at prigs and bores.' He disliked what he called 'unbalanced adulation' and the reverence with which he came to be treated in old age, and to combat it he said, 'Most of my friends think I am terribly silly.' In a way that was true, but his silliness, if it can be so called, was that of the holy fool.

James Villiers-Stuart was living by himself at Dromana when he became engaged. Emily, his bride, came to stay, and he asked Molly to be their chaperone. In fifties Anglo-Ireland this custom was still as *de rigueur* as it was in the pages of Jane Austen. Molly, with her empathy for lovers, was ideal in the role. Emily remembers her as being full of vitality and gossip during dinner, but immediately it was over she was suddenly stricken with exhaustion and said she must retire immediately. She would then disappear to her room somewhere far off in the vast house, leaving them alone.

As this story demonstrates, there is no doubt that Molly was in good form and was having fun post-*Treasure Hunt* and her return to Belleville. The loss became an underground river for us both – certainly for me. I didn't mention my father because I didn't want to make Molly cry. I began to suffer from nightmares and to transfer myself into Molly's bed at all hours of the night. I was very fearful. There were tramps in those days who called at intervals to certain houses on their route. One came to the door, and I went with Bridget to answer his ring. She passed me a shilling, and I gave it to him, touching one of his bandaged hands. That night in bed I convinced myself that his hands were bandaged because he suffered from leprosy, and I was bound to have caught it, as it was so very contagious. Bridget and I read with interest the pamphlets she picked up at church, describing the Mission's work among the lepers. Molly was having a dinner party and I sat on the stairs listening to the voices with my heart racing. Finally, I walked into the dining room among the laughing people in evening dress, and approached Molly who was serving at the head of the table. She led me from the room by the hand, and did her best to reassure me that what I had imagined was not possible. I suppose that this sort of event was why she brought me to see a child psychologist in London. I know now that he was a famous pioneer in his field called Dr Winnicott. I don't remember my meeting with him, but the letter he wrote to my mother later is revealing about us both:

Dear Mrs. Keane,

I would be interested to hear anything indicating Sally's reaction to the consultation. I realise that I have done nothing yet except to get to know about the problem, and to come into Sally's life in such a way that I think she would be able to make use of from time to time if she is in London.

I think that the only point I wanted to make in response to your invitation to give advice is that if Sally tends to be getting nearer to a more profound mourning for her father that should be looked upon as healthy rather than unhealthy. One could say that she is suffering from a delay in mourning for her father, and this may be associated to some extent with your own great difficulty with this thing that happened to yourself. You are coping with it in your own way, and perhaps Sally's way will be different from yours.

Yours sincerely,

D. W. Winnicott

For years, Molly was sabotaged by grief over which she had no control. Patricia Cockburn described arriving at the Shelbourne Hotel in Dublin with her, when one of the porters, who had not heard of Bobbie's death, enquired after him. She was shaken by the force of Molly's tears which she felt were never going to stop. Patricia, who had lost a baby son herself, was not unsympathetic, but she felt that, after three years, Molly should have been able to manage better. Molly herself was shattered by the impropriety of such outbursts, and this was not just her personal reaction but also the ethos of the time and class. In *Brideshead Revisited* when Charles Ryder goes to Morocco to find Sebastian who fails to meet him, his friend explains that he has not come because 'He's ashamed of being unhappy.' In one of her few references to her mother's death which devastated her childhood, Elizabeth Bowen wrote: 'I had what can go with total bereavement – a sense of disfigurement, mortification and disgrace.' Molly suffered from this shame. She was a social animal, intensely aware that sympathy for you ran out after a time, and one must keep certain feelings at bay behind a semi-translucent curtain of braveness and gaiety. She tried hard, usually successfully, but sometimes she was up-scuttled and could not bring it off. As late as 1956 she was still consulting her unhappiness doctor in Harley Street. He was, in fact, a hypnotist. She kept notes from him in her bible, and read them before going to sleep. She said his superficially banal axioms underlined in red ink helped her.

Sometimes at home at Belleville the beauty of summer evening light became unbearable to her. Then she was inclined to suggest going up the mountains for a picnic tea. She braced up as soon as she started preparing the basket. As the outing was impromptu she would improvise skilfully. There might be sausages in a wide Thermos, lined with wax paper, sardine and parsley sandwiches, home grown tomatoes, crusty white bread from Barrons' bakery in Cappoquin with churned butter and Marmite. The Earl Grey tea, clouded with a little milk, tasted exotic and quite different from the Thermos than from a teapot.

Going to the mountains was, for us, a trip abroad. It was a foreign landscape, almost another planet. The small lake was called Bay Lough, and it was mythically supposed to be bottomless. Its water was perpetually black and ice cold because the green shoulders of mountain prevented the sun from ever reaching it. Higher mountains were dark and stony, strewn here and there with rams' skulls, blanched bones and a few shelters, pleasingly tunnel-shaped. In the Belleville notebook, Molly described 'Little black cattle running along the tops of fences cunning as dogs, and shy mountain sheep bouncing onto and off impossible obstacles and disappearing with a rattle of tiny hooves.' The wandering dog invariably seemed to be a wall-eyed collie that fled at the sight of one, as did the rarely encountered shepherd farmers who were also wild and had no wish to speak to a stranger. We picnicked in the lost garden of Bobbie's great-aunts. Molly speculated about them. It was her favourite form of history – the shadowy people who had once lived in places she loved. They had been Harry's aunts, and he had visited them here in their summer residence and garden. She had little information about them. She deduced the rest in a novelist's way. Now their garden had sunk back into the landscape. Beside a turf-brown stream running over boulders, the grass was cropped into an undulating carpet. We sat on it, sheltered by walls of ponticum rhododendron. Molly objected to ponticum when she saw it in people's gardens where rhododendrons were meant to be perfumed and creamy like Lady Fitzwilliam or majestic and lofty like the red Arboreum at Belleville. She referred to it as an 'interloper', seeming to look on it as a despicable social climber in these circumstances. However, her feelings towards it completely changed when it covered the mountains in a mauve Himalayan mist in June. The topography was laced at every season with foreign colours that differed from the lowlands; the deep brown of winter when the hills were sometimes dusted parsimoniously with snow like icing sugar on a chocolate cake, the neon orange of the rowan berries, and the heathers of autumn. We also gathered a summer harvest of wild blueberries. They resembled a sweeter, fleshier version of blackcurrants and were pleasant and unprickly to pick, growing at ground level among their heart-shaped pale green leaves. It was not hard to understand why Molly came here. The ambience was powerful, it braced one up and brought one back to its vernal present, and connected one to something beyond oneself, something magnificent, detached and yet kind.

Sometimes we did not stop, but drove on to the point where we looked down on the Eden-like plain of Tipperary with its limestone land, which gave bone and substance to the horses reared in it and made them the best in the country. Molly talked to us about the landmarks we passed, generating an atmosphere that was nostalgic and expectant at the same time. She retold us stories we had heard the last time we came that way, about the vanished garden and the bottomless lake, giving them a mythical, magic quality that was implicit in her personal sense of place, and in the way she wrote about it. The Golden Vale of Tipperary was full of memories for her from her Woodrooffe days. She spoke lovingly of Willie and Dolly, and of splendid horses and friends, and of festive race meetings when one dressed up, bent on sport and flirtation. She described certain enchanting men, their jokes and remarks, their lovely classical clothes, and hats tipped at just the right angle. It is noticeable in her novels that when she wants to convey that a man is sexually attractive she dresses him up rather than undressing him.

Occasionally we descended to the valley in order to visit Dick and Wendy Mulcahy who lived at the village of Ardfinnan, just inside Tipperary. Dick had hunted the West Waterford hounds during the war and had come very often to tea at Belleville. He was my hero. After Bobbie died, he understood my stunned state of submerged loss, and would hold my hand and draw me to him as he did his own children. Dick and Wendy were completely natural. They expected Molly to be in tears, and as a result she felt safe and indeed happy with them and inclined not to break down. They accepted her loneliness and cherished her as they did Virginia and me. They were not Anglo-Irish but wholly Irish. They were well off; Dick had a tweed factory. His wools were washed and his dyes diluted by Knockmealdown water. His colours were influenced by the brightness and russetness of the mountain colours around him. After lunch, while Molly talked to Wendy, we children followed him around his factory. Stacked on shelves were hundreds of spindles of unwoven colours, waiting to be transformed into checked or speckled or plain cloth. The beauty and texture of Dick's tweed were sought after. Many of the stylish coats and skirts worn by Molly were made from it.

Wandering around on my own at Belleville I often visited the pig yard. It was a place where I used to meet my father mixing up pig fodder in a primitive boiler made out of a tin barrel. In the middle of the yard there was a high, open barn which threw a roof over a lot of ground, fenced in by a block wall on which I could sit and talk to Bobbie while he stirred his mixture that was particularly good for pigs, and which was supposed to result in excellent, delicious bacon. Now there were no pigs, but the seepage from their sties had made an emerald-green lake at the centre of the barn, and around it the years of rich manure had built into cliffs where great forests of nettles engulfed all. Everything in this one-time hub was deserted and decaying. It was a symbol of what was happening to the place as a whole. Belleville was retracting, slipping away. The kitchen garden was dwindling into small islands – the island of asparagus, the island of rhubarb etc., surrounded by wilderness. One of the herbaceous borders where Molly had been photographed by *Vogue* digging in her elegant corduroy slacks had been grassed over. More and more hens seemed to be succumbing to the fox. Paddy and Sheila had disappeared, so had other people. Various helpers came and went, but the energy was no longer there to cherish such a disparate universe. Molly resisted the trend. We went on trips with her after high tea to buy a Kerry cow from a farmer in the mountains, to cajole handymen, to interview an orange-haired maid, framed by the fuchsia hedges of her cottage. She was tense, keeping appointments at the bank, and we waited outside in the car quarrelling over who should hold the dog on their lap while she attempted to charm and seduce the manager in his office.

Treasure Hunt funds were running low. Molly was beginning to feel poor again – not totally poor but slightly. Her self-confidence was intermittently affected in the same way as the first frosts pinch one's bones. She was slowly coming to understand there was not enough money, and that there never would be enough money. Talk of leaving, indefinite to begin with, terrified me. I was dependent on the woods, dependent on the house. I clung to the wall on the way up the stairs and begged the house to take care of me. If it was hard for me it was agony for Molly. It is impossible to fathom what Belleville meant to her, historically, practically, romantically. It was interwoven with her psyche in a complex pattern began in childhood. Among her papers, she preserved faint carbon copies of the furniture list from the auction. They were like death warrants to her. For years she could not look at this list specifying beloved objects, bow-fronted Chippendale writing bureau, Sheraton cabinet with pierced disengaged pediment and mahogany and satinwood inlay, Sheraton serving table

Molly at Ardmore in 1945, painted by Norah McGuinness

IRISH ECCENTRICS and MURITANIAN ROMANTICS

Treasure Hunt at the Apollo Theatre and *King's Rhapsody* at the Palace Theatre

Eleven years ago, M. J. Farrell and John Perry wrote a comedy about a crazy Irish family called *Spring Meeting*. It had a great success, one that has now been followed with their second play *Treasure Hunt*. It, too, concerns an impoverished Irish family living in a house the upkeep of which is beyond their means. The late master has died leaving several bequests, but no money with which to fulfil them. The young people face the facts and plan to take paying guests until the farm has been put on a sound basis. The older generation oppose them from the first and try to get rid of the guests when they arrive. The simple story is fantasticated by the presence of Aunt Anna Rose—a great and very Irish eccentric. Dame Sybil Thorndike proves again her great talent for comedy in her creation of the part.

READING THE WILL : The scene in the first Act of M. J. Farrell and John Perry's comedy "Treasure Hunt" at the Apollo Theatre, when the lawyer reveals that there is no money left to fulfil the bequests of the late master of Ballyroden. Left to right are Anne Leon, Terence Longdon, Dame Sybil Thorndike (in the Sedan chair) ; Richard Wordsworth as the lawyer, Alan Webb and Marie Löhr

TROUBLE OVER THE P.G.s. : The younger generation, played by Anne Leon and Terence Longdon, try to solve the economic situation by taking in P.G.s. But Uncle Hercules and Aunt Consuelo do their utmost to spoil the scheme

THE TREASURE HUNT : Aunt Anna Rose (Dame Sybil Thorndike) inherited valuable rubies from her marriage, but they have been lost for fifty years. The play ends with an hilarious hunt for the jewels which will save the house of Ryall

AUNT ANNA ROSE MAKES A TRUNK CALL : Dame Sybil Thorndike plays the eccentric old aunt who spends most of her day in her Sedan chair in which she makes imaginary journeys all over the world. On arrival, she puts through a trunk call to the telephone extension at the other end of the room

Molly's play *Treasure Hunt*, on stage at the Apollo

Bobbie and Peggy
Ashcroft at Belleville

Dromana, on the
River Blackwater.
Home of the Villiers
Stuarts, and used by
Molly as the model
for the house in *Two
Days in Aragon*

Molly and John Gielgud in the
South of France in the late thirties

Sally and Adrian at a wedding

Molly and Sally in London in the fifties

Molly's passport photograph, *circa* 1957

Molly, with Tessa, at the Round Tower, Ardmore. Photograph by Kevin Brownlow

George and me at Kilcor

Molly and her granddaughter Julia at Dysert

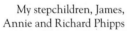

My stepchildren, James, Annie and Richard Phipps

My sister, Virginia, and her husband Kevin Brownlow, photographed by Peter Suschitzky in the late sixties

Jacket of the Abacus edition of *Good Behaviour*

Elizabeth Bowen

Molly and Diana Athill at the Booker Prize

Virago poster

Molly in old age

Molly with Hero in her sitting room at Dysert

with brass ram's head on the front, etc. She was profoundly sensitive to such items, both in what they symbolised and what they were. She and Bobbie had loved polishing them and caring for them and changing their position in rooms. The pleasing proportions consoled her when her eye fell on them in the morning, and she was endeavouring to pull herself together to face the day. These things evoked in her a sense of hope and a sense of poetry reflected in the way she writes about them in her novels. She felt she was betraying them and betraying the past and the future by selling them. Even financially, it was disastrous as prices were low at the time and lots failed to reach their real value. Peter-Patrick bought some pieces as he had just got married and he paid the full reserves in order to help Molly.

Abandoning Belleville meant letting go of a realised dream. Elizabeth Bowen, a connoisseur of loss and a subtle poet of place, writes of 'permanence as an attribute of recalled places'. Of course, this is true, but it does not seem so at the time of parting. Then the severance feels total, strangely violent and somehow more pervasive and bigger even than the loss of a friend. As well as this, Molly was ashamed because she was succumbing to a bungalow. She, a disciple of everything eighteenth century and a jeerer at bungalows, was about to move into one which was actually called the Yellow House because of its primrose-coloured walls and buttercup yellow woodwork. Snobbishly and architecturally it was a perverse downward step. Paradoxically, it also had the plus of affording her a tremendously creative opportunity. In turning the Yellow House into Dysert (rechristened from the townland on which it stood), she transformed it and gave it a beauty and glow which came from her imagination and personality, and from the house's majestic position overlooking the sea. Of course, the overwhelming advantage of this house was its situation. Ardmore was a place of happiness, full of memories of being on holiday with Bobbie, poker games at the Cliff House Hotel, Tommie and Joan, shelling with children, escape from the troubling responsibilities of one's mainstream life. It was a source of rest and fun, blessed by the sea. People returned there year after year because they loved it, as in many cases their parents and grandparents had done. By moving in permanently, Molly took the risk of losing the magic and respite it had always given her. In fact, the opposite occurred. There was a subconscious wisdom in her decision to go there. She stayed for the rest of her life, and became rooted among the people and in the landscape. Ardmore has an open quality which is slightly unusual among Irish villages. Molly was not its only immigrant. Others from many sorts of lives came from outside and felt at home. In an almost mystical sense, they adopted and felt adopted. Molly grew to love it as she had loved Belleville, and in a more grounded manner, because it freed her in all sorts of ways, not least from the stress of 'living grandly without money'.

Jack O'Brien, her builder, became her guru at Ardmore. Together they plotted and planned the reincarnation of the house. Molly was not easy to work with. Her mind raced and she expected you to grasp her ideas quite quickly. Their association could have ended in blow-up, but instead it resulted in friendship and mutual esteem. This was due to the make-up of Jack's character, which was quiet, ironic and authoritative. He was highly skilled and Molly trusted his building and also his judgement in other things. After the house was finished, she would go to him for advice for the rest of his life. This meant getting the advice of Bridie, his wife, as well. In their house, they were a team. To their sorrow, they were childless but that made them available to other people. Bridie was busy with many projects; her pony and terrier, the house they let, the bread she made and the jerseys she knitted which enclosed Jack's bulky frame, keeping the accounts, and ploughing her own furrow through the politics of Ardmore life. Jack never rushed at anything. He lit a cigarette, and thought things through. Molly felt steadied and reassured by his patience. He built a flight of beautiful, shallow stone steps leading from the road to the house, and a paved terrace around it containing old flagstones, spotted by Molly's sharp eye and pirated from a ruin.

The house, perched below the road and hidden from it, was originally reached by a corniche-like path, which became slippery in the rain. The foundations of the new arrangement were cut laboriously out of the cliff. Everything was done by hand. Jack was assisted by his nephews, Jack and Jimmy Burke, who were barely more than children at the time. Tommie Jameson, commenting on Molly's building works, said, 'When the pickaxe goes into the ground, the little boy goes into the air.' Jack was as skilled with wood as he was with stone. Inside, he made an elegant, robust staircase linking the split levels of the house, and in the drawing-room he carved and assembled a pair of Adamesque bookshelves and an eighteenth-century chimney piece which was a miniature copy of one Molly took him to see at Woodrooffe.

We left Belleville before Dysert was ready. We stayed in the house Jack and Bridie rented, and squeezed in there with

Bridget and Winkie the dog. Our new governess, Sylvia, lived in a caravan pulled up alongside. She was a Londoner, a young Oxford graduate who took the job with us because she was engaged to an Irish veterinary student. At the time we adored films. We dreamed about them before and after seeing them, and we were always begging Molly to take us to Dungarvan where the Ormonde Cinema was. She was very willing to go herself, as long as the films were not frightening. She was always trying to shield me from scary images as I was so easily haunted by them. My mother was extremely sympathetic to my plight. When *Roman Holiday* came out at this point, it was the perfect film for us. Audrey Hepburn was a new sort of actress with her natural manner and her vulnerable, deer-like beauty. I longed to look like her, and couldn't have been more opposite. Sylvia did look like her, with huge eyes and gamine haircut. We were all a bit in love with her. Tommie certainly was and he visited the caravan to chat with her quite often. She was cool, a thinker, clever and ironic. She was the best teacher I had yet encountered, and led one to reading in a slightly more analytical way. Before, I had read for the story and I still did, of course, but I was intrigued by some of Sylvia's critical views such as the idea that the symmetrical sentences of Jane Austen reflected the moral felicity she espoused, and that the whole thing was connected with the heroic couplet employed by Pope and other eighteenth-century writers. Molly, who had always encouraged one to read books beyond one's age-group, didn't give a damn about such notions. She recommended reading (the plays of Chekhov, for example) for the characters – the humanity and richness of them, for the dialogue they spoke – the truth and funniness and sadness of it, and for the ironic or tragic circumstances of their lives. Although she was involved in literary structuring herself, she did not want to talk about it or listen to theories concerning it. She structured her books intuitively out of her knowledge of her characters and her awareness of their social world where the logistics of the hunt and the hunt ball and who one sat next to at dinner were great events in people's lives.

Rather late in life, I was emerging from the era of being read to into the one of reading to others myself. Joan's collapsing eyesight meant she needed a reader and Molly offered me. She fostered our relationship and was not jealous of it. I felt happy reading to Joan in her drawing-room, curved at one end with a window looking out to sea and another facing across a rose garden to the summer house and a small wood. The sofas were luxurious and the classical furniture was slightly exotic as dictated by Joan's artist's eye, which favoured touches of Chinese lacquer and brass inlays. She collected antique Waterford glass festooned in chains of blue-tinged crystal drops, and snuff boxes and intriguing objets d'art scattered on chests and tables. Among them was a miniature bookcase, holding tiny editions of some of Shakespeare's plays which, observing my lust for it, she gave me. One of her paintings hung over the chimney place. It was inspired by the ridged potato beds and traditional thatched houses of the Curragh area of Ardmore. They were inhabited by people who still spoke the Irish language, and who lived by fishing and out of their fields. Some of the house fronts, creamed with generations of limewash, had jewel-like gardens planted with marguerites, mallows, honesty and marigolds. A path through the potato and carrot fields led to the pebbled strand full of silver rocks. It was here that we hunted for the precious cowrie shells along the edges of a receding tide or in the miniature bays between the rocks. One could lie down and stare into the gravel, and after a time they would gradually become visible. Joan was expert in this art, and if the light was falling at the right slant she seemed to be able to practise it even with her fading eyesight. She suffered from the cold and usually wore her soft red wool coat indoors and out. During the winter in town, she wore her latest mink coat. Having passed Tourin to Shane, they had bought a flat in Dublin where they had many friends, and opportunities for cards. Dublin did not really suit Tommie except that it gave him a chance of going to the ballet when it came. He loved ballet, and at Rock House he had a book of romantic photographs of dancers in their world of artifice, of flowers raining from the sky, of ghosts and swans emerging from mists, of tulle skirts and muscled, white-stockinged legs. I was enchanted by this book and he would push it towards me when I was the only child at a grown-up lunch party.

Across from Rock House, Tommie rolled his tennis court. People sat around here on cushions while others played – a social high spot, it was the Versailles of Ardmore. He carted trailer loads of seaweed from the beach to his asparagus bed. Agnes, their cook, served it with plenty of butter. Her cooking was delicious but very rich. Joan ate little of it, and Tommie tried to gather his food out of its sea of creamy sauces. However, to guests it was a treat. Mabel still went everywhere with them. Her room at Rock House and everything in it was pervaded with the fumes of her paraffin stove. She suffered from elephantiasis and wore skirts to the ground to hide her legs. In the lap of her skirts she always had a piece of sewing. She stitched as she chatted amusingly with her many visitors.

One evening we went for supper to the Cliff House Hotel. Joan was in brilliant, mischievous form. She even had an appetite and indulged in rashers and eggs and fried potato – all things forbidden on her diet. Tommie and Molly remonstrated with her, but not seriously. It was an evening of jokes and enjoyment. Afterwards we sat in the dark bar where Frank Nugent, handsome and enigmatic, poured drinks and talked in his quiet, intriguing voice. He was the owner of the hotel, and the chief *éminence grise* of Ardmore. On the way home, Tommie, a little intoxicated, miscalculated a familiar hairpin bend and embedded his back wheels in the mud of a crumbling cliff. Many people arrived to help and advise on the situation. This involved much time and discussion and Molly drove Joan home while it was going on. We returned to our rented cottage and had just gone to bed when there was the sound of a car outside, and Tommie's voice speaking urgently. 'Moll, come at once, Joan is very ill.' He had been reading to her in bed when she fell into a coma. He disappeared up the hill. Molly re-dressed and followed him, leaving me in the room I shared with the sleeping, oblivious Virginia. I leaned out of the window and heard what I thought was a banshee calling. Perhaps it was the cry of wooing cats. In the morning Molly returned and told us that Joan had died during the night.

CHAPTER 7

Although it did not vanquish it entirely, moving to Ardmore did a great deal towards tempering Molly's 'terrible value of the past' which was so rooted in Belleville. Her notebooks refer less often to 'my complete happiness' and 'the brilliant past'. Dysert was not a house she and Bobbie would have gone to live in together. It spoke to another part of her condition, and she became fascinated with it. The fact that the house required a drastic makeover absorbed her. It demanded all her resources, a situation which suited her. On this occasion she had the good luck of being able to share her difficulties with her friend and builder, Jack O'Brien.

Ardmore's distinctly different seasons benefited her. In winter the village emptied and the isolation encouraged writing. When she felt lonely she made forays inland. She always kept one foot in her old territory socially, and she also set up her household business so that it required a round trip in the car, calling to her favourite grocer's in Tallow, stopping at Lismore for the butcher or the bank, and returning via Barrons' bakery in Cappoquin. All this could have been done in Youghal, but she was enmeshed with the Blackwater Valley. In certain ways loneliness served her well. Driving in her Morris Minor and (later) Renault 5s, she was like a lone sailor on a small craft, watchful, all senses on the alert, open to adventure. It was a mood which fed into her writing. It encouraged her intense response to the natural world which manifests itself in the novels, and is one of the main sources of energy which sustains her work in both overt and hidden ways. Glimpses of a ruined stable yard, jokes, or scraps of conversation picked up as she stopped to do errands, a loaf from her favourite baker, a girl cycling past, 'the slow sly change of light' on a reed-bed woven into her mood and her palette. She is a very painterly writer. Compton Mackenzie, reviewing her in the thirties, said 'One awaits the next M. J. Farrell novel like one awaits the next Corot.'

In summer she was not on holiday but other people were so she partook of the atmosphere. Friends returned like swallows – Hugo Anson came with Annina, his Italian wife, and together with Clodagh (his sister) they stayed in a rented house in Ardmore for a month. Hugo, resident in Rome, wished to eat the dishes of his childhood. He and Clodagh would stand around a slowly steaming steak and kidney pudding, topping it up with hot water from a silver coffee pot through a hole in the pastry lid. His two little boys, Dado and Andrea, had to have pasta and would not touch steak and kidney pudding. Annina, attempting to make them fit in with the Anglo-Irish customs, sent them to bed early, but they would wake up again and come downstairs and disturb dinner parties, caressing their parents' cheeks, whispering to them in Italian and demanding to be watched as they danced in their belted dressing gowns until they fell over exhausted. It was not demeanour that most of Hugo and Annina's guests would have encouraged in their own children, but they were amused by it in these Italian bambinos. The boys disliked the cold Atlantic but they loved to be with their Aunt Clodagh. And they followed her into it screaming as their brown torsos touched the waves. The Ansons were passionate prawners. Even Annina, Latin by blood and nature, stood in the slow-moving neap tides for hours, elegant in her Italian sea-going clothes and occasionally stopping for a cigarette, which she smoked through a holder and broke in two in order to limit her intake. They did not invite Molly on these expeditions. They jealously protected their secret prawn runs. However, they frequently gave her a bucket full of the precious catch. Like most seasonal treats, it had to be processed quickly and in this case alive. She tipped the flickering mass of prawns into the boiling sea water where they rapidly changed from beige to pink. As a child, I laboured under the delusion that they preferred it that way because of the beautiful colour. For shrimp teas she arranged them in a mountain on a blue and rust Mason's Ironstone platter. They tasted deliciously fresh and extracting them from their shells was a fiddly manoeuvre, which prolonged the pleasure. They were accompanied by Bridget's buttermilk scones and cups of Earl Grey tea, later followed by a drop of the hard stuff in the drawing-room. Belleville-sized numbers crowded into the small room with its glorious view over the bay. It became like a railway carriage with people stumbling over others when they went to refill their glasses. Talk broke up into particles; we children sitting on the floor would listen to first one conversation then another. There was a feeling of timelessness, of endless summer at these gatherings. From the floor we could see the sand glistening on people's ankles above their espadrilles or sandals.

During the autumn of 1953, Molly was on the verge of going to New York for the rehearsals of a play called *Say It With Flowers*, by Marcel Aymes, which she had adapted from the French. She was looking forward to working with Cyril Richard, a musical comedy actor turned director whom she had liked when she went to meet him in London. Binkie had sent her a note of financial advice:

Fees of 1% 5000
1½% next 2000
2% over 7000
Ask for 25 dollars a day from day of arrival in America.

Her ticket was reserved. Adele was rallying her friends to attend the first night. Molly was both frightened and exhilarated at the prospect of the adventure. She was disappointed when the production was cancelled at the last moment because the backer, Mr Walter Chrysler of the car manufacturer, reneged. He had been discouraged by the failure on Broadway of another French adaptation, *The Little Hut*. This light-hearted piece about adultery from the point of view of the wronged husband (played by Robert Morley) had been brilliantly translated by Nancy Mitford from the original by André Roussin. It was a smash hit in London in 1950 and one of H. M. Tennent's longest running shows. The triumph of *The Little Hut* sent Binkie and John on frequent trips to Paris in search of plays. It was the era of elegant, witty comedies about love in France as practised by Yvonne Printemps and Sacha Guitry and others.

Several French scripts, including one by Jean Anouilh, ended up with Molly. Despite the fact that she was very suited to the task, none of her adaptations reached production. They represented hours of work. She said it was hard because French jokes often don't translate and you have to find substitutes for them. It was perhaps a wrong turning for her which distracted her (literally for years) from writing novels. She was one of a distinguished company of novelists whom Binkie recruited, among them Graham Greene, Elizabeth Bowen, Nancy Mitford, Enid Bagnold and Kate O'Brien. Molly could never resist the theatre – she was, by nature, a theatrical person. She always said it was the cheques, and of course they were alluring. If things were going well a play could earn more in a month than a book might yield in its entire career. Also, the writing of dialogue was one of her strengths and she liked the plotting involved in play writing. She often saw real life as a plot.

In 1954 she and Tommie quarrelled and their relationship collapsed. He was an enchanter not a saint and his relationships with women were complicated for them, simple for him. Something in his attitude pushed her to the brink of despair. As often happened when she felt herself at bay, she was swept by lightning-like anger, and she fell back on her genius for saying the unforgivable. How often she regretted it, how often it got her into trouble and yet how often she could not resist it. In the event she said, 'Joan was sometimes a bore.' She did not even think it but her perverse talent caused her to say it because she knew it could hurt Tommie profoundly at a time when he was still grieving for the wife he loved. The word, although not so terrible in itself, had denigrating connotations in the very social world in which they existed. Tommie himself referred to such utterances as 'Molly's iced steel filings'. Another friend described them as 'darts thrown with extraordinary lethal accuracy like the banderos of a skilled picador'.

She was not unconscious of the danger. There are laments and warnings to herself in her notebooks. 'Defend me from provocation, defend me from diminishing people.' 'The whole of life is a secret to me. It is a shut shell. I wonder at it and fail to understand it and make my own mistakes invariably at every cliff and danger. I have no nicety or skill in its situation.' Despite this awareness in certain circumstances (precipitated usually by vulnerability) you could not trust her not to attack. She could not trust herself. All sweetness, all shrewdness left her. When the storm was over she suffered. Of course, the break with Tommie had more to it than this one remark, but it was the bombing of the whole thing. Joan's death had unbalanced them. It is likely that their relationship could not have worked without her, although they had more freedom to indulge it. The upper-crust habit of being subtly subversive towards the wife of a man one is attracted to was not subscribed to by Molly. She could be said to have loved Pam and Joan as much or more than she had loved their husbands. Her 'iced steel filings' landed her in much trouble, but did not deprive her of love in life. Although in this case, love failed her and left her marooned. In old age, she gave an interview to Shusha Guppy in which she spoke of her absolute belief in love, of the masculine tendency to separate love from sex and of her own inclination to love too much, all of which were probably involved in her row with Tommie.

Following such happenings Molly tried to atone, but subterraneanly. She did not go so far as an apology. On the surface she rejected her anger and justified her words. The self-knowledge in her writings did not serve her in the feverish moments of life when she succumbed to passionate feeling put into cutting language. It was a smashing of the mould of *Good Behaviour*. Having done this reassembling, it was the only way she knew how to live. Her veiled apologies had a brittleness, a deliberate missing of the point about them that usually made matters worse, and failed to assuage the pain of words that had knocked the breath out of one like a blow.

In contrast, her other self consoled, understood and laughed with total generosity and made her drawing-room at Ardmore an oasis. Tommie and she quarrelled in that room, and for them the oasis never really returned. For a time they stopped speaking. Later, after he became ill, they resumed their friendship, but things were not the same between them.

Nevertheless, his love and Joan's had not failed her at the time 'when I was the serious victim of my spirit'. After Bobbie's death when she frequently records how arriving early at Tourin, talking and having a drink with them both before other guests arrived, and flirting with Tommie, had saved her and made her feel part of the human race again, and not a despairing outlaw from it. Although in Tommie's case, this fact became eclipsed by the painful ending of their affair.

The row resulted in moments of desolation for Molly.

Ardmore is a small place, and when she walked the dog she could see the cars of mutual friends outside Rock House and knew that before the rupture she would have been inside having fun. As had happened at Cappoquin, some people took sides and became cool towards her. The two of them were habitués of O'Reilly's, the shop and bar in Ardmore. Betty O'Reilly, the beautiful, dark-eyed, diplomatic proprietor, was fond of them both. If they coincided, she tried to keep them separate, the captain in the kitchen and Molly in the shop, or vice versa. If this strategy failed, he would buy her a drink and they would take refuge in hollow 'good behaviour'. Tommie still invited Virginia and me to tea. He would urge us to take plenty of Agnes's cake. Her cakes were magnificent edifices, covered with icing-sugar frills in bright colours, like a flamenco dancer's dress. Our attitudes to him differed. Virginia, although she, like everyone else, was beguiled by his charm, felt a certain antagonism towards him, being subconsciously aware that he was a rival for her mother's affection. I, on the other hand, in my endless quest for a surrogate father, loved him unconditionally. We were emissaries. When we came home from these visits Molly would ask us if Tommie looked well, if he was smoking or drinking too much.

Because of his smoking he developed cancer of the throat and after an operation he lost his attractive and witty voice. You could hear his voice in the notes he wrote instead of talking. He was naughty about these notes, and sometimes made mischief with them, leaving them about where unflattering comments might be read by their subjects.

His charm and sense of fun remained as powerful as ever. He was gallant in adversity. When he died in 1965, Molly was away and I represented her at his funeral. I was terrified because I knew I would disgrace myself socially by weeping all the time. I need not have worried. The church was full of ladies, many of them worldly wise and glamorous and all of them in tears.

Mrs Skrine, Molly's mother, had died in 1955 aged ninety. Her obituaries in the Belfast papers referred to her as Moira O'Neill, 'the laureate of the Glens', and spoke of the popularity of *Songs of the Glens of Antrim* and its sequel, both of which had gone into many editions when they came out in the early years of the century. To this day she has maintained her small constant place in the culture of Ulster. In *Stepping Stones: Interviews with Seamus Heaney*, the late Poet Laureate mentioned her as one of the first poets to have come into his consciousness as a child. Her verses have frequently been set to music. Molly seemed pleased when someone praised *Songs* to her. She was inclined to say 'she was really rather a good poet' with uncertainty. Something spoke to her from the poems, but she did not really respect them and give them enough time to discover what it was. She was a bit ashamed of their Victorian vernacular. They were mutually suspicious of each other's writings. The theory she most espoused about their relationship – that they hated one another – was half truth and half myth. After Molly became independent and married, and Mrs Skrine no longer felt responsible for curbing her fast goings-on, their relationship eased. When Molly went to 'the Bogs' reports about how their mother had enjoyed these visits filtered through to her in letters from Walter and Godfrey. She kept a series of letters which Nesta wrote to her when she and I were refugees at Drumnasole in Northern Ireland at the beginning of the war. They describe my progress as a new baby whom Molly was cruelly separated from in a charming and unsentimental way. She also preserved an affectionate letter from her mother on the occasion of her forty-sixth birthday.

My own Molly,

This is to wish you many and happy returns of your birthday my dear child. Please excuse the filthy little bits of paper which are all that I can command at the moment. I hope you found things all right at home when you got there. Or at least as right as they ever are after the shortest absence. Virginia is quite well and full of rejoicing at the return of her dear Uncle Charlie. I think he had his own rejoicing at the sight of her (though it didn't display itself in prancings). Last evening she came into my room in her nightdress, and something came into her head that prompted her to dance, and there she danced and danced while Brigid implored her not to catch cold – and I said not a word, but sat there and gazed at her.

Jessie Brown has gone away, she went last night. I am sorry, not that I saw anything of her, but I am sure she was good for Theo.

Theo, you know, is sociable, first and foremost she loves people, and after people she loves animals, <u>all</u> animals without exception. They are 'sweet'. I am sure this is a great thing for her. They give her company and just now that is such a help. Well, I am not sociable, and above all I am not an animal-lover. I do love a few, but very few animals. So here we are, together for the rest of our lives. But mine will not be long I think.

Well goodbye dear, give my love to Sally

Your own Mother.

In her letters it is obvious Nesta is delighted by Virginia and me. Molly could never completely forgive her for not loving her as she wanted to be loved in childhood. All her life she remained allergic to her mother's acerbity. It was a mirror image of her own, but whereas Mrs Skrine's sharpness was icy, Molly's was hot and passionate. There is no doubt that they suffered from a similar form of depression although they reacted to it differently. Molly attacked and Nesta became withdrawn and silent – all anger going inward and creating a fog of sadness and disapproval around her. Molly struggled almost to her last breath to throw off this yoke while her mother took to her bed and gave in. It was very hard to get a word out of her. Molly was uneasy with silence. She thought it was self-indulgent and ill-mannered not to attempt conversation when one was with another person. Despite the improvement in their relations in the latter years of Mrs Skrine's life, before she finally succumbed to an almost impenetrable gloom, much remained unresolved between them.

Much later, in 1981, when *Good Behaviour* was a hit and Molly would talk to journalists about her childhood, she occasionally tried to be fair to her mother and to disentangle the complications of the story. More often she found it easier, and a source of more amusing copy, to dwell on the drama of how they disliked each other. Godfrey (her only living sibling by this time) had to steel himself to read interviews with Molly because of what she might say about their mother.

When Virginia was unhappy at boarding school in Dublin, Molly went to live there during term time so that Virginia could attend as a day pupil. She rented a flat at Trafalgar Terrace, Monkstown, which formed part of a tall Georgian house fallen on hard times and divided into lodgings. I was at this time coming and going from Rome where I was an au pair. Our rooms were furnished from the flotsam of second hand stores. The sofa and armchairs were a clumsy, unpleasing shape, upholstered in brocade of a slightly shiny Gothic pattern interspersed with gloomy flowers – a long way from William Morris but remotely connected to him.

The house was let out in sections rather than flats, linked by a lovely period staircase. Our kitchen and bathroom were on one floor, the living room and bedroom on another and a second bedroom on a higher level. It was a difficult time. Molly, struggling with plays, succumbed to a series of health problems, the worst of which was viral pneumonia. Fortunately she was near her beloved Dr Wilson, but she was exhausted and her recovery slow. The house was very cold in winter. We slept in creaky iron-sprung bedsteads necessitating two hot-water bottles per person. We also had recourse to sleeping bags which had been initiated by Aunt Susan. These were knitted on big needles in soft blue wool and Susan, who spent her life working for her socialist causes and living in rented accommodation, was full of notions about how to survive in such circumstances. Urban lodgings, even if they were not permanent, brought a sense of impoverishment – a downgraded feeling of homelessness to Anglo-Irish people who were used to the country and a large quantity of daffodils blowing outside in the March wind as a sign of hope. Molly, feeling poor, bought the cheapest ingredients for her cooking, which turned out to be delicious when she got at them in the striplighted, linoleumed kitchen floating makeshiftly in a big ex-drawing-room. She made subtly flavoured broth from bones, skate wing with black caper butter, and a delicious soup of thickened milk with chopped watercress stirred into it at the last moment.

Virginia remembers another form of cooking which again emanated from Sue, and which was specifically aimed at her because she suffered from catarrh. It was called 'The Nature Cure' and consisted of endless clear vegetable soup, slippery elm porridge and fru grains. Standing in front of the electric fire being rubbed down with a rough towel was also part of it. This regime was one of a series of magic solutions espoused by Molly which ran throughout our lives. She was keen on orthodox doctors as well and tending the body probably because of her parents' neglect of it. During this time in Dublin, with plenty of doctors to hand we all seemed to get ill. Virginia was treated for numerous ailments including mumps and flat feet and weakness of the back. She was given exercises to do. Of course she loathed it all and it induced in her mild rebellions such as eating forbidden potato crisps when walking the dog and listening to Radio Luxembourg instead of the Home Service in bed. Despite this, she says 'everything was overshadowed by the vast relief of being out of the tortures of boarding school back with Mum, back in my own world and culture'.

Of course, there were highlights in this world in the shape of people, chief among them our Uncle Godfrey. He would arrive from his office in the most architecturally elegant part of town near Trinity College carrying a basket of muddy vegetables freshly dug from his garden that morning and he would drink quantities of weak China tea while gossiping with us at the kitchen table. His affection and indomitable sparkle were uplifting. He had a sense of fatherhood towards us and towards Molly. We never felt he was doing this out of duty but out of love. We went frequently to Springmount, the house he and his first wife, Dar, had built in a charming suburb called Strawberry Beds, and ate Dar's delicious meals. Virginia stayed there often at weekends, leaving Molly free to write; although they were younger than her she became close to her cousins Anthea and John and they compensated for the horrible bullies at school. Of the latter Virginia says 'We scorned them'. Molly did not attempt to broker a peace by inviting any of the schoolmates to tea, but joined heartily in the vendetta.

Mrs Ross lived on the ground floor. She was an angelic Dublin lady with white hair and a soft, amused voice. She possessed the only telephone in the building and took messages for Molly. They became fast friends and indulged in leisurely talks and sips of Tio Pepe from tiny crystal glasses in Mrs Ross's drawing-room. It was a dark room but her personality lit it up. She was an ideal mixture of compassionate gentleness and wit. Like many people of her generation her temperament had been conditioned by edgy Dublin repartee and by exposure during long summers to the softness and feyness of the West of Ireland.

Molly's most startlingly beautiful and original young friends were Desmond and Mariga Guinness. They had recently married and were living at Carton while they looked for a house. She took us to meet them there for tea in the library. Desmond loved Molly's books (then out of print) and cultivated her because of them. This was before they founded the Irish Georgian Society and before Mariga became stylised and welded to the eighteenth century. Back then she often dressed in an Aran jersey and jeans. Her beauty had an extraordinary freshness. Her skin was almost transparent and her eyelashes very dark. She bowed her head with a graceful, shy gesture and her charming, close-lipped smile would flood her eyes with amusement. She and Desmond were an almost conventional couple in those days. Their baby Patrick lay on the sofa occasionally opening his eyes, which were of Desmond's blueness surrounded by Mariga's lashes. Desmond came in after hunting in his socks and elegant waistcoat and told us about the terrifying fences he had just jumped. They loved Trafalgar Terrace and felt it was waiting to be transported back to its eighteenth-century glory. When the Gas Company at Dun Laoghaire produced *Spring Meeting* Molly cooked her osso buco stew for Desmond and Mariga before the performance which they took Virginia and me to see. She herself did not accompany us, fearing the play would be embarrassingly performed by unsubtle amateurs. In fact the Dubliners' flair for acting came through and I remember it as being rather good and funny.

When Molly went into town, Norah McGuinness's flat in Fitzwilliam Square was a place of refuge. The thrilling scent of oil paint and turpentine emanated from her studio onto the staircase. Norah said she had once met a ghost on this stairs. Sometimes she worked at night decorating the windows in Brown Thomas's shop. Returning late she encountered a lady in evening dress. She stood aside to let her pass and the stranger smiled in acknowledgement and walked into the flat on the lower landing. It was not until she was turning the latchkey in her own door that the thought struck her that this person had not opened the door but had passed through it. Although Norah was very definite and down to earth, she completely believed in the apparition and felt an affinity with her. She thought that by her dress this was a lady from eighteenth-century Dublin who had lived in the house when it was first built. She said that after working so long in the shop she was in a state of extreme tiredness to the point of feeling almost disembodied herself and perhaps this had enabled their encounter to happen. Framed in its architectural setting it was a meeting of two Dubliners. The shadowy belle from the elegant English-enslaved town of the Pale, with Norah, who was a very modern person even for her own time.

Norah lived, worked and travelled alone. She loved her family, and had admirers and lovers and many friends but independence and solitude were essential to her although she was very social. She had been married briefly in her youth. She knew all the creative people of her day – and had a painting of Jack Yeats's in her drawing-room which she had swapped with the artist for something of hers. She had Byzantine eyes and a wonderful smoky voice and earthiness and impatience. She knew all the gossip and was very funny and intolerant of fools or deviousness. (She had plenty of experience of the latter in her role as one of the queens of Dublin.) Molly's barbs and hers sometimes became entangled like stags' horns but they recovered from these bouts and remained friends. They trusted each other. When Bobbie died and Molly did not want to know where he was buried, she asked Norah to get his headstone made. Norah chose a Celtic cross with 'Robert Lumley Keane of Cappoquin' inscribed on it and it stands out in the huge London graveyard where he lies. Norah herself when low turned to Molly. At a time when her painting was blocked she wrote, 'I long to see you, you always do something to me which helps.' Molly loved her paintings and bought them when she could afford them. Norah looked Mediterranean although she was born in Northern Ireland. She had a glamorous, dignified heaviness. She moved in a proud way and dressed with an artist's sense of colour. She exuded certainty and self-confidence in all she did; in her style of cooking and the way she smoked cigarettes staining them with the bright lipstick with which she painted her wide, expressive mouth. Her certainty came from her work; her belief in it and her absolute dedication to it. On the rare occasions when she experienced difficulty painting she became cross and low.

She illustrated the jacket of Molly's book *Loving Without Tears* and Elizabeth Bowen's *The Shelbourne*, among others. She left you in no doubt of her affection or disapproval. She didn't mind telling friends what to do. When the writer Denis Johnston bought a home on the island of Albany she was furious and instructed him to sell it at once, and also wrote to Molly urging her to write and tell him 'it would be sheer suicide to go there'.

During her time in Dublin, Molly began collaborating with Mícheál Mac Liammóir on a new play called *The Bagges of Heaven*. She fetched him from Harcourt Terrace where he lived with Hilton Edwards. She would light a fire and put out the best Bewley's coffee before she left to pick him up. She found him an inspiring, imaginative collaborator. After work they would emerge from the drawing-room and prepare lunch together. The paella he had cooked in wartime Belleville re-emerged and he taught her how to make lasagne. He lifted the heart and created an atmosphere of fun. On the way home they would stop for shopping; special ingredients for cooking or for a bottle of what he called 'my secret', which was his hair dye. Their play, which was destined for H. M. Tennent, was never produced. The title referred to a family who live in a house called Heaven. This echoed some of the poetic names that existed in Ascendancy Ireland, such as the 'Moones of the Doon'.

Because of Mícheál and Hilton, with whom he had worked and toured when young, Orson Welles brought his production of *Chimes at Midnight* to Dublin. It was an adaptation of *Henry IV* and *Henry V* in which he was Falstaff and Molly's friend Keith Baxter played Prince Hal. The theatrical note was like a silver thread running through the Trafalgar Terrace era. Many friends, or friends of friends, came on tour with plays. *Chimes at Midnight* was the most exciting of these and was directed by Orson Welles with his characteristic panache and imagination. The relationship between Falstaff and the Prince was very moving. There was a rapport between him and Keith and when he forgot his lines he would say 'Cans't help me, lad?' Keith's face was brightly mischievous and beautiful, and at that time in his life everyone was slightly in love with him and he was enjoying the ambience. He sensed that Molly was low. He brought her freesias, and walked arm in arm with her, confiding in her and recounting interesting gossip. We went to the play twice and he came to meals, and walked the dog with us on Dún Laoghaire pier, and was guest of honour at one of Molly's lunch parties at the Zoo.

She had taken out a family membership of the Zoological Society in Phoenix Park, which meant that one could dine in the restaurant quite cheaply. She often invited friends there. She felt it was festive with the animals thrown in, and it got everyone away from the Formica kitchen table of which she was ashamed. The Zoo was part of the imaginative, plucky way she adjusted to living in the suburbs. Virginia remembers her attitude with appreciation. 'I don't remember Mum ever complaining about Trafalgar Terrace life. It was so different from anywhere she had lived before but she engaged with life in two rooms with vigour. She went to Dublin entirely for my sake, and lived creatively with such different circumstances.'

In 1960, John Perry suddenly had the idea of writing a sequel to *Spring Meeting*. Margaret Rutherford, who had had her first great success as Aunt Bijou in the original play, had a special affection for the character. Since then she had become one of London's most beloved actresses frequently working for H. M. Tennent in classic and new plays. She had recently starred in the first Miss Marple film, and John felt she would draw in the public. She was an extraordinary actress, sensitive, wild and original. John Gielgud said of her, 'Margaret was almost mad and that was why she was so good.' He agreed to direct but he was in a hurry to get away to do an avant-garde play in New York and the production had to be rushed out quickly. His heart was not in it and he really only did it out of friendship to please John and Binkie and to assist Molly. She was physically and mentally exhausted when she wrote it; the strain shows. It makes depressing reading today with heavy-handed jokes and no sparkle. It is almost unrecognisable from the work Molly had done in the past and would do in the future. She was conscious of its weakness but felt it might be pulled together in rehearsal. Nobody bothered to do anything much to it in rehearsal, but nothing could have saved it. Perilously entitled *Dazzling Prospect*, it met a firing squad. There was a revolution starting in the theatre at the time. The Royal Court was beginning to produce the works of Samuel Beckett, Arnold Wesker, John Osborne, Harold Pinter and others. H. M. Tennent's stranglehold on the West End was gradually loosening. The era of drawing-room comedies was over. They had produced much besides these, elegant presentations of the classics and Shakespeare and plays by Eliot and Robert Bolt, Jean Anouilh and Peter Schaffer among others, but it was felt by the new generation of critics that they had become decadent and incestuous. *Dazzling Prospect*, co-authored by John Perry (known to be Binkie's partner) was the catalyst. John and Molly's idea of Woodrooffe in the play was blunted by nostalgia and time and not real, as it is in *Spring Meeting*. On the opening night, due to the rage against H. M. Tennent the applause was punctuated by the booing of planted groundlings. The critics were rough. Ken Tynan wrote a scathing review in the *Observer*, in which he said (among other things) that he distinctly heard the neighing of horses from members of the audience seated around him.

Molly felt it was all her fault because she was such a bad

writer. She bravely went down to Knots Fosse, Binkie's house in the country, the weekend after the catastrophe feeling very shaky and found it extremely painful. John Gielgud, who took failure as he did success, calmly, might have helped her but he had flown off to America. John Perry was somewhat shellshocked and Binkie ambivalent and withdrawn, caught up in the wider troubles revealed by the attack on this slight play which was like the crushing of a gnat by a tank. At the Fosse, Molly was comforted by Keith Baxter and Dick Clowes. It took her years to understand that she was merely a pawn in a revolution and that what happened would have happened anyway with some other Tennent production; but this play, weak in itself and carrying all the connotations that it did, was the ideal opportunity for the critics of the time to attack what they saw as the sick lion.

The play closed, everyone else picked themselves up and went on about their business but Molly brooded on it. We stayed close to her and were affected by her pain, bobbing about on it like corks on a wave. The downside of Molly's ability to adore life and make it hum was this way of drawing one into her sorrow as she did her joy. Eventually she began to recover and to heal herself, with plotting and planning. Plan 1 was that she would never write again. Her day was over. Ten years of fruitless work ending in agony and disaster was enough. The battering from the critics had wounded her to the core but she referred to it in a brittle, brave 'good behaviour' way. 'My writing is dated. This is the end and there is nothing I can do.' The grief and shame she had experienced was followed by relief.

Plan 2 was to plunge into her passion for domesticity

which brought in its wake friendship and social life. There was the problem of earning money but a solution of sorts came out of these very things. A small invasion was taking place in the Blackwater Valley at the time: chic Americans were beginning to buy houses there. Phyllis Mitchell, who was to become a close friend of Molly's, bought Fort William. The Merril family came to the rectory in Villierstown; both had friends who wished to rent summer houses. By this time Molly had given up Trafalgar Terrace. Virginia had moved to a crammer in Sussex, the only school she had ever liked – because the first essence of hippydom was apparent there. I was studying and working at various jobs in London. The letting of Dysert became Molly's new career; it supplemented her modest private income and made her many new friends among her tenants. Her house was her alter ego. She warmed to those who loved it and hated anyone who complained. Above all, it allowed her to lavish care on her home and make improvements, not out of self-indulgence, but because it was good for business. She was just as disciplined about this work as she was about writing. She was almost French in her love of discipline and her love of pleasure. The perfectionism of small things delighted her. Her cooking became better and better. She found it more fun than writing and it seemed to take its place. She took immense trouble to get it right. Her food tasted like no one else's. It had a definite style, balancing sweet and sour, like her prose.

When Dysert was let, Molly became a nomad, moving from friend to friend in her Morris Minor, accompanied by her dog. Zephi, her latest dog, was the mongrel offspring of one of

Daphne Hall-Dare's troop of Dutch barge dogs – not sleek like a true-bred Schipperke, she was spikey in coat and temperament, and tiny. She was originally meant to be Virginia's pet, but she only loved Molly and Bridget, who conversed with her especially when there was a technical hitch with one of the modern installations she hated at Dysert in Ardmore. Molly said she once overheard Bridget saying, 'Excuse me, Zephi, I couldn't hear what you were telling me with the old cylinder boiling.' Nobody minded one bringing one's cross dog to stay but country house visiting – a pleasure and a tradition of Anglo-Irish life – was a tricky art which had to be practised. Molly, from years of experience in her youth, was particularly good at it. She felt it was a sacred duty to be amusing and she was really interested in her friends' lives. She loved talking for hours and helping with sewing and the picking of flowers and the chopping of vegetables. She resisted the temptation of interfering with the cooking and diplomatically learned new tricks from her hostesses.

During this time she frequently returned to Wexford to stay with Charlie. Theo, after years of courageous struggle with rheumatoid arthritis, had died. She had kept her interests up manfully, breeding her poodles, caring for refugees and smocking lovely frocks for her godchildren (including Virginia) until her thumbs twisted almost backwards and she couldn't sew any more. Charlie, who had been totally involved in Theo's struggle, was lonely and depressed without her; keeping him company was for Molly a new and unirritating way of being in 'the Bogs'. She adored Statia and Paddy who ran everything there. He was the groom and Statia cooked and also nursed Mrs Skrine until her death, and then Theo. Statia spoke in the Wexford accent and employed its beautiful archaic phrases. She was full of love and wit. All the Skrines were devoted to Statia and Paddy; their little girl, Bernie, became a close friend of Virginia. Molly began enjoying herself with her friend Daphne Hall-Dare again, and dipping into the wasps' nest of Bunclody social politics. She also brought Jack the pony there, and was very proud of Virginia's performances out hunting. Virginia was an excellent rider, unlike me, but Charlie thought it boastful to mention such things and disapproved of Molly doing so. In the past she had commented on her relationship with Charlie: 'I do regret the intense boredom I experience sometimes with people I love like Char. I can try harder with the most ghastly men against whom I can find some sort of challenge.' Despite these views, they were devoted and understood the cocktail of perfectionism, depression, sharpness and kindness in each other. Eventually Charlie's twinkle won out over his sadness at Theo's loss and he married in his sixties a young wife, Rosemary Barrett, and had two children.

In a surprise move, Molly bought a house in London in 1965. She was able to afford this because Walter (selflessly) had decided to make most of his small amount of capital over to Molly and Godfrey (his poorest siblings) to help with their children. Molly began to talk about 'making a home for the girls in London'. She felt strongly that we should have a background, a place to bring young men and girlfriends home for a meal or a drink. That was something she had wished for which her parents had never given her. Sadly, this plan did not quite work out. We were, in different ways, bent on escaping from our background, even though it was such a vivid, interesting and creative one. We regretted the vein of snobbishness running through it which we demonised in an oversimplified way. We embraced the new age of working-class heroes and hippy romanticism, which we meshed into our passion for the Irish landscape and for reading aloud Yeats and Wordsworth.

This move entailed long drives back and forth from Ardmore in the rickety Morris Minor loaded with belongings. There was a small space scooped out in the back for one of us to sit. Zephi in her cross old age growled from her perch of bundles. Once we met Robert and Joan Morley as we were passing through Henley, and we pulled in to talk to them. Robert teased us about how long ago we had left Ireland. Virginia and I chorused, 'But you see Mum drives so slowly.' After we parted from them, I looked in the mirror, and saw large tears rolling down Molly's cheeks. For once she said nothing, but years later told me how painful she found our beastly jeering attitude to her driving when she was exhausted almost at the end of her marathon. We also gobbled her delicious picnics without a word of appreciation, and provoked rows with our vague, bad map-reading when she was facing into the English traffic after the quiet, familiar roads of home.

One of the reasons she chose to live in Barnes was because it was near to the Froebel Institute where Virginia was studying. Molly had no interest in the course about which Virginia was passionate, and she thought teachers were boring, though she tolerated me doing a Montessori course in Hampstead at this time (I never practised my teaching). She hated the Froebel concept of 'creative play' because it meant that, on top of the usual teenage disorder of Virginia's room, there were piled egg cartons, pipe-cleaners, rags and cardboard boxes, coloured papers and much other rubbish out of which the children's lessons were constructed. Serious conflict cut between them and this was a great shock to both. Molly's brand of snobbishness was theoretical; if there was a linking space she forgot it. She liked the Liverpool accent of her actor friend Victor Spinetti but complained about 'common' regional voices of Virginia's fellow students. This was one of the counter-productive ways in which she manifested her suffering at the eclipse of their close relationship. She wanted us to be happy and to marry the sort of young men with whom she herself had been such a success. My failure as a girl distressed her because she felt it was all my own fault, caused by my shyness and over-romanticism. I dreamed of what she called 'the fairy on the top of the Christmas tree', who was always in love with someone else – occasionally someone descended towards me from the Christmas tree, but it didn't last and I would often succumb to depression. Molly was extremely loving when this happened. She would take me to the theatre, to a beautiful exhibition at the V&A or buy me something new to wear.

My girlfriend Adrian was her consolation for my egocentric romanticism and for the alien accents of Virginia's boyfriends. Like Molly, she loved society and got a lot of fun out of it. She was an original, brilliant at flirting, and much involved in labyrinthine love affairs, about which she sought Molly's advice.

Adrian and I spent hours gossiping and sewing. She made ball dresses, cutting the bodices lower to display the gold sheen of her décolletage. I made miniskirts and shifts, feeling that my legs were my best feature. I wrestled with *Vogue* patterns on the floor, and then stitched the result by hand, sometimes when driving with a possible suitor. Molly said she suspected I sewed in these circumstances to fend off the young man from making a pass at me. I denied it, but there was a grain of truth in the remark. She always encouraged one about these outfits, and the way one looked. At the same age as I was then, she had been writing novels and hiding the fact. She felt that the masque of frivolousness was best. This policy was partly responsible for turning me into an intellectual snob for a time, and a bookworm permanently. I started to harbour fantasies about going to university but Molly was not keen on this idea. She had only marginally more respect for university than for teachers' training college. She cited Sue's bluestocking existence as an example of disaster. 'Although she is cleverer and much better looking and better dressed than I am, she has had no love and no fun. She has never had a house of her own, and lives in lonely, ghastly lodgings.'

This sort of talk, of course, carried me further in the opposite direction but I was some years in London before I came to any definite conclusion about it. Meanwhile, she had to contend with my depression, and Virginia's defiance. We sisters were drawn together by talking about her behind her back. It must have been a cold wind after the failure of *Dazzling Prospect*, yet she sailed her own life on vividly, despite the domestic storms between us. She put her energies into transforming the surroundings which were unlike anywhere she had lived before. The house was newly built, and we were its first occupants. Everything was modern and a complete contrast to Trafalgar Terrace. It had central heating and was open-plan with sliding windows which were a struggle to open. Molly brought her Anglo-Irish background and artist's eye to bear on the whole thing and translated it into something it was never meant to be. She curtained the plate glass with mattress ticking lined in red flannel and with chintz in the bedrooms. A sofa table from Belleville became the dining table in the tiny eating area beneath the stairs. She placed her two favourite Georgian chairs in the drawing-room, and hung Norah McGuinness's painting of a couple of hungry ladies and a child of fifties Dublin picking through a rich household's dustbin with a rose thrown on top in Fitzwilliam Square. It was wonderful what she made of such an alien place. The narrow garden ran in a straight strip to the railway line. I would wake up imagining I heard a waterfall, but it was a train rushing to Waterloo. She met another Anglo-Irish exile, Philip Somerville-Large, who had a small gardening business in the area, and together they created curved beds filled with scented plants and shrubs and raised trellises to keep the neighbours at bay. She tried unsuccessfully to cultivate the chic French family next door and their handsome baby. They were in the rag trade, and rather tough. They complained we made their pictures shake when we ran up and down the stairs. Chicken Lindsey, a charming, rich Scottish lady from a few doors down, made up for this. They shared lots of cocktails and dog talk and fun. Virginia and she temporarily reconnected when they went to a neighbouring junk shop which they both loved. The owner was a fence for stolen goods and he had a vast shed where Virginia found materials for her creative play, and Molly discovered many treasures and indulged her penchant for camp Victoriana.

Barnes Common, where she walked the dog, was not an alien place. Blackberries grew there and rough grass, and even a few rushes. There were some magnificent trees, including a huge weeping willow which could be seen from our estate. A visionary Samuel Palmer-like light shone through it on summer evenings. I have heard that murders have been committed on the Common, but in our day it was safe, although Molly was nervous of us being raped. She thought that red hair was dangerous and she urged both us redheads to wear a scarf when crossing the Common. The station was in the middle of it.

She parked the Morris there when she visited the West End. She went to the theatre often and to the old Italian Lina Stores in Brewer Street, Soho. The latter brought inspiring new elements into her cooking, such as basil, dried mushrooms and expensive olive oil that was to be kept for special occasions and not splashed about by Virginia and me. As she wasn't writing, she entertained a lot, cooking for one or two friends at a time because of the limited space round the sofa table.

Sometimes she went away for country weekends, particularly to Knots Fosse. H. M. Tennent was down but not yet out. Binkie, struggling, was drinking more. When Elvira opened the door to Molly at Lord North Street, she would simply say 'The Boss . . . ' and raise her eyes and lift an imaginary glass to her lips to convey her worry about it. John Perry was indulging in an Indian summer of naughtiness. Dick Clowes, writing to Molly in Ardmore, informed her 'Our dearest mutual friend is living entirely for pleasure and flattery.'

Friends from Ireland arrived to stay; she fed them sumptuously and took them on jaunts to plays, to Kew Gardens and Osterley Park (an Adam house in the midst of the motorway) and to race meetings with her brother Walter, who lived at East Molesey in Surrey. He was very important to her during her years at The Elms in Barnes. They saw a lot of each other and their mutual affection deepened. It had always been there despite the unfortunate incident of dragging him in a cardboard box when he was a baby. She kept the eloquently expressed letters he wrote her over the years from the time when he had been a dashing young subaltern during the thirties in India, obsessed with racing: 'I wouldn't mind getting married,' he wrote, 'but the girl would have to understand that horses come first.' Women were attracted to him, to his thoughtfulness and his slow, mischievous smile. He was always networking in the army manner, but on behalf of others, never for himself. He had a dread of personal power. He was brave in an extreme way – like T. E. Lawrence, with whom he also shared the desire to live as an outsider, and a penchant for motorbikes, and a possibly homosexual tendency which, in his case, would have been forever resisted. There were many reasons why he never married, among them a complex lack of self-confidence, which does not show in his steady, elegant handwriting. His youthful correspondence from India manifests a passion for life and an ironic humour. In these letters he is sometimes quite critical of others and not thinking of himself as the lowest of the low, and deserving the worst, as he did later on. It is as though his later experiences undermined his psyche and produced a strange meekness and despair. From early days he had confided in Molly, feeling that she understood the human heart and that he could learn something about how to live from her. She responded very creatively towards him, building him up as she did the people she loved.

All his siblings regarded Walter as a hero because of his purity of heart and the quality in him that evoked love in his fellow men, from the great and the good to the people he sat next to on the Green Line buses which were his chief mode of transport by the time Molly came to Barnes. Godfrey summed him up in two phrases: 'Wallah is a saint' and 'Wallah has lived a buggered-up life', the latter referring to his habit of turning down the splendid opportunities he was offered, or retiring from them. The Skrines, an impoverished, well-connected family, believed it was one's duty to seize opportunities and make an effort to get on in the world.

They also responded to Walter's saintly side, loved him unconditionally and came to his aid when he broke down mentally or physically. Although they did not discuss it, they were aware that there was a tragic aspect to him that they would not face or help him to face. It was a Skrine element that they all partook of but he was burdened with an extreme version of it. He respected Molly's toughness and ability to struggle on and not lose faith in life for long when knocked down. He also admired her ease and enjoyment in the social world. He, too, could muster social skill when it was needed, but it was an effort. He was by nature shy and reclusive and not 'mustard for a party', as he admiringly described some 'blithe young chaps' under his command. These people loved him, as did his superior officers who, after the war, were always offering him jobs he was eminently qualified to do, but from which he always expected to get sacked. If not sacked, he was inclined to retire early, convinced that someone else would do better. The certainties of military life were completely wrong for his gentle, enquiring temperament and prevailing sense of wonder. The army's idea of a man of action was not someone he could ever be. At the same time, he had an inordinate respect for the whole thing and was very good at it until the moment came when he hit what he called 'a wobble' and could not go on.

He came out of the war broken in body and, to a certain extent, in spirit and too brave for his own good. Wounded in Sicily, he lay among his dead comrades. He only avoided receiving a bullet to the head because the retreating enemy thought he was already dead. When the war was over he went through painful innovatory operations to repair his wounded leg and shorten the good one so that he could continue to ride in races. He had quite a successful racing career but in his letters to Molly he described the occasions when he fell off, or unbalanced his horse, Martin M., when riding into a fence and seldom mentioned his wins.

He was not enthusiastic about his last army post, that of a lieutenant colonel on a Selection Board: '... the work has a certain interest in a way, but I am not too happy about holding it down. I dislike being in a position of judge of my fellow-men and would have preferred the T.A. which does not involve too much fault-finding and criticism on paper or otherwise. One is liable to become self-righteous and self-important when doing this kind of thing ...' He was tired and decided to leave the army and set up house with Sue, who had retired from her teaching in India. This modest dream ('Neither of us has big ideas') went wrong in practice. They got disastrously on one another's nerves and couldn't cope with the Skrine in each other. Walter was driven mad by Sue's fussing and health diets. They gave up with a feeling of guilt and failure.

After that, he abandoned any idea of owning a house and began to live like a William Trevor character in lodgings on the fringes of London, eating in restaurants that smelt of unappetising gravy. His landladies always loved him. He talked to them and took a helpful, uninterfering interest in their lives. He would emerge briefly and stay with relatives or smart army and horsey friends, all of whom welcomed him delightedly. He always departed before people wanted him to and dived back into his burrow. He adored stamps. A new Irish issue on a letter from Molly in September 1969 aroused his admiration. 'What a striking and attractive stamp. I would love a corner block of six stamps with numbers in the margin (like the one on your envelope). More than that would be too much on a page.' After his retirement he cultivated this hobby seriously. He began to attend stamp auctions. He became a freelance agent for Robson Lowe, a well-known firm in Pall Mall run by a friend. Towards the end of his life he joined their office officially – work he embarked on with slightly more confidence than usual. 'I really think the project is going well and that they will not sack me at least for a while. I was working too long hours at home. This was due to anxiety about the future as well as the present and quite unnecessary of course, but that is it. One is made as one is made.'

Walter had always looked on Molly as the success of the family and himself as the failure. After *Dazzling Prospect* and her abandonment of writing, he felt that circumstances had altered and that she was in need of his support psychologically and financially. He was beginning to make a profit from his stamp dealing and felt in a position to give it away. He wanted to pay for various things for her, including Virginia's wedding.

Molly, although going through a down time, was reluctant to accept his offers because he had already given his savings to Godfrey and herself. Now that she felt unable to write her way out of them, her money problems were a constant source of anxiety. Walter would write on her behalf to someone called 'Mr Pollard' and send her on letters from this guru with notes from himself saying things like 'Don't forget to act on this matter'.

They enjoyed going about together. She pared down the richness of her cooking when he came to lunch because of his heart condition and ate without complaining in the bleak cafés he patronised. They went racing usually quite modestly down the course where they could get a good view of the horses circulating before the start. Occasionally a jockey recognised Walter and called him in to settle his girths, as he was known to be an excellent saddler-up – sometimes Lester Piggott would wink at him. This favour from the taciturn genius was a source of pride to Walter, and he would actually mention it when it happened. Every now and again they indulged in a small touch of luxury. When planning to take Daphne Hall-Dare to Windsor with them, Walter is disappointed that it is flat racing not jumping and, to make up for this, he suggests going to a non-greasy spoon restaurant beforehand. 'I would love to give you lunch at an hotel I know. It is by the station and very nice, on the river, and we could probably get down to the course by boat and spend the afternoon in the usual way.' Racing was an elixir to them both. Molly also took trouble to charm his landlady and East Molesey mates in the same way she set out to enchant his grand friends when he took her to meet them. She basked in his reflected glory. He had a sort of magic which carried him far beyond his diffidence and pain.

Virginia married the film historian Kevin Brownlow in the summer of 1969 and I went as a mature student to Reading University to read English that autumn. Even though it was not what she would have chosen for me, Molly had a great generosity of spirit and understood what I was doing. She sold The Elms and returned home to Ireland. Tessa, her first chihuahua, came into her life. She trembled inside her thin velvety skin and had the noble overbred head of a fairy's race horse. Molly adored her lion-like courage and sensational smallness. She hid her under a scarf in her handbag when travelling by air and let her wander round the table at the end of dinner parties so she could lap up the wine left in people's glasses. Thomas McCarthy in his memoir *Gardens of Remembrance* describes Molly at this time as living 'in a kind of twilight zone of reading and gardening and caring for the pig-like Chihuahua that always accompanied her in her old Morris Minor'. She was rather contented in her twilight zone which involved much cooking and 'chums' and polishing up of the house for letting. It seemed that her writing sleep would never end.

CHAPTER 8

t was snowing on the day of Elizabeth Bowen's funeral. It was
22 February 1973. The small church at Farahy was crowded.
People from the disparate threads of her life gathered, practically all of them in a state of grief because they had lost a
friend of a rare essence. She was seventy-four. The congre-
gation included her family, members of the literary world,
her neighbours, people who had worked for her at Bowen's
Court. Charles Ritchie, her lover of thirty years, was there, a
romantic almost legendary persona glimpsed now for the first
time in the flesh by many of her other friends. A tall figure,
he walked up the aisle with calm dignity, the shoulders of his
blue overcoat dusted in snow. The Anglo-Irish had picked
their scarce winter blossoms for Elizabeth, aconites, snowdrops
and the green Christmas hellebore. Molly had forced the stiff
branches of her *Hamamelis mollis* with their tiger-coloured
scented flowers into a bouquet. The church smelt of the first
narcissus of the year. One of Elizabeth's closest friends, Ursula
Vernon, lofty, aged and still as beautiful as Garbo, bent over

the bouquets arranging them around the coffin and then sat down and wept. After the service Elizabeth was buried with her husband Alan Cameron, who had died twenty years previously. At the end of the land leading to the church people queued up to offer their sympathy to Audrey Fiennes, her cousin and closest friend from childhood who knew the whole story and greeted each person who approached her with a consoling awareness of their relationship to Elizabeth. Later some people walked across to the house where her cook at Bowen's Court lived. At first she offered tea but had to stop as the crowd increased in her kitchen. She spoke of her former boss with love and said, 'She was a mother to us all.' Elizabeth was childless but the epitaph fitted – her friendship had unconditional generosity about it. She left a hole in people's lives. Molly was shaken but she never cried at funerals. She treated them as parties and put her best foot forward. Later at home she experienced the sting and despair that recalled Bobbie's death. We were stricken by Elizabeth's death.

The loss probably drew Molly closer to Nora Preece. She was a cousin of Eddie Sackville-West, who had loved Elizabeth to the point of wanting to marry her even though he was homosexual. He had died suddenly in 1965. Nora adored them both – unlike Molly she wept at funerals, in private or any time she felt like it, and expressed her feelings in all ways, notably in her romantic, literary, indiscreet letters. Writers were drawn to her. She herself was a writer manquée who put her wordsmithing into her correspondence and conversation.

When she gave up Barnes, Molly continued to let Dysert in the summers and spent a lot of time visiting 'chums'. She often stayed with Nora at Kells. This romantic house beside the sea was protected from Atlantic storms by woods and laurels. Within the shelter, Nora's husband, Roland, had made a beautiful dark garden for shade-loving plants and ferns. He was also a brilliant embroiderer and his carpets were sought after. It was through him that Molly came to do petit point. He taught her some of his stitches and drew up elegant repeating patterns for her – not sentimental roses, which she despised. She was clever at treading the difficult line of conversing with Roland and flattering him for his superb gardening, sewing and woodwork and sympathising with Nora who found him irritating. When an expedition was planned Nora would say, 'I think we will find a task for Roland.' They would drive off, leaving him with some smashed-up item of furniture to mend.

When they had to sell Kells and move back to England, Nora wrote to Molly: 'I think of you a great deal as part of something like fun and things being unworrying which one has known before and must one feels know again – I do wish Elizabeth and Eddie weren't dead, do you?'

Nora's strictness and glory in words echoed her own and may well have softened her hatred of writing and subconsciously influenced her to try again. It is certain that after *Dazzling Prospect* she felt she had no public left. Having first seen this as the end, she began to realise that it gave her a freedom to write something to please only herself: '. . . a book that truly involved and interested me . . . black comedy perhaps but with something of the truth in it, and the pity I feel for the kind of people I lived with and laughed with in the happy, maligned 30's.' She started to follow the thread of her wicked imagination and allowed the darkness which she had used sparingly in previous books to become the main current of this one. Doing so required courage because it meant exposing the cruel, wounded side of her own psyche which she was ashamed of and which the natural kindness and romanticism of her nature struggled to keep in check. This nasty aspect of her temperament, which had frequently got her into trouble, suddenly had a useful purpose. In *Good Behaviour* she is very aware of the link between individual darkness and that of society. She knew the small world which she inhabited and loved and hated to the bone. 'I do send my Anglo-Irish background up rather I know I do, but sometimes I am conscious of the courage and glamour that has sustained its existence.' She disliked abstract discussion but if it came to it she was inclined to defend the Anglo-Irish robustly. Art, however, is not opinion. She would never have referred to her society as decadent, but her characters prove that it is, by the lengths of treachery and self-deceit to which they are prepared to go in order to get their own way even in quite small matters. While living the life of her background with passion and conviction she knew about its cruelty and absurdity and decline. It was a world where denial becomes betrayal, and where the tough, successful, indifferent ones do better than the compassionate (Mrs Brock is brutally treated for her kindness). In *Good Behaviour* charm buys spoiling, and love between parents shuts out children. The result of childhood pain on the grown-up and what the journalist Mary D. Kierstead in the *New Yorker* described as 'the lasting effect of small cruelties' was deeply understood by Molly. Her main character, the spinster Aroon, wounded, warped and misguided, is the bad bank of her own psyche; she is shepherded to disaster by a social code where 'Tears are such rotten behaviour', where feelings are mostly expressed obliquely and where good manners can swiftly become a mask for all sorts of dubious goings-on. Profound grief was sidestepped and lesser pains converted into jokes. It was a way of not being a bore and avoiding despair. Molly was a master of the art in real life and in the book she carries it a step further and creates a brilliant black comedy. She does not deny the starkness of tragedy as her people do but she presents the story through a filter of humour. Laughter is the lifeboat that carries you across a rough sea of cruelty, hypocrisy and sorrow but does not shield you from them. This view is very much of Molly and the way she felt. She was passionately sensitive to suffering whether it concerned herself or another, sometimes to the point of becoming unhinged. Except in moments of extreme depression she never forgot that her ability to see life as funny was what saved her sanity. The skilful, ironic comedy of *Good Behaviour* came from self-knowledge, her forte in writing rather than living, and years of observing people. Together with its unsparing quality (in matters such as Papa's wooden leg and Aroon's largeness, etc.) there is also enjoyment of humanity and generosity and fun.

She always said her plots were character-driven. She would start with an idea but the characters developed and carried it in quite different directions from its original intention. With *Good Behaviour* she took a greater interest in the technique than she had ever done before. She fractures the narrative and breaks up time, and she creates a heroine who is an unreliable narrator. In the past she had frequently got fun out of characters that were askew to reality in flashes but she had never done it in such a full-blown way before. Aroon is the linchpin and seed of the whole book. Molly said that she was suddenly struck by the idea that it would be interesting to write about someone 'who really never knew what was hitting them – like in the theatre when the audience shouts "turn round William is going to shoot you . . . " ' Suppose one wrote about somebody who behaved like that throughout life, who simply couldn't see what was happening.' In Aroon, Molly's acceptance and understanding of 'the pretences which support people' and her scorn of denial are delicately balanced. Anglo-Irish society itself was very ambivalent about such matters, jeering at certain pretensions while respecting others. Molly herself sometimes partook of this ambivalence and sometimes was enraged by it. Aroon is her revenge; in her she lets rip about denial. All the characters are perceived with exactitude and relish. They are mosaics of herself and people she had known, burnished in her imagination – although she maintained that she had no imagination and that it was all sharpness and observation. Despite its darkness one's remembered impression of reading the book is colourful and vivid. One is dazzled by the rightness and reality of details and the way they are woven together – the rooms, the food, horrid and delicious smells, the generosity and betrayals of relationships. It is a hymn to the beauty and harshness of the natural world, where she noticed such things as 'blackbirds scuttling low about their love affairs'. One critic wrote, 'the beauty of the book is its prose stitched together like fine lace'. An extraordinary skill with detail was something she had always had but in *Good Behaviour* she took infinite time over it, polished it and strictly whittled it down to the essential word so that the writing shone with a jewel-like, controlled exoticism. 'The men were the flowers in these mysterious forests, sleek and orchidaceous in their hunt coats, the facings and collars pale, thin gold watch-chains crossing meagre stomachs, white ties as exact as two wings on a small bird's back, long legs black as cypripedium stems, hands sometimes gloved, eyes focused distantly, as if a fox stealing away from its covert was still the thought in mind.' The originality of her writing and her character came through in this book. She was always a bit ashamed of its ruthless quality even after it was a success and much praised for this very reason. She discouraged certain friends from reading it, feeling they would hate it. Some of them did.

Writing in secret benefited her. Having a secret always bucked her up. She broke her silence with one person, Stephen Vernon. He was a writer manqué, widower of Ursula Grosvenor, daughter of Bendor, Duke of Westminster, and a beautiful, uncertain enchantress who died soon after Elizabeth Bowen and who had been a close friend of hers. Stephen was clever, devious and brave, and also a beauty. He had been stricken badly by polio at the age of forty. Before that his and Ursula's life was centred on horses and hunting. When he was paralysed and could no longer ride he cultivated other resources and still got fun out of life and sometimes made mischief. He was bisexual, living in smart society where good behaviour and bad meshed seamlessly and where everything was permitted so long as discretion prevailed and the shell of good manners was not shattered. Stephen knew a great deal about this situation. Molly turned to him for guidance concerning her homosexual lovers Hubert and Richard and how they navigated their two worlds. She said that without his input her treatment of the boys would have been 'crass', as she put it. In her first version she had Papa discovering the boys dancing together to the gramophone after dinner. Stephen told her that such a thing would never have happened. The sensuality and the attraction which Papa picked up was all in the atmosphere and the secrecy and risk was a big part of the magic of these relationships. They flirted with one another as they danced with Aroon. They used her and her illusions and to atone for their deviousness they gave her the luxurious presents of the thirties, Floris bath essence, a soft, sensuous Jaeger coat and even a blood horse. Stephen lightened the burden of writing for Molly. He was the first person to read *Good Behaviour* and he was an enormous supporter of it. They discussed their secret at Fairyfield, where he lived in Kinsale. It was an exotic, dark house, flanked by ilex trees with rich flock papers on the walls, furnished with the residue of Grosvenor grandness filtered down through several bigger houses. Stephen was looked after by his gentle cook, Mrs MacCarthy, and the butler, Gerard, who helped him dress elegantly and take his scented bath. Gerard was a brilliant conversationalist who had grown up in Kildorrery, Elizabeth Bowen's village, and she had sent him to work for the Vernons as a young boy. Sitting late over a dish of grapes in the friendly gloom of the dining room with its curved walls lined in green silk and with gold furniture, Molly and Stephen discussed the book. His delight in it, plus a few glasses of wine, eased her doubts. They laughed as they fished for the suitably evocative names abounding in *Good Behaviour*, which in part tell the story in themselves. This was Stephen's area of expertise. The name Wobbly Massingham came from him. He knew to the bone the England of the Cavalry Club and eccentricity and charm and confidence underpinned by majestic houses and unindebted acres. This world, encompassing as it did the richer English relations, was important to the Anglo-Irish. They sometimes jeered at it but they were also admiring of it and dependent upon it for rescue when everything collapsed, as in the case of the Crowhurst twins in *Good Behaviour*.

Once finished she sent the book off to her regular publisher, Billy Collins. Perturbed and shocked by its blackness, he turned it down. He was her friend as well as her publisher and he wanted to help her so he suggested the compromise of writing or rewriting one nice character into the novel. Molly, for once putting art before money, refused. She felt that to soften it would ruin it. She may also have been influenced by the fact that she herself was afraid of the book's ruthlessness and she partly agreed with him that it was too much for readers to swallow. Before in her books she always wished to be entertaining and funny and give her audience a good time. After the debacle of *Dazzling Prospect*, her confidence was not high. She put the script away in the drawing-room tallboy and forgot it. She afterwards admitted that after the initial disappointment she was quite relieved that her attempt to go back to work had failed, as it seemed to set her free for ever from the pain of writing. She was actually enjoying her life of domesticity and friendship in a new and liberated way and was, by her standards, almost at peace. Because Virginia and I were both married, she no longer felt totally responsible for our wellbeing.

George Phipps and I married in St Mary's Collegiate Church in Youghal. It was a very big building for a small family wedding but ancient and beautiful. Patricia Cockburn and Clodagh Anson filled it with flowers. Molly gave a lunch party afterwards at Dysert – she was joyful and full of love for me. She looked stunning and young in a flowery silk dress. In the past I had sometimes annoyed her by being in love with 'the fairy at the top of the Christmas tree' and not with somebody on the ground. When George and I got engaged her delight was total. He was her sort of man, a country person, simple on the surface but full of complexities and hidden depths. His abiding interest was the natural world, about which he was very knowledgeable. Tall and romantic, he was used to charming people and being loved but with that he was gentle and sensitive to the feelings of others. Molly loved the twinkle in his eye. She responded also to the tragedy in his life. He had lost his beloved first wife who had left him a young widower with three children. Molly did not know the children well at the time of our marriage but her heart went out to them and she longed to make them feel welcome in the rather strange circumstances in which they found themselves – at their father's wedding. The eldest, Richard, acted as George's best man. My youngest stepchild, James, was five, dressed in a grey flannel suit and knee socks. Molly handed him a bottle of champagne and he offered it around with aplomb. He was a party animal like herself.

Having a stepmother and being one has its hazards but we managed to survive them. Richard, Annie and James welcomed me with generosity and they have become my adopted children.

George lived and farmed at Kilcor, near Castlelyons in Co. Cork. It was a delightful, slightly ramshackle establishment that attracted many visitors who sometimes stayed for months.

New friends arrived with me. They fell in love with Annie, just then turning from a child into a beautiful girl, or with Mrs Phipps, my mother-in-law – and sometimes with both of them. The latter was good at persuading young people to help her with jobs. I would see them sitting with her on a wall in the yard, lost in conversation. She resembled a noble medieval figure dressed in her woollen pixie hat and long coat, with a bucket of food at her feet for the ducks and a bucket of poison for the rats.

Molly's reprieve from writing lasted until the summer of 1979 when Peggy Ashcroft came to visit and had to stay in bed with flu, offering Molly the sort of opportunity she relished of cherishing and spoiling someone she loved. She carried little trays of soup and fruit in to her friend and sat at the foot of the bed talking for hours. Peggy, instinctively the artist, ferreted out what she had been up to, and persuaded her to let her read the book. She responded to it immediately. Her temperamental, emotional affinity with Molly – combined with her actress's ability to calm and synthesise her feelings and use them – made her the ideal reader of *Good Behaviour*. She took the script back to London with her and gave it to her friend Ian Parsons, then chairman of Chatto & Windus, to read. He loved it but his second reader did not. He wrote expressing his admiration and reassurance to Molly that the book would certainly find a publisher, and regretting that it would not be himself. Despite this and other shoots of hope that were beginning to surround *Good Behaviour*, Molly was still very uncertain about it. In a letter to her friend Sibell Rowley she writes, 'Book holding its time rather. I never was all that optimistic but all may get worked out.' Around this time she met the writer Diana Morgan who, having read and admired the novel, did it an immense service by giving it to the agent Gina Pollinger to read.

Gina was the agent from heaven for Molly. A small, very attractive, hour-glass figure, passionately and discerningly literary, she fell in love with *Good Behaviour* and kept faith with it through several more rejections until it was accepted by André Deutsch in 1980. She had the further dimension of taking care of her authors almost as though they were her adopted children. She had compassion for the neurosis and insecurities and jealousies to which writers are prone. She understood the vulnerability and loneliness of their exposure every time they put a book out. She never left her clients marooned and alone in times of uncertainty and challenge. She cherished them and kept in touch. In Molly's case, she telephoned, she wrote, she sent comforting gifts, such as soft red leather walking shoes, and she welcomed her into her home. As well as this, she and her husband, Murray, were expert fighters in the marketplace. It is not surprising that their list of authors was a long and illustrious one. She was the architect of Molly's last and most successful career. They fell into one another's arms. Molly became friends with the whole family and was particularly devoted to Edmund, Gina and Murray's son.

The charmed life of *Good Behaviour* continued and gathered momentum. At Deutsch it found an ideal editor in Diana Athill, celebrated in literary circles as one of the best in the business. She retired in 1993 and has since become famous for her own writing. As her memoirs show, she is a very original, unorthodox character who is quite *comme il faut* on the surface. She is a splendidly cool, interested brave person. Her upper-class background resembled an English version of Molly's; a country life where people hunted and gardened and sewed and talked animatedly about the ramifications of cousinship. Like Molly she respected all this while being to a certain extent a rebel. Her understanding and admiration for *Good Behaviour* was instantaneous. She wrote saying she would publish, and asked for a photograph so that she could see what the author looked like. Diana said that when she first saw the picture of Molly, shielded from the sun by a hat, looking down solicitously at Tessa in her lap, she was reminded of generations of women in her own family. She and Molly were linked perhaps most closely by this inherited unconditional love for their little dogs. In time they would walk Tessa and Hannah, Diana's Shih Tzu, together on Primrose Hill. Sometimes they were discordant. When the success of *Good Behaviour* was at full throttle there were moments when Molly became intoxicated. Diana was disapproving; she had seen it all before and would experience in old age something similar herself. In a subtle, scholarly way she pricked the balloon of Molly's hubris. Commenting afterwards, Molly would put this down to 'a sort of strange school-mistressy jealousy' (an explanation for human behaviour which she was fond of) and toss her head. Despite such moments they greatly valued each other. When Molly was ill and down in 1990 Diana wrote unequivocally saying what she really thought: 'I wish they'd ask me for my hero because it would be you, a) for writing so well, b) for writing so well delicious books that are fun to read as well as showing life as it is, c) for being as brave as a lion.'

Before it appeared at all *Good Behaviour* received a well-publicised promotion. André Deutsch put out a personal press release: 'It is a marvellous novel and reappearance is a word of good omen with us. Think of Jean Rhys.' He was referring to another forgotten writer whose career had been relaunched by Diana starting with the publication of a new novel, *Wide Sargasso Sea*, based on the life of Mr Rochester's mad wife in *Jane Eyre*. Molly admired the book and recognised the usefulness of the comparison and was very willing to take advantage of it, but she sometimes got huffy, saying that people expected her to be as drunk and dysfunctional and also as brilliant as Jean Rhys, whom Diana had had to totally look after, coax writing from and frequently rescue. Although Molly had her own impossibilities, they were of a less dramatic kind.

Deutsch sold the US rights to Knopf in New York; *Good Behaviour* was printed in America and published there in the spring of 1981, a few months ahead of London. The print run was not large. It was a surprise when the book received almost universal rave reviews, from the major New York papers to the provincial literary pages across the land. *Good Behaviour* arrived in London with a fair wind behind it. The *New York Review of Books* said it might well become a classic among English novels and Walter Clemons of *Newsweek* wrote, 'This self-possessed, crisply detailed, alertly funny novel is a wonder. Silent for decades, Keane has abruptly published a masterwork. I hope it will be noticed; I'm confident it will last.'

Molly received a letter from Eudora Welty, whom she knew slightly through Elizabeth Bowen: 'I wish I could tell you how extraordinary and how crowning a piece of work I found it.

It filled me with pleasure page after page. I felt the kind of admiration for it that's exhilaration, really, something that goes right to the heart of the hope every true lover of fiction feels on opening some looked-for book. And when I finished it, totally absorbed, I turned straight back to the beginning and read it again out of the wisdom and anticipations the first reading gave me. I knew I had a masterpiece in my hands – it was the kind of meeting with a true original work that I haven't found since (I hope you don't mind) Henry Green – it was the same kind of excitement and pleasure.'

Eudora Welty was the first of many good writers who, having read *Good Behaviour*, rushed to welcome it. From this Molly began to have a new, glimmering feeling about her work – that she was a professional and writing was perhaps her real life. This was a steadying influence when she let it be. It played against her perverse tendency to regard writing as slightly unmentionable and the opposite of fun; it was lessons, it was money-slavery, it was spying.

Because of *Good Behaviour* Molly suddenly became a subject herself. Journalists began to come to see her in Virginia's flat in London and even to Dysert to interview her. She never mastered the technique of sounding interesting and yet giving nothing away, which is the mask of the practised interviewee. Her first attempts were disastrous. One in particular, with the *Sunday Times*, caused shame to Virginia and me. The young columnist was obviously not a fan of the book and she thought Molly was a terrible old snob. She sets the scene by remarking '*Good Behaviour* is about upper-class family life in those heady pre-war days when it cost perhaps £2 a week to keep a horse and rather less to keep the groom'.

Molly burbled on, ad-libbing and falling into all the abysses that can occur between people from opposing social worlds. She mentions sacking nannies, feeling sick when writing out the menu for the cook, and how her mother only loved her husband 'and cared bugger-all about us really'. Her worst faux pas occurred when she said, 'I don't think there was a lot of poverty in Ireland in those days. When I was a child I do remember seeing children going to school barefoot but they rather enjoyed it. They didn't mind at all.'

Virginia was horrified by the piece and took Molly to task about it. She rang up Diana Athill who advised her to stop worrying as no one ever remembered what they read in the papers. Molly treated the whole thing like a dinner-party conversation. If she was out of sympathy with the person she was sitting next to she was prone to falling into a nervous aggression. She became flippant and sharp, and talked off the top of her head. She always conducted interviews as if they were social encounters, but if she got on well with the journalist concerned she sounded as if she were talking to a friend and not to someone she had just met. She later devised a routine at Dysert, putting flowers in the drawing-room, sitting the stranger down by the fire and offering them smoked salmon sandwiches and Irish coffee generously laced. Roy Foster, the eminent historian, remembers coming as a very young reporter to interview Molly. He arrived bleeding from the head, having just fallen off his bicycle. She rushed him into the kitchen and poured the whiskey meant for the coffee down his throat. He was a bit worried as he thought he might have been concussed but he says in fact he felt instantly restored.

Feminists espoused Molly and dressed her up in their ideas.

She was happy to go along with it if it seemed 'useful' and sold books. It caused her to have a rapport with some young journalists whom she really liked. In opinion she was dead against feminism (believing that men should be pleased and flattered at all times) but in her independent, struggling, flourishing spirit she was perhaps the personification of its essence. Of course, these young women responded as well to her charm and to the strength of her writing. A few of them became real friends, particularly Clare Boylan, who, over the years, often came to stay a night with her at Dysert. They would discuss the craft of writing. This was exceptional for Molly who was always embarrassed if someone asked her to elaborate on this subject. Her line was 'I don't know how I do it. I just do it.' She really felt that analysis was distasteful, and dangerous, and might have the potential to undermine the whole edifice.

It sometimes seemed she was finding out about herself and saying things she would never have said in real life. There was a confessional aspect to it which was perilous but it brought out her originality. Occasionally she succumbed to an upper-class weakness of being profligate with intimacy in order to leap over shyness and sound amusing. Much depended on how the interviewer had read *Good Behaviour*. Most of these people were quite young and she adopted the role of a frail old girl telling them about the past, which was rather at odds with the contents of the book. The late Stan Gebler Davies once said to me 'the first time I met your mother I brought her a bunch of roses because I thought she was a sweet old lady. The next time I brought her a bottle of whiskey; far more acceptable.' In fact she was a candidate for both gifts.

Shortly before publication day in London, Maureen Cleeve from the *Evening Standard* arrived at Dysert having been sent an advance copy of *Good Behaviour* by Diana Athill. 'It is a black comedy, very comic and slightly rude, there is a shining brilliance, a confidence and vitality about it that suggests a book written in the prime of life.' A brilliant, subtle journalist, she quickly got the point of Molly. She understood the background and knew that a day's hunting or shooting was not a hobby but the equivalent of a hard day at the office. She did not disapprove when Molly said, 'Nothing amuses me like being nasty about people I don't like.' And she understood the subtext of the phrase 'nipping about'. She brings Molly as a person to the page. 'Meeting Mrs Keane for the first time you feel a delightful intimacy as for an old girlfriend with whom secrets may be shared. Her conversation is full of suspense, for she is always about to reveal "something"; "such a great chum of mine, what a tragic tale to tell . . . I disapprove of him most horribly because . . . that's a very wicked story and one should not tell it . . . " But she does.

'I managed to tell her a small secret and she was very pleased . . . She says she wasn't pretty but she must have been enormously attractive because she is now; she still has the voice of a girl.' The conversation she quotes evokes Molly's presence almost tangibly:

(On her childhood) 'Mother's father governed various little islands like Mauritius and she came back from there to marry my father. She loved her sons but she didn't love me. I was jolly hard to love. Totally disobedient. She feared for me as she would if I had been a hippy and taken drugs. She never stopped being a Victorian. It was a class thing I grew up with, good behaviour. Don't whine, and don't make a fuss. If you broke your neck you must pretend you hadn't.'

(On the loucheness and cosiness of the twenties) 'I didn't manage life at all when I was young; I just flung myself at it. We had such a lovely time. One of the things of first importance was pleasure; there was nothing about doing good works or having a job because no one was educated to have a job. Ireland was like a big family, you would go to a race meeting in Wexford and then to a race meeting in Dublin and all the same people would be there.

'Everyone was a bit bottled most of the time if you ask me. And we were always dancing. People didn't need such grand things as bands and discos, you just danced to the gramophone.'

(On horses) 'I've had this feeling for horses all my life. It's a frightening excitement that takes the place of everything else. When I was young we really disapproved of people who didn't ride; it was the only thing that counted. I remember once one of my books got on some kind of best seller list and I was asked to a great literary party at the Piccadilly Hotel. I thought what awful ghastly boring people – still I'd better go.

'I travelled over on the boat with this hunting gent – really rather mad and in fact dreadfully boring but how I wished I was spending the evening with him instead of at this dreary party.'

(On Bobbie's death) 'I knew I had to behave, that I mustn't bore people. I bottled it all up.'

(On Ireland) 'That terribly jolly life that was doomed. But Ireland is still the last bastion of civilization; there is leisure and there is great beauty still uninvaded.'

From London Maureen Cleeve sent her the article with a note: 'I do hope you like this. They all thought you were wonderful in the office. I hope Diana will explain about the poetic licence. Thomas Pakenham is dying to meet you. He has been reading all your old novels under the impression that you are J. G. Farrell's mother. In any case he thinks they are very good.

'With best love and best luck to the book.'

Later in the summer André Deutsch telephoned Molly and advised her to sit down before he continued. He was about to tell her that she had made the shortlist for the Booker Prize. She was shocked and gratified. She had never seen herself in that sort of context. At first she was just terribly surprised and pleased to be nominated, but as time passed and the Irish media whipped up *Good Behaviour* as almost a certainty, her competitiveness cut in and she secretly yearned to win. She remained cool on the surface. When the London *Times* interviewed each of the candidates by telephone, the conversation with Molly went as follows:

'How much is it, dear? No! They say it is bad luck to even think about winning, but I suppose if someone had to give me ten thousand pounds I would buy some new iron windows. I live by the sea and the windows are fearfully rusted. Then I'd buy a lovely china breakfast set. I'd give the girls some money of course.

'It won't make any difference to my writing. It will be just as difficult to write as it ever was. I haven't read any of the others. I should think the Indian will win. He sounds a jolly good bet.'

The 'Indian' was Salman Rushdie and he did win, with his innovatory novel *Midnight's Children*. Despite not winning, the publicity did *Good Behaviour* a lot of good and some of the judges, including Malcolm Bradbury, the chairman, reviewed it favourably afterwards. Doris Lessing, also listed for *The Siran Experiments*, was less starry-eyed than Molly when she spoke to *The Times*. 'A writer winning a prize is seldom better than others in the running and everyone feels this. If there were a lot of prizes instead of a few, it would help to get rid of what is always a faint flavour of silliness about the business.' As usual she is the voice of intelligence and truth. Molly went to the party accompanied by Diana Athill and John Perry, dressed in an elegant green kaftan handed down to her by Adele Astaire. She was gallant in defeat, and determined to enjoy herself but she was too insecure to possess Doris Lessing's sane attitude. Later she admitted, 'Prizes are all right if you win them and hell if you are listed and don't.' Towards the end of her life she remarked to me, 'If my novels are so good why did they never win anything?'

An unlikely and very deep friendship grew up between Molly and the television presenter Russell Harty. Fascinated by *Good Behaviour*, he proposed making a documentary about its author in 1982. Although he was famous Molly had not heard of him because she never watched TV, but of course she said yes at once. I asked a friend in London what Russell's approach was like. 'Well, he might take the piss,' she unreassuringly replied. Russell arrived with a film crew and spent a week jaunting up and down the Blackwater Valley with Molly and Tessa in the Renault, even filming her mixing her bedtime drink of cider vinegar and honey. The shoot ended with a lunch party at Dromana on camera, which I rather anxiously attended. I need not have worried: Russell and Molly were made for each other. They were both very talented, shy show-offs who instinctively understood the vulnerability of people who expose themselves through being creative, and their extreme need to be appreciated.

As a child Molly, like many small girls, had adored acting. She never forgot appearing in Susan's drawing-room production of *A Midsummer Night's Dream*. When the curtain came down she lay back on the grassy bank (a green velvet sofa) waiting for admiring comments about her Titania. None came. The Aunts embarked on a discussion about how wonderful little Godfrey was as Peaseblossom and never mentioned the Queen. Russell's programme was her revenge for this moment. As well as giving expression to the actress she had never entirely ceased to be, he tapped into the essence of Molly. Her complex enchantment and her natural empathy came through to extraordinary effect. Letters poured into his office from delighted viewers:

Your programme on Molly Keane was a pretty thing. You ought to be proud of your work and in love with her.

Your programme tonight was a quite fitting tribute to a patently glorious woman. Thank you all, not least the camera-man, music director, yourself but mostly the subject herself. I feel uplifted.

Dear Sir, if it would not be too much trouble to you could you ask Molly Keane for the proportions of cider vinegar, honey and water she uses to get to sleep. I am fed up of living on Mogadons.

When they met they were both on the cusp of something. Molly, in the midst of the biggest success of her life, was still being nourished and exhilarated by it and was greatly enjoying herself. Russell was beginning to be disillusioned by the barbed shadow side of fame. Fed up with being a star, he was at the same time alarmed at the idea of losing such a status. An inspirer of love in audiences and friends, he was sometimes an object of mockery and hate among the critics. There was an originality, gentleness and risk in his camp style which made him vulnerable. He said of himself, 'I know I'm not the world's most popular broadcaster. I'm much too strange.' Their meeting and the success of the programme encouraged him. After it was shown he wrote to Molly:

Dearest Heart,

. . . what an amazing amount of good you have done me.
It has been a spectacular paragraph, no, chapter, in my
little life. I send you gratitude and undying affection.
Have you read *The Tablet* in which you are a big hit?

In one way the programme caused Molly to become meshed with the culture of her times. During its most surreal moment she finds herself in a helicopter conversing with Mick Jagger, both of them politely pretending to know something about the other. She is just a name, a passing celebrity woven into the ephemeral curtain of the media. Russell understood this sort of tinsel stuff and combined it with reality. A wordsmith and a literary animal, he was initially drawn to Molly by reading *Good Behaviour* and therefore predisposed to know what she was really like. Their backgrounds made them exotic to each other. Thirty years younger than Molly, Russell was born into a prosperous Lancashire business family. He took a first in English at Oxford, taught at Giggleswick School in Yorkshire and then at the City University of New York. His brilliance, or 'strangeness', got him a job on BBC Radio where he managed to persuade the super-strange Salvador Dalí to talk to him in the arts programme *Aquarius*. The success of this venture caused him to be promoted to TV where he became one of the first of the star interviewers.

Writing about him after his death, Melvyn Bragg said, 'Russell Harty, on form, was more vivid, more fun, more lively than almost anyone I have ever met.' He goes on to mention his 'serious melancholy, sly snobberies', 'marvellous enjoyment of the outrageous' and his loyalty and helpfulness as a friend. He might have been describing Molly. Their affinity resulted in a romantic friendship. Her age and his homosexuality proscribed it but their relationship had the exhilaration of a love affair about it. They trusted each other and shone in one another's company. Molly, burdened by her long memory for betrayal, benefited from this. She spoke the truth as she saw it to Russell both in public and private. His ability to inspire her with a sense of trust and a sense of fun, and to get her to talk about herself with an illuminating simplicity, is evident in a programme (ostensibly about music) which they did together for BBC Radio.

She begins by being honest about her attitude to music. 'I'm dead unmusical. Good music really hurts me and *Top of the Pops* stuff too awful.' She is expansive when the conversation turns to cooking. 'I suppose cooking is a sort of escape. It is a disciplined skill. You have to give it your whole attention so it's a deliverance from other worries – when you ought to be writing and can't. Bills you ought to pay and haven't paid. It is a thing you can excel at in spite of advancing years. Besides it's a pleasure you can give. I think pleasing people is one of the great luxuries. Pleasure given to lovers, husbands, children, friends, belongs to the real hours of life.' When he asks her about the solaces of old age her answers are revealing of a contentment and acceptance rare in her: 'The young are so kind to me. On journeys quite tough-looking young help me along ... At Waterloo a boy said, "Keep an eye on my case while I go to the toilet." After that he carried everything for me, and I always have too much luggage and a dog as well.'

'Then bed is such magic. I'm not longing to be at a party or doing anything except reading my book till my eyes close. Sleep really is the greatest.'

'I could talk to my friends forever. I truly love my friends. I'm happy in their company. I like listening too.'

Russell, in turn, made his feelings for her public in his introduction to the Virago edition of *Loving Without Tears*. 'She is my friend, my confidante, my partner in two or eleven little personal deceits, my model, my teacher, my critic, my correspondent, my main source of Irish gossip, my social guide and my heroine.' His letters to her are less flamboyant – full of romanticism and jokes, they are also revealing of melancholy and pain:

I am sitting in a hot garden, with a lot of roses and honeysuckle, and thinking about how I miss you.

I've just poured a drink and lit a fag and started to think about you.

I despair. I don't really despair, I pretend. Oh the sound of the Kerry babies.

Dearest Molly, Are things blooming? Are you well? Happy? What? I have taken an awful pasting in the *News of the World*. They have ripped me apart and left a bleeding piece of meat. However, somebody sold their little story and they trapped me with tape recorders and things planted in dustbins. I feel like one of those rabbits that we had at school in the biology lab all cut up and laid out and pinned down. I am also supposed to have a toy-boy called Jamie, whom they say is a teenager. God help us all ... ! Long to see you. Virago asked me to write the introduction to *Loving Without Tears*, which I'd be proud to do. Hope you still love me as I do you, Russell.

In June 1988 the unexpected happened. After a five-week battle with kidney failure, Russell died, aged fifty-three. His secretary and close friend Patricia Heald telephoned to give Molly the news. She kept a rough copy of the letter she wrote Patricia the next day: 'Although I've known him for such a comparatively short time – alas – I do grieve for him as deeply as though he had been a friend from childhood. What you must feel is beyond any words of sympathy. Thank you so much for ringing me last night. I was so glad to hear your voice and to speak with someone so absolutely part of Russell's life as you were.'

It is characteristic of Molly's psyche that the three great successes of her writing life were linked to three romantic relationships: with Bobbie at the time of *Spring Meeting*, Bill Scott during *Treasure Hunt*, and Russell with *Good Behaviour*. These were moments when self-doubt left her, sharpness left her and she felt whole and able to give unconditionally in a state of happiness as she also did when a real friend was in trouble. Russell was buried at Giggleswick where he had his country home and where he had been at his most happy. Molly visited him at Rose Cottage and he had sent her a photograph taken by the writer Jamie O'Neill, his partner, of the two of them there arm in arm in the snow.

For years Molly had stayed with Virginia in London, embarking from there on tours of friends living in the country. With *Good Behaviour*, the whole thing entered a new phase. Virginia remembers returning exhausted from teaching and bumping into Molly in the street: 'She was in flying form, carrying a bag of muscatel grapes, and wearing one of those peaked caps I hated.' These hats were one of her few errors of dress sense. She had several in different colours and was devoted to them, perhaps because their jaunty style symbolised her mood. They walked together up several flights of stairs to the flat with Molly pointedly sprinting past a chair Virginia had placed on the landing halfway up in case she needed a sit-down. Once indoors, in a reversal of their ages, Virginia lay down on the sofa while Molly went into the kitchen and emerged with a tray of tea and tiny tomato sandwiches spread with the unsalted Danish butter she adored, and which was unobtainable in Ireland.

Virginia has many other recollections of this epoch. Sometimes she was annoyed by the takeover of her small kitchen, but mostly she relished the delicious results. She was less enthusiastic about presents of clothes. Molly loved to buy us things we couldn't afford, and was furious if one didn't wear them. Virginia's pervading image is of Molly's happiness and generosity. 'The bounty of success poured into our flat – people, stimulation, flowers ... She accepted the fact that the focus of my life was psychoanalysis and teaching, though theoretically she despised both of them.' She stopped making cracks about shrinks as she had done in the past. At the time Virginia had home-tuition pupils (traumatised in various ways) who came to the house. One of these became friendly with Molly. He talked to her in bed in the morning, and she stirred up Tessa who growled through the blankets and made him laugh. Although she disapproved of Virginia's job and considered it boring and unglamorous, she made a connection with this injured child. Virginia mentions her 'complete abandonment of her *Good Behaviour* shackles amongst the "common" or middle-class people she met with us – none from an upper-class background. She switched on one hundred percent to the people she liked. She never pulled class.' These young Hampstead left-wingers responded to her. They often confided in her and she was warmly affirmative of their sex lives. ' ... But darling those sea-green eyes ...' The new friends she met through Kevin and Virginia became part of her English life, together with her lords and ladies in the country and the famous and creative people and their helpers whom she loved. She was very fond of John Gielgud's Hungarian friend Martin who many people considered a mega-bore. At first she wanted to affirm what John saw in him in order to help John himself. But it brought her to a real bonding with Martin over gardening and dogs and cooking. She was amused when he gave her a present of a bottle of brandy and said, 'John did not pay for this, Molly, I took it out of the house-keeping money.'

Some time previously, Virginia had with great effort discovered the graveyard where Bobbie was buried. John Perry had attended the funeral almost forty years before, but he could not remember where it had taken place. Virginia spent hours trolling through the record books of cemeteries until she eventually found her father's name. She felt at this moment, when Molly was strong, that she should give her the opportunity to mourn in a way that she never had. With great courage she asked if she would like to go with her to the grave. 'It was a physical shock. She acted as though I had shot her. When she could speak, she said: "I absolutely will never go there. It is him alive and not in a grave that I want to remember."'

Nineteen eighty-one was a productive year. When not being celebrated in London or Dublin, she was writing *Time After Time* at home. She admitted she felt 'rather thrilled' when Gina Pollinger told her she was a 'hot property'. *Good Behaviour* was rapturously received, all sorts of offers of work were coming in, Virago was reissuing her M. J. Farrell novels. However, in the midst of so much plenitude and success the shadow of death was not entirely absent, either in the public or the private domain. John Perry casually remarked in one of his letters: 'They have discovered a new kind of cancer called AIDS.' Peggy Ashcroft wrote referring to 'your year of triumph and your year of acute anxiety'. This anxiety was caused by the fact that Virginia developed cancer of the jaw, and was faced with a series of innovatory operations involving the replacement of the malignant part with a bone graft taken from her hip. Afterwards she wrote about her experience and Molly's reaction to it:

'She was consumed by horror and fear at my having cancer. Now that I have a daughter I can empathise with her reaction. At the time I felt the need to protect and help her with her fear. It annoyed me as it didn't help me with my own terror of death. She was compelled to find a reason for my getting cancer. She always insisted that it was caused by the blow to my head in a car crash.

'The night before my first operation in 1981 she sat at my hospital bed reading me extracts from the manuscript of *Time After Time*. It transported me away from my Florence Nightingale ward filled with thirty or forty critically ill patients; away from my fear to the Ireland in the book and those powerful characters full of humour, sadness, harshness and beauty. She was strong that evening and full of warmth, humour and the feeling that life was well worth living. She was often like that in London. She always looked well dressed. Although she was a small woman, in my mind's eye she was never small. Her personality and essence were so big I had no sense that she was nearly eighty years old.

'When I was in hospital for my first operation Mum was staying with Peggy. She brought huge bunches of old scented roses from Peggy's garden. I remember a morning of bliss when a shaft of sunlight from the high windows hit them. They were a big contrast to florists' flowers. I felt they were typical of Mum and her invincible sense of the beautiful and the natural.

'My jaw was wired during the second operation. I had to suck food though the wires for 8 weeks. When I got home she spent hours in the kitchen every day preparing me delicious meals. It was hot weather; she was old and often very tired, but each meal she cooked was irresistible. One pile of meat or fish, another of vegetables, another of potatoes, delicious sauces, everything blended separately for me to suck through the wires. All the other patients with wired jaws had to suck a uniform brown sludge through their wires. She peeled grapes and blended them into fruit cocktails. She blended avocados or tomatoes with French dressing. She made soups, sorbets and ice creams. Having a wired jaw is a frustrating thing. It can make you feel like a grotesque helpless baby. Her beautiful food made me feel normal and raised my morale. They were a potent example of her combination of love, determination and skill.

'She made friends with the butcher and fishmonger. She became so friendly with the greengrocer that he visited her in Ardmore. He talked about her for years afterwards. Every day she climbed three flights of stairs to my flat carrying bags of fresh ingredients and bunches of flowers. It was an example of the strength of her love, creativity and self-discipline. She was as ruthless with her own aged body in her pursuit of excellence as she could be with other people for the same reason.

'I was in the Intensive Care Unit for some days after the second operation. I had tubes to my stomach and lungs. I couldn't speak. I was attached to various machines. I was in a lot of pain. It was very hard for her to bear. I think her great courage failed her then, although she visited me every day.

'At home she showed great hospitality to my visitors, giving them drinks, feeding them and feeding Kevin.

'Something I grasped as a stick to beat her with in my youth was the theoretical racism of people of her generation and background. During my second long stay in hospital when the crest of my hip was grafted with my jaw, I was in a ward with a black American senior nurse called Maggie. She was a remarkable woman with an outstanding capacity to help and cheer the many seriously and often terminally ill patients. Mum developed a delightful, humorous relationship with her which was full of respect and admiration.

'Mum tidied the flat, made my bed, washed up, filled my hot-water bottles. Despite her tiredness she was endlessly patient and sympathetic to me. It was heavenly to feel like a perfect cherished child during my convalescence.

'Her focus on the senses when my body was so battered was very helpful.

'The experience of having cancer and three major operations at the age of thirty-six was highly traumatic. Her practical love often felt like a safe ship in a stormy sea.'

'This account is testimony to their love for each other and to their mutual ability to be creative in very harsh circumstances. During the first operation Molly stayed with Peggy and was sustained by her and by 'Nan' who lived with her and who had been her children's nanny. Peg's home in Hampstead stood in the middle of a walled garden scented by the old-fashioned roses that seem to love the soil of London. It was a haven for Molly. She knew she did not have to hide her fears from Peggy 'who understands all about tears of every sort'. As the prognosis became good and Virginia started to emerge from her frightening entanglement of pain and tubes and wires, Molly's anxiety receded to the point where she could write a jokey letter about it all to her 'beloved safety-valve' Sibell Rowley: 'Meant to ring and tell you all but the telephone here too publicly situated for details of the worst. I spend my days making mousses and soups out of everything and solid food for Kevin and seed and sand for the budgies. There is a carpenter in the flat too, constantly requiring tea and biscuits.'

Stoically and gradually Virginia made a complete recovery. She returned to her life with renewed energy and with the sense that it was more precious than it had been before. The only outward sign of the drastic treatment she had been through was that she no longer wore her hair long but cut it to shoulder length so that her curls puffed out and hid the unevenness of her repaired jaw.

CHAPTER 9

M olly was in good spirits while writing *Time After Time*. *Good Behaviour* was about to be published and she was beginning to believe in the fair wind surrounding it, although she would not have admitted so for fear of bad luck. She began this next book in a pragmatic mood: ' . . . when darling Deutsch accepted [*Good Behaviour*] I thought I'm so old that as soon as they set eyes on me they will know I can never write another, so I quickly wrote half the next one'.

Although ostensibly about hatred, *Time After Time* has a light-hearted quality. It is the flower of her Indian summer and is, in my view, her funniest book. She is brilliant on the nuances of selfishness. She evokes the predicament of her elderly siblings – having to live together although they loathe each other – in a way that is strangely life-enhancing. There is something gallant and very Anglo-Irish in their attitude. Egotistical and sly, they lock their bedroom doors against each other, but they make everyday life work because it has to. They do not sulk. They talk animatedly over lunch, although the conversation can carry a barbed agenda often expressed through bickering remarks attributed to their dogs. Finally, blood proves thicker than water when they are under threat. Molly's treatment of her villainess is theatrical. She is potent and accompanied by a whiff of sulphur in the manner of a pantomime fairy but she is still believable. Her power succeeds as the power of the enchanting outsider nearly always does in doomed hermetic Anglo-Irish enclaves (held together by the frayed strings of waning energy, obstinacy and love of place). This is especially so if the enchanter returns from the land of youth, when long-relinquished dreams seemed possible and strength was rising not ebbing.

Her portrait of Jasper, the only brother among three sisters, is impeccable. When questioned by a French journalist on how she came to invent such a person she replied, paraphrasing Flaubert, '*Mais Jasper, c'est moi.*' His perfectionism, cooking and fastidiousness resemble Molly's. He is meticulously house-proud and at the same time capable of grabbing an ingredient out of the dog's dinner to enhance a stew (almost certainly she had done the same thing herself but her dog's dinners were canine haute cuisine and the dishes carefully scrubbed every day). She didn't share his love of cats or his lack of passion, instead rather despising both tendencies. Her sympathy lay with his secret grief, his longing to be 'a complete human being'. She found people like him difficult in real life. Their elegant reticence discouraged her and her charm often failed with them, causing her to feel cheap and cold-shouldered.

The deep vein of pain and savagery running through *Good Behaviour* is absent in *Time After Time*, although Molly did try to drum up savagery in various ways. All of the characters suffer from a psychologically wounding physical disfigurement which she rather harps on. In fact, she was in too hopeful a mood to trawl her own depths as she did in the previous novel and would do again in *Loving and Giving* – some critics thought this was a weakness and that *Time After Time* was a backward step. V. S. Pritchett, writing in the *New York Review of Books* did not see it as a lesser achievement. 'The ingenious narrative is always on the move and has that clean athletic animation that one finds in Anglo-Irish prose. Mrs Keane has a delicate sense of landscape. She is robust about sinful human nature and the intrigues of the heart, a novelist well-weathered in the realism and evasions of Irish life. No Celtic twilight here, detached as her comedy is, it is also deeply sympathetic and admiring of the stoicism and the incurable quality of her people. So Irish realism with the solace of its intrigues dominates this very imaginative and laughing study of the anger that lies at the heart of the isolated and the old and their will to live.'

Despite Molly's optimistic state of mind and the comparative ease and speed with which she completed *Time After Time*, she was not without her habitual anxieties while she was writing it. She kept up a steady stream of complaints in letters to her friend Sibell Rowley:

'Pegging away at awful book yesterday when hit by awful head-ache and boredom followed by misery and sickness. (I thought it was a stroke ...) ... I must get on with this travail, I do so wish I was Alain-Fournier and could write *Le Grand Meaulnes*.'

'I am working away at awful book copying and altering such a drag. I don't know what to think of it – not much.'

'I'm getting on better with book but one never knows. Really at it. The exhaustion and the misery and the day gone. No time for any sports not even making marmalade.'

Molly and Sibbie confided in each other in a way that would have been considered dangerous by some of their mutual friends, but they loved and understood each other. The friendship between them was close and free, and they told each other everything (almost). They were well-suited.

Sibell was Ursula Vernon's first cousin and they had met at Fairyfield. When Ursula died she and Molly became Stephen's most frequent guests and honorary domestic lieutenants. Sometimes they ganged up on him like horrible schoolgirls, but both were very fond of him, and rushed to his aid when he was ill or in trouble. En route from Gloucestershire to Kinsale, Sibbie stopped off at Dysert and Molly often went to stay with her. She was the best company in the world. Attractive to look at with white hair that grew in a compact flower-like shape, she would sit, Pickles her beloved terrier companion at her feet, knitting some comforting gift for a friend while regaling one, poker-faced, with fascinating, indiscreet gossip. She was brave, funny, well read, an ex-Master of Hounds and a brilliant cook. She possessed the gift of confidence and the burden of suffering which being aristocratic can bestow. Madresfield, her family home, is the house Evelyn Waugh took as a model for Brideshead. The shadow of scandal surrounding the father in the novel was rooted in the experiences of Sibell's own father who, accused of homosexuality by his brother-in-law, was obliged to abandon his family and live abroad for the rest of his life. Molly's description of herself in a rare moment of self-forgiveness as 'a woman bad in word and good in deed' certainly fitted Sibbie. Her sister Lady Dorothy Lygon said, 'She was rather a stormy petrel – and a great wielder of the wooden spoon; if mischief was going to be made, she made it.' Molly agreed with this but it did not prevent her from being inspired and exhilarated by Sibbie's friendship. 'I can't think of anyone alive to compare with Sibbie. She is a sacred monster whose mind works like magic.'

They both knew what it meant to live with the uneasy bedfellows of a serpent's tooth sometimes dipped in poison and a compassionate heart. Although far from discreet in their letters, they had a habit of ending them 'I can't wait to see you to tell all'. Sibbie never complained; she was tough and much less emotional then Molly. They could sometimes criticise each other in letters to other people but despite this betrayal their friendship was stalwart and mutually beneficial.

They complained to each other about having to go to Fairyfield to keep 'the Major' company. In fact they had great fun there. Until he ran out of health and money, Stephen wove a magic carpet, and Fairyfield was a bit like being in a Ronald Firbank novel. He loved to spoil his visitors with breakfast in bed and leisurely cocktails over stimulating, imaginative talk and jokes which stirred things up. To both Molly and Sibbie, who worked hard in their lives at home, the luxury was restful and delicious. One was treated like a beloved child home from boarding school. Molly enjoyed delightful gossips about life and cooking with Mrs MacCarthy when she brought her breakfast up, and she loved being driven by Gerard in a big comfortable car. Although she was herself an intrepid traveller in her little Renault she was never quite free of anxiety about having a puncture.

All sorts of people came to Fairyfield, the chic and the homely, the academic and the horsey with a generous sprinkling of artists and the warm, ironic people 'who understand'. Stephen's favourite guests were actresses, beautiful young men and nuns and priests. Molly noted with amusement that when a group of novice priests came with their professor they had difficulty choking down their cups of aromatic China tea. She wrote to Sibbie describing a visit to Stephen's favourite convent: 'I've had a field day with the nuns on my last visit when a dog fight broke out during the rosary and Stephen and the sisters continued to pray and make the sign of the cross through the uproar.' Meanwhile Molly, ever practical, rushed to get a bucket of water to throw over the combatants.

Though she laughed at Stephen's theatrical brand of 'holiness', she also envied a faith which brought him consolation and fun. Molly threw herself onto her knees by her bedside every night and read from her blue leather-bound Bible, but it is difficult to ascertain what this meant to her. In her diaries there are occasional references to prayer: 'I cry out to a sort of God but not with any hope that it will help me.' 'If I do say a prayer or remember a collect and recite it it is more like composing a little poem than praying.' 'How nice to be a Catholic and believe unquestioningly.'

Through *Good Behaviour* Molly became friends with Diana Petre, who wrote *The Secret Orchard of Roger Ackerley*. This book was about growing up off-piste in an unorthodox demimonde. Diana's father kept two families; the children of both tended to creativity and brilliance, and they knew nothing of each other's existence until they were quite old. Evidently this was not an unusual arrangement, and the meaning of the expression 'secret orchard' was quite commonly understood. Diana's upbringing had gifted her as a writer and wounded her as a person, especially as, like Molly, she did not have the sort of mother she longed for. Although her mother manifested her shortcomings in a very different way from Mrs Skrine: a princess of the demi-monde, she abandoned her family (sometimes without enough to eat) while she went off with her lovers. Diana lived in a literary world and devoted herself to writing and to helping other writers if she respected their talent. She had been married to James Sterne, and her closest friend was Francis King. When she read Diana's work Molly recognised at once that she was the real thing, and often wrote to encourage her. When Diana was commissioned to write a book based on interviews with old people she sent an early draft of it to Molly, who wrote back: 'I don't wonder you find writing a killer. It is so intricate without being pretty. I feel rather jealous.' Diana lost faith in the project and decided that she would turn her research into a base for short stories. Molly urged her to keep going: 'I feel you are mistaken in giving up longer works ... because you are such a perfectionist in the rest of life you are dissatisfied with your own unusual ability. You are quite unable to write a boring word.'

Diana, like Molly, had an intense interest in keeping house. Her cooking was delicious and light. Molly met many writers at her table, including Bruce Chatwin, who was all the rage having just published *On the Black Hill*. After reading it she wrote to Diana, 'writers like that make me feel I'm hardly fit to write for *Woman's Own*. Oh the enjoyment, but perhaps one shouldn't read them.' She meant one shouldn't read them with one's own work in progress. The sparseness of his style made her uneasy with her own intricacy.

A French journalist interviewing Molly in Paris noted that 'la folle jeune fille' was very much alive in her. She still possessed a sort of frivolousness, a wildness which demanded fun as a reward for the disciplined hours of writing which she kept with exactitude and never shirked. She felt she deserved to dance a bit. Certain people, particularly the Fairyfield friends, danced with her. Mostly elderly, they were exhilarated by her Indian summer. They shared the thrill of success with her and provided sanctuary from its rigours.

Although she was good at it, the worst rigour was TV. She was terrified of making a fool of herself. Convinced that publicity was 'good for sales', she forced herself on as though she was out hunting. When the strain became too much for her eighty-year-old body she fled (for a cure of rest and fun) to one of her 'nests'. A favourite one was the home of the artist Billie Henderson. From there she wrote, 'A marvellous nest here. Bed all day if required as I rather do . . . ' After collapsing with Sibell Rowley, she said in a thank-you letter: 'It is wonderful what care and kindness and laughing and whiskey can do for an old one.'

She also took refuge with John Perry. He had lost interest in cooking and the food consisted of too much coleslaw, ham from the fridge and Chambéry instead of whiskey, which did not suit her fragile digestion, but their affection for each other came through and made up for it. She described a visit to Knots Fosse in a letter to Diana Petre: 'I do rather love John though he is hardly ever funny now and seems to have lost height and has skin cancer on his once pretty nose. Oh dear age. Obviously in a stew of regret at having suddenly sold this house. I feel bad about it too. The garden very creepy and resentful and all our talk is about the ones we knew. All ghosts now. I think Binkie's ashes are in the air we breathe. A lot of birds' wings at my window last night.'

John's eclipse preoccupied all his friends. John Gielgud and Molly telephoned and conferred with each other about it. Both still engaged with the life force themselves, they found his abandonment of it upsetting. They wanted him to go on being the chic, waspish dilettante they had always known who sparkled and made mischief and loved cooking and tennis.

After the sale of Knots Fosse John moved to a flat in the village and almost never left it. Friends took themselves down there a little reluctantly because of the food, parsimoniously rationed heating and John's subdued mood. The relationship between him and Molly moved into a newly peaceful era. The old jealousies had worn away. He was truly delighted with the success of *Good Behaviour*. During her impoverished years he had sent her air tickets to stay in London and at Knots Fosse, prising her off her Ardmore rock where she was 'stuck like a sea anemone'. Now their positions were reversed. She was the one coming with treats and news from the wider world. They had shared so much for so long. She was superficially disparaging about their talk of ghosts but they needed their ghosts as much as their living friends. John was stoical, more loving, less prickly. Molly complained, 'he is hardly ever funny now', but of course he sometimes was. He was pleased with telephone calls and visits. Having lived in the theatre world for most of his life he was interested in the gossip and flotsam of success which Molly reported on from her post-*Good*

Behaviour life. She was especially bucked by becoming a member of the Groucho Club; it made her feel dashing, as the Shelbourne had in youth. She joined in order not to bother friends when she needed a bed in London, but never stayed a night there, though she enjoyed proposing 'a succulent lunch at the Groucho' to people. She was delighted that one of her heroes, Jeffrey Bernard, was an habitué. She admired his exquisite prose in the *Spectator*. I don't think she ever met him but he reminded her of friends from Woodrooffe days: serious drinkers whose natural habitat was the racecourse – people who were dissolute, humane and funny.

A tremendous blessing that came with her last career was a relief from money worry which proved to be miraculously permanent. This was something Molly was not expecting in her old age, after a lifetime of surviving generously and grandly in the Anglo-Irish way on uncertain funds. Success with a book or play would transform her money scene for a time and then dwindle. She always felt guilty about not being able to master the art of saving despite instructions from John and Binkie and Walter. Her friend Clare Boylan said, 'Spend everything then begin writing the next book. That is how it should be.' Clare was young and full of energy; after *Dazzling Prospect*, Molly had experienced a writing block and she was anxious about the inevitable desert of old age. She was always anticipating dottiness and worked very hard, taking on almost any job that came her way with the harvest of *Good Behaviour*. Revenue coming in meant peace of mind and festivity, more frequent champagne cocktails at home and delicious lobster and sole-on-the-bone lunches at

Aherne's restaurant in Youghal, and the Arbutus Lodge in Cork. The post brought parcels of books from John Sandoe's shop in Chelsea and boxes of chocolates from Charbonnel et Walker. Cheques were sent off to Daphne Hall-Dare and Mecha Cazalet and other friends in need. Jack and Jimmy Burke, her beloved builders (the now grown-up little boys who had flown through the air when the pickaxe went into the ground during the original Dysert renovation), were summoned for ongoing improvements. She wrote very generous cheques for Virginia and me although she complained of the former spending 'every penny on that appalling shrink', and of me frittering money away. She bought another Renault and gave me her almost-new one. She delivered it driving in tandem with her friend Phyllis Mitchell. She jumped into Phyllis's car and they disappeared down the hill before I knew what was happening. There was a label of explanation tied to the steering wheel.

Hugh Leonard, the playwright, did a great deal to stabilise her financial affairs when he proposed her as a member of Aosdána. They got on from the moment they met when he arrived to spend a night at Dysert to discuss the script of *Good Behaviour*, which he was adapting for television. She described him as 'pure magic'. He had the Dublin wit, a tremendous interest in food and cooking, and although he was extremely talented and successful he understood all about the pain and uncertainty of writing for a living. An adopted child, he suspected that his natural father might possibly have been Denis Johnston, another very good writer, author of the play *The Moon in the Yellow River*. This idea added to Hugh Leonard's allure where Molly was concerned as she had loved Denis and his second wife, the actress Betty Chancellor (who had given a wonderful funny performance in *Spring Meeting*). They had often stayed at Belleville.

Molly was proud of becoming one of 'Ireland's Treasures' which was the translation of the name given to Aosdána members. The honour came with a grant of five thousand pounds a year. The Irish Arts Council had been set up by the then Taoiseach Charles Haughey as a generous, imaginative gesture towards his country's artists. Molly, previously not keen on Mr Haughey ('too IRA') became very appreciative of him. In a note attached to the anthology *Molly Keane's Ireland*, written with real feeling in her ninetieth year when her powers were failing, she said, 'Under the auspices of Mr. Charles Haughey, the word Aosdána has been revived and applied to an Irish Government institution which takes under its wing creative artists who have made a significant contribution to the visual arts, music and literature in Ireland. Before the new Aosdána, such artists pursued their lonely and often despairing ways in and out of galleries, concert halls and publishers' offices, the older among them often breathing their last in undignified circumstances. The revival of Aosdána brought encouragement to the young and a blessed lull in the anxieties of the old.'

Also during the years of her Indian summer Edsil Roe arrived at the Allied Irish Bank in Lismore. Molly invited him and his wife over to Dysert as part of the charm campaign she directed at every new bank manager, but this relationship proved different from any other. In Mr Roe – later 'Beloved Edsil' – she had found a financial guardian angel, and a true friend in every way. Edsil was a low-key, intelligent person from Northern Ireland and after a career at the bank dealing with their charm and intransigence, he was slightly suspicious of the Anglo-Irish and inclined to steer clear of them socially. Despite this, the friendship between them blossomed. Molly took to having tea with Edsil and his wife in their house under the shadow of Lismore Cathedral. There they cultivated an extensive garden surrounded by ancient cut-stone walls and Gwen was a beekeeper. Molly drove home from there with baskets filled with tomatoes, pots of honey and bunches of sweet peas. Her fears of always taking unwise decisions about money were soothed by Edsil's advice and his attitude to life which was steady and not excitable like her own. When he retired he became her trustee and during her very old age he was a terrific support. In her last diaries, appointments with him were marked with kisses.

Throughout these years Molly still adored parties of every sort, but added to the qualms she had suffered from all her life (What shall I wear? What shall I say?) were new anxieties. 'I am too old, too tired, the effort will kill me.' However, she seldom turned down an invitation.

Becoming the Grand Old Lady of Irish Letters had introduced a new terror into Molly's life, that of having to draw from her handbag a painstakingly crafted speech which she read out in her light Skrine voice at various public events. She wrote a ruefully funny one for what she referred to as a 'feminist jamboree' in Dublin.

I think I'm a bit of a fraud as a feminist. For eighty years I have been sneaking my rights rather than grabbing them. I found out early on that a little yearning isn't such a dangerous thing really.

I am always being asked why I wrote under a pseudonym when I was twenty: and it's always the same dotty answer: the boys would have nothing to do with me if they thought I was a literary type. Today what a happy change! The most outdoor fellow living would be proud and enchanted if your writing appeared in the dailies or the weeklies or the glossies or the hardbacks. He'd say you were dish of the world wouldn't he, when you brought home the lovely bread?

Not a lot of bread in writing when I was young. You never got one penny beyond your advance unless you were Rose Macaulay or Margaret Kennedy. My first advance was seventy pounds and I was over the moon. I gave a party for about twelve people in the Shelbourne in Horse Show week, and it cost all of fifteen pounds.

I do admit one thing, my stupid and irresponsible nature has never prevented me taking a profit and a bonus from the efforts of those splendid and dedicated women who have won so much for us writers ... Remember Anna Wheeler born two hundred years ago, fighting like a tigress for women in a world where justice had not yet come down from the trees. Look back even fifty years and you find Virginia Woolf parcelling up the books for the Hogarth Press, besides being the great inventor and innovator for the novel. In publishing today think of Carmen Callil [founder of Virago Press] – a tiny bombshell vibrant without stridency. Success seems to be ready and waiting for her round every corner she turns, wherever she adventures.

In Ireland we have had our great and polite crusaders. Lady Gregory is a prime example writing and working for The Abbey and fighting for the Lane pictures. I count her a true wonder for all time. Nearer to us unforgettable Nora McGuinness. A strong and gifted painter and tireless in her encouragement of all the arts.

I won't go on, except to say it is my pride and my pleasure to declare this exhibition open.

Her tendency to make fun of her great age ('I'm practically senile') or to flatter the young for being clever and modern in a way she could never be herself was partly based on the changes she had seen in her lifetime and was partly a ploy she made use of. When she tried it on Desmond Guinness, who had known her for years, she recorded his response with amusement in her diary. 'Molly you are far too young for that racket. Come and be my au pair girl.' After a late party she was very white the next day and sometimes stayed in bed, but in an uplifted, lightened mood. She would ring up and tell me about it. The joy and absurdity of people inspired her. She was intrigued by the vulgar clothes of the nouveau riche. In a letter to Sibbie she writes, 'Imagine tight gold trousers at lunch!'

She scooted around in a robust new Renault to familiar houses in the Blackwater Valley. In a notebook she describes driving to a party given by her friend Io Merril at her rectory in Villierstown. Io was American, married to a diplomat and giving parties was almost her profession and her joy. She knew how to impart a sense of happiness in these circumstances; coming through her door you entered a graceful, slightly exotic environment where conversation could be wild or learned. She wandered about in bright, floating scarves dispensing cocktails and delicious curry biscuits. When she was driving towards one of Io's parties Molly jotted down a rough note that I find illuminating. She makes no reference to the party itself in it but the mood that it evokes in her is deeply implicated in her creative response. Her note is interesting because it seems to distil a moment when the paradoxical threads of her existence (the feeder streams of her inner and outer life) appear to merge; aloneness and sociability, wildness and civilisation, the companionship of a beloved dog, chic (high heels *de rigueur*) and, above all, empathy with the outsider and a feeling for place beneath which her writer's instinct lurked. 'A starveling little wood – wild strawberry leaves at its edge, a short-cut to somewhere – a trodden path showing the way. The ghost tinker sitting on the side of his cart, the piebald donkey and the fat white and tan terrier. The tinker had his arm around his dog. He beat his ass lightly with the ends of his rope reins. We waved.

'I stopped opposite the little wood and gave my dog a run and changed my shoes for the party. I heard wheels on the road and the tinker drove past. He did not wave. I watched as I saw him turn the ass and disappear down a side road or lane. I felt curious to see where he had gone. When I came to the place there was no road, no gap, no gate. No sight or sound of the happy tinker. No sound of wheels.'

Had the tinker really been there, or was he a figment of her imagination induced by the heightened mood of her arrival at Io's party?

After a visit from Josephine Slater (Godfrey's daughter), to whom she was devoted, Molly wrote to Sibbie, 'I have had my dear little niece and the lorry driver husband and 2 babies staying for the last 5 days. She was so nice and so unhappy and so much cleaner and tidier than my children. Perhaps nieces are best.'

Except for our mutual untidiness Virginia and I annoyed her for different reasons. My introversion and secrecy upset her. She said certain situations caused me 'to shoot backwards like a prawn' (undoubtedly true). She was infuriated by my unpunctuality, comfort eating and laziness – all very unSkrinelike traits. Also I reminded her of her mother in my disapproval of some of her social manoeuvrings and good put-downs – if she aimed one at me I was inclined to sulk and fall silent. There were times when I could have done much more for her by chatting and not nursing my wound, forgiving in other words. I give up too easily on social intercourse and she put enormous effort into keeping it going.

Once, when I deeply annoyed her and she was feeling very low, she declared, 'I don't want you to come to my funeral, Virginia can arrange it all.' Hurt, I retired in tears to the kitchen where Norah did her best to console me. 'Sally,' she said, 'she doesn't mean it, it's only words, they can't hurt you like stones.' The trouble was words were so important to both of us. Later, when things had calmed down, I told Molly how much she had upset me. She looked rueful and said, 'Just think of it as some awful schoolgirl remark.'

She was annoyed by Virginia's left-wing views. They both adored BBC Radio 4 but frequently disagreed about what they heard on the news. She found Virginia's indulgence in psycho-analysis threatening and a deliberate slight on her as a mother. Virginia maintained that the opposite was true and that the analysis gave her insight and enabled her to put herself in Molly's shoes. Their relationship was warmed by distance and the honeymoon atmosphere of her visits. Occasionally their honeymoon ran out of steam as when Virginia and Kevin took a short trip to the West, which caused Molly to feel cross and lonely as they had come from London to be with her. She tried not to show it and despatched them with the loan of her car and a delectable picnic, waving them off with the tight smile she affected when feeling bereft. The part of her which believed passionately in the idea that we were so lucky to have men in our lives and that it was vital to please and divert them supported these expeditions. Although he came from an artistic, middle-class background horrified by hunting, and she from an Anglo-Irish one which revered it, her respect and admiration for Kevin increased over the passing years and with every visit she made to Belsize Park Gardens. He sometimes found the emotional undertow at Dysert mindblowing and took refuge in his natural introversion and hard work on whatever book he was engaged in at the time.

If Molly sometimes caused tears, she was also a dispenser of understanding and laughter. Her generosity and love could cut in as quickly as her fury. Everything depended on her inner state. When depressed she could play Virginia and me off against each other (if one was the favourite she was seductive and hard to resist). When either of us was in trouble she dropped all politics completely. She always encouraged me to write. Although she referred to writing as a curse, she knew it was my salvation, as it was hers.

There is no doubt that, freed from the deep-running history, emotional currents and psychological stumbling blocks that existed between the three of us, she found fulfilment in her many relationships with outsider children and they with her. It was an extension of the gift for friendship which lit up her life. Nick Burke, son of Phyllis Mitchell (also a difficult, magical character), said to me after they had both died, 'At least we got on well with each other's mother.' He hit on an infrequently acknowledged truth that, liberated from the loaded love affair that can exist between parents and children, this other love is a blessing that feeds the heart if one is prepared to accept it.

Phyllis Mitchell was a very important person in Molly's life. They met in the late fifties when Phyllis bought Fort William. The splendidly restored house and extensive lands reaching down to the River Blackwater had passed from the Duke of Westminster to another American family, and then to her. Phyllis was an aristocratic American with a deep love of Ireland. She understood the pain and complications of the country, and was interested in them. Politics and diplomacy were part of her life since she had lived in Washington from the time of her marriage to Murray Mitchell. He was one of the administrators of the Marshall Plan after the war, and she went with him to Paris. She was refined, sensitive and intelligent. Molly minded her Ps and Qs when conversing with Phyllis. She didn't 'scandalise' and 'tell all' as she did with Sibbie but she told a lot in a different sort of way. Phyllis loved the natural world and was knowledgeable about it. She moved in a graceful, wavery manner when tending her roses, or one of her animals, or pouring a drink for a friend. She was beautiful and original looking with dark hair cut in the flat bob of the thirties. She had a gentle voice and a hearty, mischievous laugh. I once went with Laurent, a French teenager, to have tea with her at Fort William. He didn't drink tea so she rang the bell for one of the servants to bring him Coca-Cola. He was a Parisian from a chic communist family and as we were driving away he remarked, 'That was a nice lady but she must be very to the right because she has *domestiques*, and she rings for them.' Appearances can be deceptive. Phyllis was to the left in many ways.

Molly and she had vulnerability in common. If something hurt them they were haunted and did not easily forget it. They were both perfectionists who expected much of their children and were sometimes disappointed in them. They spoke about this to each other although they would not have mentioned it to other people. They were embroiderers, readers, observers of human nature. They were drawn to outsiders and artists.

In some of Molly's novels grand ladies have acolytes and 'slaves' whom they exploit. Her relationship with Phyllis was not like that. She saw her as someone whose riches gave her time to relish life in all sorts of small ways and she loved relishing it with her. They tended orphaned hedgehogs (a favourite animal of Phyllis's), feeding them in an outhouse and releasing them at a later stage. They took picnics to special places – sea rocks and woods. The Fort William picnic hamper came from America. It was luxurious, containing strapped in plates and cutlery, cold wine, consommé spiked with sherry and neatly cut sandwiches. They discussed clothes and sometimes indulged in the beautiful, romantic suits designed by their Italian friend Michelina Stacpoole. They were keen on baskets made by the legendary basketmakers at Tallow, the Quinlan brothers. On trips they filled these with wild spinach, mushrooms, blackberries, *moules* and many other things. Molly took these seasonal treats home for processing.

Phyllis, who never cooked, brought them to Maureen, her housekeeper, another perfectionist who turned them into delicious soups and tarts.

In the evening at Fort William they sat in front of the fire and clinked the ice in their glasses filled from the loaded American drinks trolley, and became gently tipsy. They looked forward to this interlude when they let go of a certain underlying anxiety (natural to both of them) and conversation soared in various directions. Phyllis's low, melodious laugh echoed round the room. When someone came to announce dinner they emerged reluctantly from their comfortable boat-like sofas and wended their way, slightly unsteadily, across Fort William's immense beautiful hallway to the dining room where they ate under the gaze of Mary Walker, an Abbey actress painted by John Butler Yeats, father of the two more famous sons and a brilliant artist himself.

Virginia and I were also close to Phyllis. She was a most helpful friend. She wanted peace but she was aware that its opposite existed. She could have made mischief as we all three confided in her but she never did, even by mistake. She was delighted by Good Behaviour and Molly's literary success. She had sat at Yeats's feet as a very young girl in New York, and this had drawn her to Ireland. Over the years she and her son had built up an Irish library at Fort William. Many of the passages in Molly Keane's Ireland came from there.

When Molly heard that Virginia was expecting a baby she shot off to London immediately to cook and help her to take life easy. This arrangement did not last long as her anxiety was too much for Virginia, who was made to feel as though she was suffering from an illness. Molly decamped to Peggy's, who consoled her, as always. She was so delighted at the idea of a grandchild that she did not find the rejection overwhelming. She hopped in and out of Manor Mansions in a joyous visitor's mood, leaving delicious cooking behind her.

Julia was born on 17 November 1984. She was a beautiful child with a serene expression and we all fell in love with her from the beginning, especially her father, Kevin. He was not expecting this to happen. He had resisted the idea of a child, feeling it would disrupt his cinematic life drastically. He was working in his study when Virginia, hurrying to a scan, shouted out to him, 'This evening I may know if the baby is a boy or girl.' 'Send it back if it's either,' he answered, without stopping typing for a moment. Once Julia was born he was full of tenderness for her. He sat next to the washing machine rocking her in his arms as the murmur of the motor sent her off to sleep. Virginia threw herself into Julia's life with complete love and happiness, and a certain amount of anxiety. Molly and she had differing ideas about motherhood. Virginia believed in breastfeeding on demand. This resulted in almost constant sleeplessness and abandonment of everything else in her life except Julia, who seemed very happy with the situation. Molly, who had been cut off from her own babies by nannies, and had suffered because of this, nevertheless felt that Virginia's approach went too far and led to slavery and exhaustion. She went to stay with Sibbie (one of the few she confided in about these matters) and then back to Ardmore. She never did *not* love Julia and she understood Virginia's exhaustion. She was stirred up by denied regrets and unadmitted instinctive forces in herself, but her generosity prevailed.

She sent me over to help Virginia although she longed to do so herself, but recognised the impossibility of it. To Diana Petre, she wrote, 'I feel I am a ghost Granny.'

Despite a rocky start, her relationship with Julia was the chief joy of her declining years. There were occasional abysses, as when she bought her a present of two black rabbits and had an expensive pen built for them (two, in fact, as the first was too near the house, and attracted rats, and caused smells outside the spare room window). Julia, a London child, was horrified by the rabbits. She turned her head away and politely ignored them. Molly, who had been deeply attached to her own pet rabbits in childhood, was disappointed. Julia grew more used to them over time but never to the point of picking up one of these plump creatures with their soft black coats and scratchy claws.

Later, after her second stroke, Molly often said she was living much longer than she wished (her feelings were ambivalent about this) but the great plus of her longevity was her developing friendship with Julia. She respected her beauty and her reserve, which was unlike her own Latin emotionalism at the same age. She entered easily into her imaginative world and her fears and laughs – like all writers her own childhood was never far away from her, and she mined it for the last time and perhaps most brilliantly in *Loving and Giving*. Nicandra was the knowing child desperate for love who she saw herself as being, but in her there are also elements of Julia, who Molly was watching with delight at the time of writing and who was not guilt-ridden and lonely as Nicandra had been.

CHAPTER 10

In one of her rare observations about her own writing, Molly said, 'Does one get perverted by success, does it fatten the mind? Is there a despairing quality? . . . I can never do it again, that follows a peak achievement. You must go back to the beginning. Be as diffident as you were before you knew you were good.'

Knowing she was good was not something Molly experienced much. When she attempted to reread one of her books she said, 'I feel slightly sick as though I had eaten too much.' These feelings are familiar to many writers. You venture into the wilderness each time. This was true of *Loving and Giving*, her last and darkest novel.

Diana Athill considered it her best. While she was working on it Molly suffered a slight stroke and had to go into hospital. On her return home after what seemed like a fairly slight setback, she abandoned the book and set about writing to a deadline an introduction to a new edition of *The Real Charlotte*, a work she greatly admired. In an interview in the *Irish Times* with Clare Boylan, she admitted, 'It was the hardest thing I have ever written. I did feel unwell – somehow diminished.' The task took her all summer, by the end of which she found herself back in the 'Bons'. This time she was in Intensive Care, attached to machines. When she was eventually allowed home, she was on oxygen. ('Very expensive my dear. To think I have been breathing it free for eighty-four years.')

She was like a winged bird, wavery and lacking in confidence. She was physically and emotionally weak, and stayed in bed a lot, but she was determined to finish her novel. She panicked when the manuscript could not be found. She had no idea where she had put it. She wept in her bed and accused herself of losing her mind and being no good and 'finished' while Brigette and Norah and myself searched through cupboards and drawers and stared at many notebooks filled with her elegant, slightly indecipherable writing. The manuscript was eventually discovered in a hat box under the spare-room bed. When she saw it Molly said, 'Why does anxiety go on forever and blessed relief last such a short time?'

She worked propped up on pillows, wrapped in her peacock-tail dressing gown. She chewed her pencil a great deal, and Brigette or Norah came in silently at mid-morning bringing a cup of awful stuff called Complan with a little whiskey or lemon zest in it to disguise the taste. She looked ill and pale but intensely focused on this painful, beautifully written book which she was struggling to draw out of the muddle in her head. The language is more pared down than is usual with her. It shines with the beauty and fragility of the life force which still possessed her and is darkened with a sense of loss. She accepts mortality in this novel with a controlled despair.

The heroine is given the outlandish name of Nicandra after her father's racehorse. Diana found for the cover of *Loving and Giving* a wonderful Gwen John painting of a little girl which personifies the dilemma and tragedy of Nicandra's childhood. Outwardly beautiful and composed beneath her big hat, the child in the portrait wears a slightly twisted expression. She seems secretive, resourceful and troubled. Molly herself felt stricken at this time and she put that and her vivid recollections of the bleaker aspects of her own childhood into Nicandra, who is hopelessly in love with her glamorous mother.

'... she saw Maman coming down the drive. She wore her lilac coat and skirt, braided with deeper lilac; the skirt widened at the hem and floated out over thin boots, the tidy laces criss-crossing on shadowy ankles – there was something playful in Maman's way of walking, something jaunty that swayed her hips, and made her straw hat tilt up on her frizzed curls ... From the shrubbery side of the avenue fresh wet heads of lilac bowed over her, heavy in their prime flowering. She lifted her arm to catch at a branch and, as she held it down, rainwater fell on her face – her eyes were shut; it was as if she was drinking the scent of lilac.

'Nicandra ran towards all that beauty ... "Where are you going? Can I come too?" "Oh darling, perhaps not just now."' Maman is on her way to meet her lover with whom she subsequently disappears and is never seen again. The hurt she leaves behind is too unbearable to talk about and she becomes unmentionable in the family.

Her mother's betrayal is the shaping wound of her life but she is also obsessed with other unmentionables.

She is troubled by an overweening sense of guilt. She felt she was living 'on the edge of a nasty secret' as Molly had done. Growing up at Ballyrankin surrounded by the natural world, perpetually seeding and mating and breeding, she was fascinated and curious about sex and the body. Sensual by nature, she sought a reality and an explanation which was not forthcoming. In her Victorian household these matters were accepted but not mentioned. One's stomach was referred to as 'your little inside' and the loo was called 'the place'. Taboo fuelled Molly's interest. The locked door of Bluebeard's cupboard was always seductive to her. Childish guilt stayed with her for life triggered by differing causes. It was perhaps justified in her tendency to put out her thorns like Saint-Exupéry's rose with uncontrolled sharpness when cross. Sometimes she was guilty about things for which she should have been self-forgiving – as when the mayonnaise split or she stayed in bed for a day, or if she failed to succour someone who needed help. This last was a rare occurrence. Her kindness was always there, more powerful than her sharpness or her guilt. Very occasionally she gave herself credit for it. In a diary of 1980 she notes: 'I was feeling anxious and inhuman walking up Belsize Park Grove when the thought of Sally enjoying my car came over me like a burst of light.'

Her sensuous, exploring nature clashed with her upbringing and saddled her with lifelong guilt. In one of her diaries Molly writes: 'It is not kindness or generosity this giving. I would do anything to please, betray anyone to please. Pleasing is my pleasure.'

She is being too hard on herself in the Skrine way. Flattery and the notion of pleasing to get something back was anathema to her parents – it was one of the reasons they rejected society. They didn't need people as she did. They were inclined to dismiss most outsiders as being either 'too fast or too dull'. Their attitude infuriated Molly, and fed her passion for getting on with people and being a success with newcomers. She did sometimes betray in order to be funny and 'pull her weight at the dinner table'.

Her desire for approval and love, too, was overweening. It was the reason why she was so sharp and unlovable at times. Love mattered too much to her. She saw this as a weakness which she camouflaged with sharpness. Her natural ability to sparkle and adore people and enjoy life swept her out of this state of mind but it was a recurring stumbling block.

Nicandra, her heroine, is good and Molly's attitude to her goodness is ambivalent. Her kindness constantly backfires and she is betrayed. She falls for a man who does not appreciate it, in fact he finds it irksome, although he takes advantage of it whenever it suits him. He marries her for her beauty and her money but he is not really drawn to her. He prefers her best friend, Lalage, a taker not a giver. She is a predatory trollop, but extremely seductive. Molly notes her 'sun-burnt heels' and understands the attraction between her and Andrew, also very glamorous, 'evasively elegant as a departing swallow' with his 'lovely looks and quiet ways and proper manner'. They are untroubled by one another's selfishness and sexually at home together. As with Maeve in *Taking Chances*, Molly sees Nicandra's love as being too much for this man's character – too raw and unplayful and too engulfing. In a diary she writes,

'What I deplore in myself is over giving.' She condemns it in Nicandra too – Nicandra is not perfect, there are moments in the novel when her kindness disappears. She uses Willy as a whipping boy (Molly, too, had her whipping boys in a verbal sense), and she appears not to notice the immense kindness towards herself of Robert the grocer, although she flinches at the vulgarity of his too-broad hatband). She can lapse but mostly her reaction is innocent and self-giving. With this she is not clever like Molly. She suffers from 'a blind obstinate energy' – she cannot learn from life. She can only be constant and keep going. She is afflicted with a disastrous lack of a sense of self. Giving is all she knows; give and take does not exist for her. She can lose herself in the beloved, in riding or cooking, or dogs, but she is almost never happy, although looking back she deludes herself about this. Her self-delusion and lack of humour and sparkle are totally unlike Molly.

Nicandra's destiny is cruel. One is forced to ask oneself: is goodness no good? Is it stupidity, unreality, powerlessness? The failure of kindness in the book is harsh. The story is so exquisitely observed and imagined, so beautifully and economically written, but it is hard to read and its view of life is depressing, despairing even. When I said this to Molly she said, 'Look at Tossie'. Tossie is indeed the hope of the book. She is compassionate towards people without expecting too much from them. She is 'Maman's (Lady Forester's) elder and widowed sister, widowed for two years but still wearing full mourning regalia. She knew it became her. She enjoyed nearly everything, even widow's weeds . . . perhaps most of all widow's weeds, as her married life had not been as exciting as she might have wished, and besides, they were so graceful and pretty.'

Her money kept everything going, and after her sister's elopement she does everything she can to console her brother-in-law. 'By the end of the thirties, Aunt Tossie wondered for how many years she had been paying for interesting yearlings, and with very uninteresting results. It had been worth it. There was a time when Dada could have done something really silly, like ... well, like shooting himself. Time passes. Tragedy gets tidied away – mortal injuries subside. No point in saying money doesn't help.' When Aunt Tossie gave or spent she was as exuberant as a child tossing a ball into the air. 'All right,' she said, 'but don't be silly about it.' If she could not provide a remedy for life's major troubles she accepted a way round.

There is an extraordinary scene in the book which, in its dramatic combination of inner and outer circumstances, could only have come from Molly's pen. On the terrible day of Maman's departure Nicandra and Tossie are preparing to forget their troubles and enjoy themselves cleaning the latter's valuable diamonds in a solution of hot water and bread soda. They have been planning the operation for some while and are both looking forward to it. Tossie unlocks her jewel case and opens the smaller boxes in which the diamonds reside. They are all empty, the jewels are gone. She realises at once that Maman has stolen them because they are of higher quality than her own. She stares into the jewel case, in shocked silence. 'Nicandra felt a growing impatience, "Can't I start?" she asked, "the water is getting cold." Aunt Tossie took a long pull at her drink. Then she shut the jewel case and took out the key. "You haven't locked it," Nicandra said helpfully. "Not much use now ... look darling let's do this job tomorrow shall we?" She wavered a little in her words, "Aunt Tossie is rather tired – silly old thing I know. Done in actually. Have to think things out." She fell back among her pillows, one narrowly white-cuffed hand still held the glass of whiskey erect – there was a magnificence in her yielding.' Tossie's decency and humour and steadiness illuminate the novel. Over the years Sir Dermot wonders (although he is too polite to ask) why when money is needed his sister-in-law does not pop some of the legendary jewels she doesn't wear instead of dipping into her investments. Tossie never divulges the reason in order to spare his and Nicandra's feelings.

Molly wanted to be like Tossie, 'who never made difficulties about small things'. She did not always succeed in this although when it came to big things her gallantry was equal to hers. There is quite a lot of Molly herself in Tossie, especially in the detailed equilibrium they both cultivated in the face of the losses of old age. Molly put energy into inventing her own luxuries as Tossie did. Enjoyment and duty were combined in tidiness and caring for things. I see Molly clearly in this description: 'she had fits of putting things away in their exactly proper places thus leading to the postponed satisfaction of finding them again, laying a hand on them without a thought. At those times night-dresses were folded and piled, sachets between each, camisoles threaded anew with narrow ribbon after washing – all glimmered secretly in a deep drawer. Gloves were important, always made of chamois leather, white with black stitching, or faintly primrose coloured, soft as kid from careful washing. They were soaped and stretched on hands and ivory glove stretchers while drying. Shoes were kept on wooden trees, never to lose their shape or seam across with age. Shoes should be ageless – good shoes made by the right house were beyond any whim of fashion.'

Referring to the writing of the book, Molly said, 'It was very tough – I have always found writing very hard. I have always had to work against myself but now, in addition, was the search for words. I couldn't remember ordinary adjectives. I suppose it was one of the things that made me press on, the fear that one day I might lose it all.' The agonising effort was rewarded. The novel was highly praised except by the few who found the sharp tooth of its pain too much. It got a bad review from William Trevor who always disliked Molly's novels as she did his, although she admired his short stories. Peter Schaffer, an habitué of Ballymaloe (where he often spent time writing), visited and she gave him a script of *Loving and Giving* to take away with him. He later rang her in the middle of the night from New York to tell her how good he thought it was. She husbanded sleep, and was usually cross if woken by the telephone but this call filled her with relief and joy.

The publisher Tom Rosenthal had bought Deutsch by this time and he gave a dinner party to launch the book at his house. Molly was not quite up to the fanfare any more – celebrity was becoming tougher and less exhilarating, but she was determined to survive it. Her voice sounded tired in interviews. Even her Gloucestershire 'nests' alarmed her. She dreaded tumbling down and breaking something or being too exhausted to speak. Virginia had rung people to ask them to get oxygen in for her, which annoyed her. She sniffed at it like scent. Fun was had despite her anxieties. Her friends were old and understanding of one another's frailties, but grit ('not being a nuisance') was engraved in all of them.

Part of her knew that it was the last time she would come on a royal progress bearing the gift of success. *Loving and Giving* itself was a literary wow and received rave reviews. It was almost impossible to believe that the frail old lady who spoke in a slightly muddled way about it on the radio had actually written it. Clare Boylan, reviewing it for the *Guardian*, wrote, 'Molly Keane is astonishing ... *Loving and Giving* is perhaps her richest work yet, an exquisitely written black comedy with a shock ending. The language is eloquent and original, the descriptions divine.' Auberon Waugh called it 'Quite the best book she has ever written.'

In the late eighties, Molly gave an interview to Shusha Guppy for her book *Looking Back*. It was one of the last she did and it is important from the point of view of Molly's ideas and feelings. She had just emerged from hospital after her third and most serious stroke. It is as though she had found a certain clarity in weakness and she wished to leave these thoughts behind. Feeling very fragile in body and mind, she makes a great effort to express herself and say what she really meant. She did the same thing at the beginning of her *Good Behaviour* career when she was on top form in conversation with Maureen Cleeve. It was as if, in both cases, talking to another writer inspired her. She actually gave the interview in her dressing gown over two days. Virginia, myself and Sibbie, who was staying with her at the time, did our best to stop it, but she and Shusha were both hell-bent on going ahead. Overexcited, weak and determined, Molly got very cross with us. Sibbie was having a dreadful time staying with her instead of their usual convivial one. Molly, trying to muster energy, went to bed at seven o'clock for some days before the event, and seemed to expect Sibbie to do likewise. Sibbie was patient about this although she said it was gloomy sitting in her small room knitting and looking out at the rabbits, which were still domiciled outside her window. She said Molly did give her a big drink before retiring and that helped. She came to visit me in order not to be underfoot when Shusha was there. We were both annoyed with Molly and frightened for her, thinking the stress of doing an interview so soon after suffering a heart attack might kill her. Both smarting from her anger, we discussed her foibles rather disloyally. 'What makes her behave in this awful way?' Sibbie said. I suggested that it was to do with her childhood when she had felt unloved by her mother.

'She should have got over that long ago. My mother had seven children and she only liked one of them.'

Sibbie had hunted hounds and got on with her life. Molly, too, got on with life but when she wrote she remembered the pain. The 'lasting effect of small cruelties' informed her work and mothers did not get off lightly.

Although I tried to stop Shusha coming I am glad to have her interview now. Like Molly, she believed that life was all about making efforts. She had had a hard struggle after leaving Persia. The whole family did. One of her brothers who settled in Paris, Nasser, was a divine painter and a very noble character. I once brought him and his wife, Isabelle, to see Molly at a time when she was recovering from an illness and not keen to meet anyone new, but she could not resist Nasser with his gentleness, and intelligence and charm – no one could. Shusha herself was much more than a pusher and shover when it came to literature; she was talented and sensitive and passionately engaged. Her understanding gave Molly the confidence to dig deep to find answers to questions she often preferred to avoid.

Although she was a devoted listener to Radio 4 she had a sort of horror of political discussion. If one disagreed with her she was inclined to take it personally and it easily became a fight. She explains her attitude more clearly to Shusha. 'What affects me is what goes on in the world. When I read your book [*The Blindfold Horse*] and saw what was happening in Iran and now what is happening in China, I feel wounded, devastated – I am not political but I am horrified by what happens to people.'

Death was another taboo subject. It was not so much that she was afraid of death as that she was deeply attached to the life force and it was incredibly hard for such a social, domestic and earth-bound creature to give up on it. In fact, she took violent offence for some while and refused to speak to Godfrey after he referred in a letter to 'the great reaper coming for t'other or which'. With Shusha she talks openly about death. She calmly admits 'sometimes I am conscious of life departing from me'.

During the course of their conversation she says, 'I would like to write one more book about old age – not a sad one but a funny one about the small pleasures of old age; for example finding a handkerchief in a pocket which you thought you had lost – that sort of thing.' The interview ends in this way:

Shusha: Don't be sad. I am excited about your new book.
Molly: I don't know if I will ever be able to write it. A bird twittered in my head and now it has flown away.

Shusha: Not so. It will return soon and sing. You will write
    the book about the joys of old age and give pleasure
    to your readers. Promise?
Molly: I promise.

This was a pledge she failed to keep, though she tried hard to honour it. She left many notes for the book. The plot concerned two elderly sisters, very different in character – like herself and Susan. They live together in mutual annoyance and each harbours a secret which they are determined to keep from the other. There is a younger character who visits them who seems to be the hopeful element of the book as Tossie was in *Loving and Giving*. Her persona is linked to Penelope Hamilton when Molly first met her after she arrived at Blarney in the forties. She describes 'the pine-needle path' that Penelope created there and how in this heavy Victorian castle she 'substitutes grace for conglomeration'. She also mentions the grace of her character and her 'magical sympathy'. The book is about the practical situation of the loss of one's powers, and it is a tragic comedy in big and small ways. As her own powers slipped, her diaries are full of ironic observations of her predicament which might have informed the novel. She chronicled her decline and saw it through lenses of sorrow and humour. 'My dear house has become dangerous to me ... taps running ... electricity ... masked raiders are my latest worry.'

'A strict exactitude necessary if one is to see biro, toothbrush or key again.'

'I gave myself the dangerous treat of staying in bed all day and eating nothing. The luxurious collapse, breakfast ignored.'

At one point she meant to turn the idea into a play in collaboration with James Roose-Evans who at the time was renovating a cottage beside the sea at Ballywilliam with Hywel Jones. His presence gave her confidence, as did his knowledge of the theatre and faith in God. He was the director of *84 Charing Cross Road* and of many other plays, and also a priest without a parish with very open views. He had conducted Julia's christening with a mixture of faith and theatre that reassured Molly, who had been fearing a pagan Hampstead celebration. In the end, their play was 'stillborn' but planning it lifted her spirits, and cemented their friendship. She asked him to come and preside over her funeral service.

In 1986 Peggy Ashcroft left her house in Frognal Lane and moved into a flat at the top of a charming robust nineteenth-century house in Belsize Grove, near where Kevin and Virginia lived. Leaving her house, one of the most agreeable in Hampstead with a country-sized garden, was a hard decision. She had lived there since before the war and her marriage to Jeremy Hutchinson, the father of her children. She had driven to hundreds of performances in the West End where the natural, unpretentious person that she was had become wild, passionate, tragic, exotic, wicked, heartbroken, mad, funny in the person of Cleopatra, Hedda Gabler, Queen Margaret, to name but a few of her roles. To her delight her granddaughter Manon had learned the piano at Frognal Lane, and many children with whom she had a special rapport had played beneath the apple trees. In the past she had spoken about making it into an old people's home for friends. Once in a letter she asked Molly, 'Do you feel like up-rooting?' She was inviting her to perhaps share the house with her. Being with Peg, being near Julia, might have tempted Molly with old age looming but she was too deeply rooted in Ireland and completely addicted to her home in Ardmore which she was still able to manage with the help of Brigette and Norah.

Molly talked a lot about old age but she didn't really believe in it. Peggy, finding her knees refusing to support her on stage, had more of an idea of what it was about. She took to making films with success and inspired creativity but she did not like it nearly as much as acting in the theatre. She won an Oscar for her performance as Mrs Moore (a very subtle part, full of weariness, crossness, and an unexplainable spiritual force) in *A Passage to India*. She found making the film difficult and fraught. She and her friend Alec Guinness were troubled by David Lean's interpretation of Forster's book.

Because of their mutual understanding the high risk of these two emotional people living under the same roof might have worked. The only thing they could not discuss was politics. Peg was a lifelong socialist, rooted in the traditions of history and Shakespeare and English liberalism. She never lost her youthful hatred of injustice – Binkie referred to her as 'The Red Dame'. Molly respected her as such. Their relationship went far beyond politics; it was rooted in their personal lives. Peg had known her and Bobbie from the early days of their romance. Molly loved talking to her about him and the fact that she had been charmed by him and that her memories of him were full of love. Once, staying in the South of France, they had taken Peg, weeping because of an unhappy love affair, into their room. Peg knew that practising her art was vital and the centre of her life, and she kept Molly (always ready to forget this in her own case) up to scratch about it. When she came to live beside Virginia and Kevin it brought a new dimension into their relationship. She delighted in Julia, she empathised with Molly in the joy of *Good Behaviour* and in the fear and pain of Virginia's illness. They both knew the rawness of emotion when it was unstoppable and the situation of loving too much. This had been the case with men in their youth and now this passionate, sometimes thwarted love was focused on their children. They both got on best with the younger ones, Nicholas and Virginia, feeling that they were able to deal with life and they need not worry about them. When it came to Eliza and myself, they loved us but agonised and sometimes got furious about the abysses we dug for ourselves. They had more fun and less anxiety with the others. In 1991 Peggy had a stroke and was brought to St Mary's Hospital, Paddington, in a coma. Although very fragile, Molly went to her bedside. Eliza asked her to come and sit with her mother. She thought that the unexpected sound of the voice of an old friend might get through to her and bring her back. Struggling with her own weakness, Molly put everything she had, her courage and humour and love, into this encounter, which meant a great deal to her herself, although it failed to revive Peg, who died shortly afterwards. Eliza wrote to Molly from France: 'I'm no good about letters but dear Molly I don't forget you and will always remember your beautiful visit to Peggy while she was dying.'

John Gielgud and Peggy had acted together since their youth and their love for each other was rooted in their work. He described her in his inimitable manner – 'she's terribly ordinary in a way but with this wonderful distinction of attack – like a little bull-calf hitting you with his head – she has a strong instinct about a part and a clear idea of what she wants to do with it'. In his obituary of Peggy in *The Times* Trevor Nunn wrote: 'I began to see that irreverence and flirtatious fun were every bit as fundamental to her art as her instincts about heightened language – Peggy was always more of a girl than a lady.' He says that actors only become great in old age when life has tested them and they have come true and achieved a quality 'in which acting becomes wisdom and you simply lose yourself in the largeness of her spirit'.

Virginia, waiting for Peg's funeral service to begin sitting beside Molly and John Gielgud, remembers being slightly embarrassed by the former's Anglo-Irish funeral party mode. Molly chatted away while John struggled to answer her through his tears. Peggy's career was later commemorated at Westminster Abbey in a service full of music and Shakespeare and the marvellous tradition of English letters which she had graced all her life.

When I read Molly's letters to Mary D. Kierstead I sometimes wonder if she wished to pass the baton to her and inspire her to write the novel about old age which she failed to do herself. The letters range from the last years of her Indian summer, through the struggle of her decline until just before her death. They end with a note from Virginia saying that Molly has broken her hip and is very weak. Mary-Dee was a contributing editor on the *New Yorker*, and she came to interview Molly for the magazine in 1986. She was a close friend of Bill and Joan Roth who lived in Tipperary and who were also friends of Molly's. In her first letter to Mary-Dee, Molly writes, 'I'm really fainting at the idea of "The New Yorker" having any interest in me. Perhaps I am glad you are not Dorothy Parker.' She sort of fell in love with Mary-Dee from the moment she walked through the door, stunningly dressed with the sleeves of a beige cashmere jersey knotted around her shoulders against the Irish cold. She came from the *New Yorker* and she had actually known E. B. White (the tormented *New Yorker* wordsmith and an exquisite stylist) who was one of Molly's chief mentors.

If that was not enough, it turned out that her maiden name was Devereux and her ancestors had emigrated to America from Wexford. Molly, wandering round the churchyard in childhood, had often remarked on this French name on their gravestone and been intrigued by it. There was vulnerability impeccably masked by her style and grit in Mary-Dee that Molly responded to. She came to love Will Kierstead, her husband, who was laid-back, a knowledgeable gardener and a gentle person. Brigette also admired Will, she gasped at the wonderfully sharp creases in his New York trousers and adored ironing his shirts when they stayed at Dysert. He was the sort of man Molly loved to spoil. Actually he was unspoilt by such indulgence although he accepted it smilingly. Later on in shaky health she went with the two of them (Will drove) to Wexford for the day. This trip, postponed several times because of illness, was important; subconsciously she knew it was her last time at Ballyrankin but the bleakness was diluted by the fun of showing Mary-Dee the landscape of her forebears.

Mary-Dee summed up their relationship simply. 'We just got on,' she said. They did from the beginning as one can tell from the piece, long and detailed as *New Yorker* articles always are, which she wrote about Molly having just met her. Her acute, skilled writer's eye focused on Molly with an uncanny understanding. It was as though they had known each other for years. Afterwards, Molly wrote to her, 'Talking to you was a kind of liberation. I don't mind at all if you have to send me up rotten.' Mary-Dee was, of course, a very perceptive reader and before meeting Molly she had read her novels carefully. Molly for her part trusted her as she trusted Sibbie and Diana Petre but in a different way. Her letters to all three have a different atmosphere. When she wrote to Mary-Dee she was in communication with a writer who worked with her own tools of sharpness and worldliness and knowledge of vulnerability and courage. That is why I think she chose to chronicle in her letters to Mary-Dee her experience of 'the poisonously sly advance of time'.

Over the years after Molly's death I would meet Mary-Dee occasionally at the Roths' house. Once when I went to New York she gave me the letters Molly had written to her, dated and catalogued in meticulous *New Yorker* style. Her eyes were fading but you would never have guessed it from her elegant, quick stride around the city she knew so well, and the colours she put together in the way she dressed and the wit and precision of her conversation.

In letters to Mary-Dee the pain and pragmatism are always there. Molly knew that her correspondent had a horror of self-pity, as she had herself. The grief is not sidestepped, but it is not naked; it is clothed with a writer's detachment and a certain coolness. This is so, even in the last letter she wrote to her.

November 20 1995

Dear Mary-Dee

Brace yourself to read my complaints. Mind blank,
sight for reading and tapestry weak. Still struggle with
both. Avoiding arthritic pain and sleep. Two luxuries.
Still greedy pleasure to indulge this vice. Still love and
value my friends but pleasure of their company can be
exhausting. Callers break the monotony. Phyllis Mitchell
a great loss ...

Virginia and Sally both well and happy with their men.
Both writing hopefully. It was a different Molly who loved
you and was very conscious of Will's great personality and
irresistible charm. This letter for Christmas, with every
loving wish and gratitude for so much.

A low point occurred at the kitchen door. Molly was wavery
in her peacock-tail dressing gown, tightly belted around her
small waist with a shawl inside it, barely noticeable, because
of her thinness. There were shadows under her eyes which
were bright in an unhealthy way, with anger and inner pain.
I was setting out for a walk feeling quite bad myself. 'Everyone
gets depressed,' I said, 'I know I do often.' My words were like
a match to petrol. 'What bloody nonsense you talk Sally.
You're not approaching ninety and on the verge of death.'
She slammed the door in my face. They were hard words, and
I wept as I walked along the road. I thought she was being
cruel and unfair and she was. Now that I am nearer to the
age she was then I see it differently. The feeling that the time
to repair mistakes and recover from darkness has gone and

the experience of happiness is ending saps the power to enjoy anything. One is stigmatised, different from others who still have time. It was particularly terrible for someone of Molly's temperament who hated to be left out. She felt that her body and her mind were crumbling, and she was becoming what she terms 'a load', 'a burden'.

In her diary she writes: 'The bright day and evening are both without me now. Or I am without them ... I am jealous of my past lives ... I wouldn't be able for the ecstasy now. I should be glad that is so.'

In a more ironic mood, she notes, 'I can't bear being Moll without her knacks of observation and wits busy with comment not always fortunate.'

Around this time she developed a habit of not answering the telephone. Probably she was dozing and thought the ringing was a dream. Once I was so worried that I called Jackie Burke, who had a key to the house. He went up there immediately and, getting no response to the bell, he entered and, knocking on the bedroom door, woke Molly up. She was charmed to see him and sent him out to the hall to fetch a drink for himself. He sat on the end of the bed and they chatted. He rang to tell me this when he got home. She was, however, very angry with me for my interference. She telephoned Billie Skrine (Godfrey's second wife), a great friend and confidante. 'I think Sally has gone off her head,' she said, 'she actually sent up the builder to see if I was dead.' She hated all inroads into the independence she cultivated so successfully over the years. At the same time she was frightened by her weakening and that is why she did the Duchess when she was speaking to Billie. The next time I called Jackie in a panic we decided that he would try not to go into the house but just peer through the window. He rang back in triumph, 'Don't worry, Sally, I saw her walking into the drawing-room with Hero.'

Because she could not combat depression with practical life as she had done in the past, it was gaining power over her. She fought it tooth and nail, cooking sometimes with the help of Brigette or Norah.

In her diaries she sought to accept losses and remind herself of her blessings. In a sort of prayer she wrote, 'Give me recognition and pleasure and gratitude for all the wonders I have had from my life which could have been so circumscribed.'

In the struggle just to survive, her great fear was losing the power of loving. She who had loved dangerously and emotionally all her life, embracing the joy and trouble that it brought her. To Shusha she said, 'I believe absolutely in love.' Here she was referring to sexual love, but she was equally passionate about the love of all close ones and friends. Bleakly, she wrote: 'I am losing the power of loving with each stroke.'

She mentions taking to her bed with a sense of relief when friends cancelled. Awakening refreshed, she wishes they were coming. 'I feel lonely, I need people,' she says. It was a dilemma. She feared becoming a bore, and no longer being able to delight friends with her conversation, and her cooking. But she did need people. She adapted the menu she had offered the journalists, and gave teas with smoked salmon sandwiches, orange cake, China tea and plenty of booze. People did not let her down. Many sustaining friends visited. They telephoned also and wrote, among them George, Michelina and Hassard Stacpoole (for each of whom she had immense affection) and Ruth Annesley (who, with her sympathy and intelligence, never failed to calm her agitation). Many members of the Keane family (including Richard) came, and the Shane Jamesons. Robin Oliver (Norah Preece's delicately subtle son), was her last house guest. She was bucked by people she had known as children, Andrea Jameson and the Cockburn boys in particular. After the deaths of their parents, the boys took it in turns to come with their families to Rock House in Ardmore where Claud and Patricia had lived. Molly was fond of Alexander who had been my childhood friend (as all the Cockburns were). Alexander (who died tragically early) was clever and domestic and more fun than practically anybody one has met. He and Molly never discussed politics (they were on different sides). They flirted (they were both experts at it) as they sat beside the drawing-room fire, indulging in indiscreet gossip and cooking talk.

She was devoted to Caroline Walsh, her lawyer, and above all to 'the Brigadier', Denis FitzGerald. She adored his company, and didn't mind when he corrected her if he thought she was being over the top sharp. He spoke of her 'little forked tongue' which suddenly shot out when you were least expecting it. He was very fond of her and they understood the social aspect of each other's characters. He gave lunch parties and picnics beside the Glenshelane river where he lived, in a charming house that had once belonged to Bobbie's great-aunts. He was the sort of Anglo-Irishman who is almost extinct now. He was highly principled and brave (decorated for his part in the tragic battle of Arnhem). He knew Molly romanticised the FitzGeralds. They had arrived in Ireland with the Normans and they are a remarkable family who have thrown up some extraordinary people over the years.

(The art historian and writer Desmond FitzGerald is a case in point. If I was asked to nominate the most remarkable Irishman of my generation it would be him.) Molly loved the portrait of Edward FitzGerald, the eighteenth-century patriot and martyr, in Denis's dining room. He often served 'Lord Edward's pudding', a sort of custard, the receipt of which had come down to him through the generations.

Denis was cultured and he loved talent. He introduced Molly to Thomas McCarthy, one of our best poets, who has become a preserver of her reputation as he admires her writing and often teaches from her books when he lectures in America. He came to work for Denis as a gardener when he was young. Denis encouraged him and sort of adopted him. They both loved gardening. Tom wrote a poem entitled 'The Brigadier Burning Leaves ... '

How many autumns. Maybe nine or ten
 since we raked the first leaves
 and had them stacked for burning.

This evening there was woodsmoke again,
 leaving its taste on walls and eaves,
 carrying the burnt year into October.

Denis had the gift of engaging with the person you really were. He understood Ireland in its many manifestations. The FitzGeralds had been Normans and chieftains and Catholic Irish and Anglo-Irish. Those of them who were interested in history were imbued with the whole story since at least the twelfth century.

He attended the Anglican Cathedral at Lismore, and he was very friendly with the monks who were his neighbours at Mount Melleray. He was proud when a FitzGerald became Abbot. Molly was fortunate to have him as a close friend. In the last phase of her life she was dependent on his sophistication and his simplicity and his honourable and amused character consoled her. He visited regularly and often brought bunches of the herbs he grew. She would sit after he left, holding his little bouquet and inhaling its scent.

She was blessed in the regular team of people who looked after her in the last years. Joe Meehan was her doctor. He lived in Ardmore and was just beginning his practice when they met, so he was very young but born wise with an interest in people's inner world. Despite his scientific training, he was devout. 'One needs faith in my profession, there is so much suffering in it,' he said to me. His compassion is combined with an ironical wit. He describes being rather thrown by Molly when she first called him to the house. She was in bed and when he went to examine her, Hero, her dog, burst growling from the blankets. She poured a huge whiskey and insisted that he drink it. He remembers thinking 'luckily I'm on foot, if the guards found me driving after this I'd be struck off'. Over the years they became close friends. She accepted it when he said she must go to the Bons Secours because she knew he did his utmost to keep her out of it. He loved her and understood the complications of her character and she trusted and loved him. As her eyesight worsened, he managed to pretend to drink the whiskies.

When sewing and mending became difficult Josie Morrissey, her dressmaker, did it. She was another beloved person who could make you a wedding dress or upholster a sofa. She was skilled and serene and she and Molly were very close.

Brigette Foley arrived to work for Molly in 1976, and she is still a great friend of both Virginia and myself. They shared over the years a tremendous interest in domesticity and clothes. They brewed home-made furniture polish that smelt of beeswax, and rubbed it vigorously into the furniture which shone as a result. Brigette had a talent for cooking and appreciated Molly passing on recipes to her. They made marmalade together every February. This note fell out of *Le Grand Meaulnes*, one of the last books Molly had been reading before she died: 'Well-being returns when I see sun-light glittering through a new batch of marmalade on the kitchen table.'

Once when they were sorting stuff into black plastic bags in the tiny east bedroom at Dysert, Molly, although very aged, took a flying jump like a good horse over one of the bags, landing nimbly on her feet. She was in a temper about something at the time. Brigette said, 'It was pure sauciness gave her the strength.'

After the era of tiny strokes began, Norah came to work. At first she just cooked for lunch parties but over time she did more and more. Molly described how waking from a doze and seeing Norah standing at the end of the bed brought her an instant feeling of peace. As with Josie, she benefited from the calm of Norah's character. She was consoled by her youth and vigour and her ongoing motherhood. Molly was godmother to her youngest child, David.

She was frequently on the telephone to Godfrey and Billie. Godfrey, like herself, was failing. He suffered from the Skrine heart problems. In fact, he fell from his horse with a heart attack and died just before she did. She got on extremely well with Billie, his second wife. She admired the verve, authority and sympathy in her character. Billie was one of the rare Scottish Catholics, and this gave her an empathy with Ireland as did her brilliance with horses. She bought wild Connemara yearlings and turned them into disciplined, spirited, beautifully mannered ponies which were sought after when she sold them. She never hurried them but understood their different characters and treated them accordingly. Molly noted her success with all animals and her love for them, and when she was no longer able to take him for walks she gave Hero to Billie. This was a hard decision for someone who had always had a little dog to indulge and scold and be loved by. She grieved for Hero after giving him up, but she did it out of generosity to him.

As her head and body weakened, offers poured into Gina Pollinger's office for Molly's writing, and she was sad and disappointed at not being able to fulfil them. Gina helped her by passing on assignments that were not too taxing. One of these was the anthology *Molly Keane's Ireland* which we compiled together.

Neither of us found the collaboration easy and we both turned to Gina complaining about the other. However, it got done in the end and was quite well received. Molly embarked on it entirely for my sake. She felt undrawn to the idea personally, being unable to read and research much with her failing eyesight and having to rely on her memory which was becoming misty.

Born as we were into diverse times in Ireland, our views differed but also overlapped in our love of literature and Yeats, and in our love of the country. We both had a romantic view of it. This Ireland exists but it is getting weaker and scarcer and even then it was dimming, diluted by television and the bustling capitalist state, which came a cropper but now seems to be rebuilding itself, one hopes in a different way. Dublin is an important factor in Irish culture and we sought to include it but we were both drawn to rural Ireland and until fairly recently it was considered an agricultural and fisherman's country. For generations our poets and writers have relied on the reality and metaphor of the natural world as the Celtic monks and Yeats and Heaney and Molly herself did. In the years since we put the anthology together, much has changed; rural, spiritual Ireland has retreated and been damaged by scandal. It can still be found in the landscape (also diminished by bad planning), in the music and the writing, and sometimes still in people's talk. The old bachelors of Connemara, who used to be the best people in the world to hold a conversation over a gate with and who spoke a beautiful Irish-English honed by loneliness and imagination, have become extinct. The language has been diluted by Americanisms and technology. Irish people are keen on the web and are very good at it. They are more likely to see their history on a screen than in the ruins of a castle or an abbey. A country must evolve or it becomes moribund but it is important to preserve our thinning culture (sometimes commercialised in a false manner). Our roots and essence and the soul of Ireland reside in it.

In her introduction to the anthology, Molly spoke of the link between the artist and the landscape which was still strong although in her own case it was now limited to what she could see from her bedroom window at Ardmore: 'Sometimes after a night of wild storms and floods, I wake from a heavy doze to see gleaming sun on the farthest headlands and distant waves, silent as the spread of a gull's wings, breaking behind each other on the shining sea. It is a liquid, bright scentless morning, all colour spread with a full wet brush. Such contrasts, as startling as they are swift, are peculiarly sustaining to the creative artist, and in a life-enhancing way, mirror the romance, poetry and drama which have been part of Irish life since the first Celts wandered westward across Europe.' The landscape retains a mystical quality which is as powerful a source for writers today as it has always been.

We wanted to draw attention to the strength and originality and strangeness of the Irish imagination which Yeats compared to 'a bough held down by a weak hand which suddenly straightens out'. Elsewhere, he spoke of the Ireland where 'a man can be so battered, badgered and destroyed that he is a loveless man'. And the country in which 'all things hang like a drop of dew upon a blade of grass'. I had seen a print by Bob Ó Cathail depicting a bleak accordion player, seated on a kitchen chair lost in a music of ecstasy and pain. I mentioned him to Lucinda McNeile (the editor we were lucky enough to have at HarperCollins) and he is responsible for the linocuts which gave so much to the book, especially the feeling of Yeats's two extremes – the sense of struggle and the sense of glory involved in being born Irish.

Two artists helped us with the project, Bob Ó Cathail and Derek Hill. Derek gave us permission to put his painting *The Back of Tory Island* on the cover. He lived partly in Donegal and he spent long years painting Ireland and its people, and his understanding of the country is evident from his art. Molly and Derek were friends and he would sometimes invite himself to stay for a night and say on the telephone, 'We will have a wonderful time giving everyone a good put-down.' They were both accomplished at it, as well as being artists and very sensitive people if anyone gave them a put-down. Molly loved his work and Derek himself.

She enjoyed the unrespectable secrets, sometimes tragic or louche, or bitter, hidden in the faces of his portraits but most of all she admired his landscapes: 'The smell of a dark cottage is behind a dwarfish geranium leaning into the mean sunlight which comes through a small paned window. He observes and transforms the sea's spite and anger to follow it in his masterpiece *A Quiet Wave* – the whole of an evening in its placidity.'

Both of them were devoted to the Prince of Wales. Molly admired him from afar but Derek was close to him and they went on painting holidays together. When Prince Charles came to Ireland, Derek asked him to telephone Molly, and he told her how much he liked her books. She was very pleased and bucked by his call. She partly longed to boast of the compliment to friends but she restrained herself and only mentioned it to Denis. She was haunted by the old loyalties and Sinn Fein days, and she thought that the royals must be protected by discretion at all times.

John Gielgud sent Molly *The Life of Trollope* by Victoria Glendinning, and a letter, probably in reply to a wail from her about the horrors of ageing, imploring her 'to try and rejoice in your longevity'. This was hard for her to do. She was born busy and not contemplative. She tried to make a success of old age and she managed it sometimes but she was frequently despairing. Other people died: Godfrey, Johnnie

Perry, Stephen, Phyllis, Clodagh and (both young in her eyes) Shane and Didi Jameson. These people were close friends and her attitude to their deaths was strange. It was as though the struggle of survival took every ounce of her energy and there was none left for grief. This was untypical of her hitherto. Her desire to comfort the bereaved was undiminished and she picked up the telephone to them.

The prospect of her own death was like a gathering storm on the horizon in front of us all. We wanted her suffering to stop but we did not want her to stop. In the autumn of 1995 George and I went on two holidays, which was unusual. It was as if I wanted my strength reinforced for the ordeal ahead. Molly's health was going downhill, her eyes were a mental and physical disaster because she had always depended on reading and sewing, and they had helped her. Driving was an unrealistic dream she held onto as a sort of symbol of hope. Eventually Dr Condon could do no more for her eyes and he told her so. Eating was an effort. George sent her a snipe. I think it was the last meal she enjoyed. I watched her sitting up in bed eating it with relish. Like Tossie, she sucked the brains out of the tiny head.

One evening she rang me in a state of strange energy and agitation. I felt she wanted me to come over but I had just left that afternoon and I was coming back next day. She was not alone, one of 'the ladies of the night' was with her. Shortly after this she went out into the hall and fell and cracked her hip. Alison got her back to bed with difficulty. Once in bed she was not in pain – only when she moved. She refused to ring me until the next morning. When I got there Joe had sent for the ambulance. He came to support her when she was leaving home. Getting her onto the stretcher was painful and hard to bear.

Much later I left her in the hospital ward. They had decided to operate the next day with an epidural. It had been a hard day. A young doctor came to take blood. She made one of her last 'jokes' to him. 'Do you think I might have AIDS?' she said. 'I'm too old I suppose.' She was all charm to him but overwrought and exhausted with me. He (used to the desperation and anger of old people at the end of their tether) noticed her annoyance. I felt his silent sympathy and tears came into my eyes. When people came in to see other patients, Molly welcomed them as she thought they were visitors entering her drawing-room at Dysert. She was very confused. We were both in a sorry, stunned state. When I left she was peaceful, drugged against the pain with the nurses taking good care of her. It was my birthday. I arrived late at the Barn at Ballywilliam where the people I most loved were waiting, George, Ken and Rachel Thompson and Paddy Rossmore. We ate smoked salmon and brown bread and drank champagne sent by Mum. We all felt we were on a cliff edge but the cocktails made by George according to the recipe he had learned from Molly were a knockout elixir that made one feel artificially all right.

The operation went well but she slipped in and out of confusion. After the hospital she was supposed to stay in a nursing home for two weeks to convalesce. This was not a success. She was terrified she was going to die away from her own home. She behaved badly and invented stories about ill treatment for her visitors and waved her stick at the nurses (normally she loved nurses). She was desperate. We decided to bring her home early. The last morning there she sat up in bed wearing a pretty jersey looking rather young and well and wrote a cheque for the nursing home, totally clear-headed.

Once home she relapsed into a world of half-light. She, who had always made efforts, made almost none about learning to walk again. Nurses came and one of them helped her to the half door. She leant on it and took in deep breaths of sea air. All her life she had been revived by breathing in this way. It was her natural elixir. This time she went back to bed and didn't return to her front door again. It was like her farewell to the life force.

When she was not in a trance, she was often confused. Now and again she became quite clear-headed. Once I was sitting beside her and she put out her hand and took mine, and in a brittle social voice, but as if she knew the importance of the remark, she said, 'You and I are such different cups of tea that I think sometimes I have been very nasty and unfair to you.' It was not easy for her to admit this and I was moved that she forced herself out of the mists she was embracing in order to say it. She was slipping away. I rang Virginia who had just returned to London. She arrived back with Julia – I remember washing Molly's shawl in Lux to make her shroud. The Brigadier came and went leaving his prayer book covered in soft leather, embossed with the Duke of Leinster's crest. We read Molly the 23rd Psalm written in the old language out of this. I don't know if she heard. I have been told that the sense of hearing is the last to leave us. When I was alone with her at one moment I said in reply to her earlier remark to me that I loved her and that I knew she loved me.

One afternoon Andrea came to sit with Molly to give us a break. I went for a little walk and breathed in the air thankfully as she herself had done. She would have been happy to leave this world beside her beloved Andrea. In fact she died later that night. It was like a scene from one of her books. She was surrounded by people she was unaware of, visitors kept calling in the Irish way as though it was the eve of a wedding. Norah and Brigette were there and they repeated the Hail Mary at intervals. We all joined in. 'Holy Mary, Mother of God, Pray for us sinners now and at the hour of our death.'

She was not in the throes of anything, she was at peace. When she left us it took us some time to notice. One had the feeling that she had triumphed in some way. Grief did not come till later. We were too tired to be sad. Dawn was breaking. After a long silence Joe said, 'She would have wanted us to have a whiskey'. We sat around her dining-room table and raised our glasses to Molly.

INDEX

Agate, James 88
Agnes (Jamesons' cook) 198, 207
Aherne's restaurant, Youghal 278
Ainsworth, May 170
Alain-Fournier, *Le Grand Meaulnes*
   270, 316
Alberta, Canada 4–5
Allende, Isabelle 28
Anderson, Judith 92
André Deutsch (publishers) 246–7,
   248, 254, 268, 299
Anglo-Irish Treaty (1921) xiv, 35
Anna (Lord North Street cook) 169
Annesley, Ruth 312–13
Anouilh, Jean 204, 219
Anson, Andrea 201–2
Anson, Annina 201–2
Anson, Clodagh 99–101, 118, 134, 201,
   202, 244, 321
Anson, Dado 201–2
Anson, Hugo 201–2
Arbutus Lodge, Cork 278
Ardavoo (wing of Cappoquin House)
   147–8, 149–52, 154–5, 171–2, 175
Ardfinnan, Co. Tipperary 190–1
Ardmore, Co. Waterford 101, 108, 111,
   117–19, 131, 136–7, 197–9, 201–3;
   Rock House 134, 136, 137–8, 197–9,
   207, 313; MK moves to Dysert
   193–6, 200; Cliff House Hotel
   194, 199; O'Reilly's in 207; *see also*
   Dysert (MK's house in Ardmore)
Army & Navy Stores catalogue 14

Ashcroft, Peggy 71, 120, 245, 263–4,
   266–7, 289, 304–7

Astaire, Fred 94, 96
Athill, Diana 246–7, 248, 250, 252,
   254, 255, 293
Austen, Jane xv, 172, 185, 196
Aymes, Marcel, *Say It With Flowers*
   203–4

The Bagges of Heaven (unproduced
   play, MK and Mac Liammóir)
   216–17
Bagnold, Enid 204; *National Velvet* 92
Ballymaloe 299
Ballyrankin House, Ferns, Co. Wexford
   ('the Bogs') 5–6, 10, 29–30, 83, 112,
   129–30, 208–9, 222–3; burning of
   during Civil War (7 July 1921) xiii–
   xiv, 33–5, 36–7, 38; the 'Wild Wood'
   15, 16; workforce 17, 18–19, 23,
   26–7, 46–7, 107, 222–3; landscape
   around 29–30; New Ballyrankin 36,
   40; MK's final visit to 308
Ballywilliam, Co. Cork 304, 322
Bankhead, Tallulah 92
Bar S Ranch (Alberta, Canada) 4, 5
Barnes Common 227–8
Baxter, Keith 217–18, 220
Bay Lough 188
Beaumont, Binkie 74–5, 125, 129,
   167–9, 181, 183–4, 203, 204, 276;
   house at Lord North Street 142,
   167–9, 228; and *Treasure Hunt* 166,
   170; and alcohol 169, 228; and
   Dazzling Prospect 219, 220
Beckett, Samuel 219
Bedford, Sybille, *Jigsaw* 163
Bell, Miss (governess) 17, 18–19, 27

Belleville (house in Cappoquin) 79,
86–7, 98, 109–11, 117, 119–20,
131, 140–1, 171–2; drawing-room
at 104–5, 106, 108–9, 110–11, 177;
gardens 111, 121–2, 149, 175, 189,
191–2; MK's writing room 113, 114;
MK's rows with Bobbie at 119–22;
Bobbie's family at 123–5; sub-let
to the Scotts 147–8, 157, 171, 175;
monastery farm beside 148, 181;
MK's return to (1949) 171, 177–8,
185; and memories of Bobbie 177,
185, 188, 191, 192–3, 200; decline of
191–2; sale of 192–3, 195–6
Bernard, Jeffrey 277
Blackstairs Mountains 29
Blackwater River 99, 134, 150, 156, 286
Blackwood's Magazine 35
Blarney Castle 178, 179, 303
Bogarde, Dirk 160, 164, 165
Bolt, Robert 219
Boothe, Evelyn 59
Bowen, Elizabeth 34, 39, 87,
110–11, 177, 193, 204, 237, 242;
on the Anglo-Irish xiv, 163; on
bereavement 187; funeral of (1973)
235–6; The Shelbourne 48, 216; The
Last September 66
Boylan, Clare xi, 251, 277, 292, 300
Bradbury, Malcolm 255
Bragg, Melvyn 258
Bridget (MK's cook) 109, 112, 148, 151,
155, 170, 185–6, 196, 202, 222
Brooke, Peter 74
Brown, Irene 166
Brownlow, Julia (daughter of Virginia)
289–90, 304, 306, 323
Brownlow, Kevin 180–1, 234, 262, 266,
267, 285, 289, 304, 306
Brownlow, Virginia (daughter of MK):
MK pregnant with 138, 139–40;
birth of (1945) 104, 140; christening
of 94; as a baby/young child 102,
104, 140–1, 150, 151, 209, 210;
childhood of 63–4, 157, 179, 181,
207, 211, 212, 213, 214, 218, 221;
MK's note to over Bobbie (1944)
131, 132; and grandmother Nesta
210; horsemanship 223; and creative
play 224–5, 227; at Froebel Institute
224–5; conflict with MK 225, 284–5;

288–9; wedding of (1969) 232,
234; and MK's media interviews
249, 250, 300; MK with in London
261–7; and psychoanalysis 262, 278,
284; locates Bobbie's grave 263;
treated for cancer of the jaw 264–7,
306; left-wing views 284; at Belsize
Park Gardens 285, 288–9, 304, 306;
birth of daughter Julia (1984) 289–
90; at Peggy Ashcroft's funeral 307;
at Dysert for MK's last days 323
Bunclody (Newtownbarry) 35, 41–6,
223
Burke, Jack and Jimmy 195, 278, 311–12
Burke, Nick 286

Callil, Carmen 281
Cameron, Alan 110, 236
Cappoquin, Co. Waterford 97, 123, 130,
147–55, 175, 207; Bacon Factory 90,
119; Barrons' bakery 188, 201; see
also Belleville (house in Cappoquin)
Cappoquin House 147–8, 149–52,
154–5, 171–2, 175
Casson, Lewis 166–7, 183
Cavendish, Adele 93–7, 99, 109, 134,
255
Cavendish, Lord Charles 93, 96–7, 106
Cavendish, William, 6th Duke of
Devonshire 95–6
Cazalet, Mecha 146, 278
Cazalet, Robin 146
Chancellor, Betty 279
Charles, Prince 320
Charleston (dance) 64
Chatto & Windus (publishers) 245
Chatwin, Bruce, On the Black Hill
274–5
Chekov, Anton 174, 196
Chrysler, Walter 203
civil war, Irish (1922–3) xiii–xiv, 33–5,
65–6, 98
Cleeve, Maureen 252–4, 300
Clemons, Walter 248
Clowes, Dick 129, 220, 228
Cobb, Gladys 165–6, 183
Cobh (Queenstown) 90–1
Cochran, Jean 79
Cockburn, Alexander 313
Cockburn, Patricia 187, 244, 313
Cockburn, Patrick 101

Cockburn boys 313
Colette, *Gigi* 76
Collins, Billy (publisher) 18, 120, 243
Collins, Michael xiv
Colthurst, Sir George 178
Condon, Dr 321
Cooper, Gladys 90
Coward, Noel 88, 127, 181–2
Cullen, Jimmy 65

Dalí, Salvador 258
Dare, Zena 90
Davies, Stan Gebler 251
Dazzling Prospect (MK play) 218–20, 226, 232, 237, 243, 277
de Valera, Éamon xii, 140
Devoted Ladies (MK novel) 71, 80
Dickens, Charles, *Our Mutual Friend* 167
Dick-John (horse) 98
Dromana (house in Co. Waterford) 121, 156–7, 158, 185, 255–6
Drumnasole, Co. Antrim 38–40, 102–3, 130, 209
Dublin 48–9, 140, 141–2, 179, 187, 198, 211–18, 277, 281
Ducks and Drakes (MK play) 125–7, 161
Dungarvan, Co. Waterford 196
Dysert (MK's house in Ardmore) 202–3, 206, 244, 251, 271, 278, 279, 284–5, 305; MK moves to 193–6, 200; MK's renovations 193, 194–5, 200, 221, 278; letting of 221, 234, 236; press interviews at 249, 250, 252–4; and MK in old age 1–2, 308, 310–13, 315–17, 319–22, 323–4; MK dies at 3, 324

East Molesey, Surrey 229, 233
Easter Rising (1916) xiv, 35
Eden-Roc, South of France 181–2
Edwards, Hilton 141, 142, 217
Eliot, T. S. 219
Elkin Mathews & Marrot (publishers) 44
Elspeth (Swiss governess) 150–1
Elvira (cook) 168–70, 228

Fairyfield (house in Kinsale) 242, 271, 272–4, 275
Falkiner, Ninian, 140

Farahy, Co. Cork 235–6
Fiennes, Audrey 236
First World War 31–2, 49–50, 162
FitzGerald, Denis 313–15, 320, 323
FitzGerald, Desmond 314
FitzGerald, Edward 314
Foley, Brigette 292, 305, 308, 312, 316, 324
Fort William (house near Lismore) 123, 154, 221, 286–8
Fortune, Paddy 18
Foster, Roy 250
Fraher, Mrs 153–4
France 181–2, 183, 203–4
French School in Bray 32–3
Freud, Sigmund 56
Froebel Institute, London 224–5
Full House (MK novel) 22, 57, 76–7, 82–3, 88
Furze, Roger 81

Gas Company Theatre, Dun Laoghaire 214
Gate Theatre, Dublin 141, 142
George VI, King 87
Gerard (Fairyfield butler) 242, 272–3
Gerard, Brother 179–81
Gibraltar 126, 129
Gielgud, John 71, 72–3, 109, 170–1, 182–3, 184–5, 262–3, 276, 320; directs *Spring Meeting* 74, 183; directs *Treasure Hunt* 165, 167, 170, 183; summons for soliciting 183–4; directs *Dazzling Prospect* 218–19, 220; on Peggy Ashcroft 306–7
Glendinning, Victoria, *The Life of Trollope* 320
Godfrey, Dood and Kid 173
Good Behaviour (MK novel) 48, 206, 237–43, 245–9, 263, 268, 276, 277; MK's press interviews 8, 210, 249–54, 300; characters 10, 32, 50, 101, 156, 173, 178, 238, 239–40, 241–3; success of in USA 92–3, 248; Billy Collins rejects 120, 243; darkness in 120, 237–9, 240; and Peggy Ashcroft 120, 245, 306; writing of 237–8, 240–3; shortlisted for Booker Prize 254–5; and Russell Harty 255, 257–8, 261; adapted for TV 278
Grasse, South of France 182, 183

Greene, Graham 204
Gregory, Lady Augusta 13, 281–2
Groucho Club 277
Guardian Angel (MK play) 141, 142
Guinness, Alec 305
Guinness, Desmond 214, 282
Guinness, Mariga 214
Guitry, Sacha 204
Guppy, Shusha 206, 300–3, 312

H. M. Tennent (production company)
    74, 125, 142, 169, 203–4, 217,
    218–20, 228
Hall-Dare, Daphne 41–6, 48, 59, 130,
    222, 223, 233, 278
Hamilton, Adrian 178, 179–80, 181,
    225
Hamilton, Penelope 178, 303
Hamlet (dog) 169
Hannah (dog) 247
Hansy (dog) 136
Harty, Russell 185, 255–61
Haughey, Charles 279
Heald, Patricia 260
Healy, George 175
Heaney, Seamus 208, 318
Henderson, Billie 275
Hepburn, Audrey 196
Hero (dog) 312, 315, 317
Hill, Derek 319–20
Hutchinson, Jeremy 304

India 25, 51, 229, 231
Irish Arts Council 279

Jack (pony) 223
Jackson, Pam 152
Jagger, Mick 257
James, Henry 56
Jameson, Andrea 313, 324
Jameson, Joan 134, 135–7, 144, 194,
    197–8, 206; death of 199, 205
Jameson, Julian 136, 151
Jameson, Shane 136, 137, 198, 313, 321
Jameson, Tommie 134, 135–6, 137, 194,
    195, 196, 198, 199; collaborates with
    MK to deceive Bobbie (1944) 131,
    132; and death of Bobbie 144, 146,
    206; break with MK 204–7; death of
    (1965) 207–8
Joe (stable boy) 20–1

John, Gwen 293
John of the Rocks (fisherman) 22
Johnston, Denis 216, 278–9
Jones, Hywel 304
Josephine (Lord North Street cook)
    169

Keane, Alice (mother-in-law of MK)
    123–4, 130–2
Keane, Bobbie: love affair with MK
    84, 88, 305; at Belleville 86–7,
    97–8, 105, 106, 110–11, 114–15,
    116, 117, 119–22, 139–40, 177,
    191, 193; personality of 87, 89–90,
    140; stammer of 87–8, 117, 123;
    marries MK (October 1939) 88;
    background of 89, 90, 107, 123,
    154; and Cappoquin Bacon Factory
    90, 119; honeymoon in New York
    90–3; and Clodagh Anson 99, 100;
    and Second World War 117, 132–3,
    139, 140; and Ardmore 117–18, 119,
    137–8, 194; MK's rows with 119–22;
    mother killed by Guards' Chapel
    bomb (1944) 130–2, 139; MK
    deceives over England visit (1944)
    131–3; and the Jamesons 134–5,
    137–8; and MK's jealousy 138–9;
    Quidnunc profile on (1944) 141–2;
    death of (1946) 86, 142–4, 145–7,
    150, 185–8, 190–1, 206, 216, 253;
    funeral of 143, 158; MK's mourning
    for 86, 114–15, 145–7, 149–50, 153,
    185, 187–8, 190–1, 200, 216; location
    of grave 143, 216, 263
Keane, Charles 143, 148, 172, 173
Keane, David 173
Keane, Diana (Diana Macdonald,
    sister-in-law of MK) 123–4, 125, 131,
    132
Keane, Feargal 108
Keane, Frida (Frida Delmege, sister-in-
    law of MK) 123–5, 131, 132, 139
Keane, Harry (father-in-law of MK)
    123, 189
Keane, Molly, character: wit and 'talent
    to amuse' xiii, xv, 2, 9, 17, 45, 155–6,
    164–5, 222, 239; paradoxes of xiv–
    xv, 30, 45, 54, 65, 113, 132, 206, 223,
    238, 272, 283, 285; kindness and
    generosity xv, 65, 79, 133–4, 157–8,

165, 206, 234, 238, 262, 278, 285, 294–5; stiletto sharpness xv, 8, 30, 65, 88, 124, 138, 164, 173, 210, 294, 295, 313; anxiety 2, 102, 117, 133, 138–9, 140, 179, 233, 264, 277, 288, 292; excitability/volatility 2, 3, 11, 13, 28, 30–1, 39, 94, 124–5, 138–9, 210, 245; feelings of loneliness and exclusion 3, 14, 16–17, 24, 30, 32–3, 84, 116–17, 172–3; need for demonstrative love 3, 9, 10–11, 15, 25–6, 28, 58, 138, 295; rebellious/subversive nature 3, 8, 13, 19, 21–4, 26, 45, 52, 55; love of fiesta/parties 9–10, 28–9, 38–40, 42, 47, 48–9, 152–4, 190, 253, 280; passion for domesticity 10, 67–8, 87, 109, 112, 212, 220–1, 226–9, 258–9, 265–7, 269; sense of guilt 17, 23, 60, 63, 67, 72, 88, 116, 138, 294; depression 30, 62, 68, 103, 116, 210, 239, 285, 312; verbal assaults 30–1, 204–5, 206, 284, 296; overvaluation of social success 33, 60; talent for flirting 38, 42, 49, 58, 59, 62, 66, 82, 83, 159; nervous ills 40, 133, 134; and the 'good put-down' 65, 108–9, 284; absolute belief in love 77, 87–8, 206, 312; mourning for Bobbie 86, 114–15, 145–7, 149–50, 153, 185, 187–8, 190–1, 200, 216; genius for saying the unforgivable 94, 109, 204–6; passion for flowers 105–6, 147, 149, 189, 264–5; powerful anger 120–3, 204–5, 206, 210, 284, 285, 300–1, 310–11; deceives Bobbie over England visit 131–3

Keane, Molly, life: childhood 3–4, 6–7, 8–12, 13–27, 28–32, 52–3, 252–3, 256, 294, 301; lack of formal education xv–xvi, 7; pupil at French School in Bray 32–3; social scene in Ireland xiii, 41–4, 46–7, 48–50, 59, 62–5, 134–5, 151–7, 222; and theatre people 71–5, 92–7, 109, 120, 141–2, 159–60, 164–71, 181–5, 203–4, 216–20, 245, 275–7, see also Ashcroft, Peggy; Beaumont, Binkie; Gielgud, John; Perry, John; children of, see Brownlow, Virginia (daughter of MK); Phipps, Sally (daughter of

MK); sewing 1, 108, 109, 222, 237; physical appearance of 3–4, 76, 77, 94; and feminism 8, 250–1, 280–2; media interviews 8, 210–11, 249–54, 275, 291–2, 299, 300–3, 307–9; Aunts of (Lou and May) 21–4, 40, 62–3, 66–7, 130, 161, 175, 256; and French language 33, 150–1, 203–4; fox-hunting 40, 41, 46, 47, 48, 52–5, 59, 62, 64–5, 84, 175, 285; money 40, 47, 64, 113, 133–4, 147–8, 170, 191–3, 204, 212, 221, 232–3, 277–80; horses 41, 42, 52–5, 233, 253; religion 44, 145–6, 167, 175, 182, 273, 304; first sexual affair 55–6, 59; and homosexuality 71–2, 78, 80, 241–2; marries Bobbie (October 1939) 88; success 88–9, 133–4, 165, 170, 173, 247, 257, 261, 263, 277–8, 291, 300; honeymoon in New York 90–3; Quidnunc profile (1944) 141–2; feud with Richard and Olivia Keane 171–4; affair with Bill Scott 174–5; slipped disc 178–9; lives in Dublin 211–18, 221; buys house in London (1965) 223–9, 234; return to Ireland (1969) 234; TV and radio appearances 255–7, 258–9, 275, 300; and Russell Harty 255–61; with Virginia in London 261–7; Groucho Club member 277; Aosdána member 278, 279; political views 284, 302, 305, 313; as a grandmother 288–90; letters to Mary D. Kierstead 307–8, 309–10; asks Sally Phipps to write biography xiv–xv, 1–2; old age 1–2, 81, 113, 174, 259, 275–90, 291–3, 298, 299–304, 305, 306–24; ill health in old age 30, 290, 291–3, 300, 307, 310–13, 316, 321–3; death of xiii, 3, 324

Keane, Molly, writing: MK as last of the Anglo-Irish writers xiii, xvi, 3; accuracy and preciseness xv, xvi, 8, 116, 240–1, 296; autobiographical elements xv, 2–3, 31, 44–5, 57–8, 70, 83, 84, 113–14, 173, 182, 197, 238–41; houses and objects xv, 37, 48, 92, 105, 156, 162, 177; opposing forces in xv, 30, 45, 54, 65, 113, 132, 238–43; sense of place xv, 36–7,

Keane, Molly, writing – *continued*
87, 105, 177, 269; MK's rejection
of analysis 3, 197, 251; landscape
and natural world 7, 201, 240, 270,
318; feelings of exclusion in 16, 82,
116–17; childhood theme 18, 21,
25–6, 30, 290, 293–7; servants in 18,
21, 163–4, 178; debt to the Aunts
24, 161; gardening spinsters 23–4,
50, 76; brothers as leitmotif 25–6;
pseudonym (M. J. Farrell) 41, 53–4,
55, 141–2, 263, 281; secrecy of early
writing 41, 46, 70, 226; parties and
hunts as set pieces 47, 53–4, 55, 56,
197; English ladies in 50, 158–60;
and the failure of kindness 50, 295,
296; identification with hunter and
hunted 54, 113; sexual love in 55,
56–8, 295–6; and homosexuality
80, 241–2; comedy elements 89, 127,
155–6, 159–65, 237–43, 252, 268–70;
pain of the creative process 90,
113–14, 118, 165, 243, 246, 278, 299;
dialogue as strength 92, 127, 204;
marriage in 116–17; and widowhood
158–9, 160–1; adaptations of French
works 203–4; *see also* entries for
individual books and plays
Keane, Olivia 147–8, 172–3
Keane, Richard 147–8, 171–4
Keane, Vivien 143, 148, 172
Keane, Lady Eleanor 143–4
Kells (house in Co. Kerry) 236–7
Kew Gardens 228
Kierstead, Mary D. 238, 307–10
Kierstead, Will 308
Kilcor, Co. Cork 244–5
Kildare, Co. 5, 6, 20–1, 28–9
Kildorrery, Co. Cork 242
King, Francis 274
The Knight of Cheerful Countenance
(MK novel) 23, 40–1, 48
Knockmealdown Mountains 156,
188–90, 191
Knopf (New York publisher) 248
Knots Fosse (house in Essex) 220, 228,
275–6
Kokoschka, Oskar 93

La Terriere, Tighe 76
Lamb, Lady Caroline 95–6

Laurent (French teenager) 286–7
Lawrence, T. E. 229
Lean, David 305
Lenaire (society photographers) 80
Leon, Anne 164
Leonard, Hugh 278–9
Lessing, Doris 255
Lillie, Bea 92
Lina Stores, Brewer Street, Soho 228
Lindsey, Chicken 227
Lismore 99, 123, 150, 200, 279, 315
Lismore Castle 93, 95–7
Lismore Cathedral 97, 280, 315
Lizzie (servant at Belleville) 139, 141
Lohr, Marie 166
London 73–4, 88, 129, 142–3, 166,
216, 221, 223–7, 261–7, 277; Guards'
Chapel bomb (1944) 130–2; Lord
North Street 142, 167–70, 228;
The Elms (house in Barnes) 223,
224–5, 226–9, 234; Brewer Street,
Soho 228; Belsize Park Gardens 285,
288–9, 306; Belsize Grove 304
Long, Denise 182
Loving and Giving (MK novel) 30, 57,
138, 270, 293–300, 303; Nicandra
in 23, 25, 30, 50, 290, 293–4, 295–6,
297–8; writing of 291, 292–3, 299
Loving Without Tears (MK novel) 141,
216, 259, 260
Lygon, Lady Dorothy 272

Mabel (Joan's lady's maid) 144, 198–9
Mac Liammóir, Mícheál 109, 141,
216–17
MacCarthy, Mrs (Fairyfield cook) 242,
273
MacCarthy's Bar, Fethard 83, 84
Macdonald, Donald 125
Mackenzie, Compton 201
MacNeice, Louis 103
Mad Puppetstown (MK novel) 13–14,
18, 19, 21, 25–6, 54, 57, 98
Madresfield Court, Worcestershire 271
Maggie (American nurse) 266
Mary-Josie (maid at Ballyrankin) 19
Martin (Gielgud's friend) 262–3
Martin M. (horse) 231
Mary, Queen 170
Masters, Sivie (Sivie Perry) 69, 77–81,
85, 118, 134

Maugham, W. Somerset 127
Maureen (housekeeper at Fort
    William) 288
McCarthy, Thomas 314; *Gardens of
    Remembrance* 234
McGuinness, Norah 214–16, 227, 282;
    painting of MK and Bobbie 137–8,
    147
McNeile, Lucinda 319
Meehan, Joe 315, 321–2, 324
Merril, Io 282–3
Merril family 221
Mills & Boon 40
Mitchell, Murray 286
Mitchell, Phyllis 93, 221, 278, 286–8,
    321
Mitford, Nancy 203, 204
Moiseiwitsch, Tanya 165
Molly Keane's Ireland (anthology, MK
    and Sally Phipps) 279, 288, 317–20
Monte Carlo 137
Morgan, Diana 246
Morley, Robert 203, 224
Morrissey, Josie 315–16
Moth (donkey) 25
Mount Melleray, Monastery of 86, 97,
    106, 156, 179–81, 315
Mulcahy, Dick and Wendy 190–1
Murphy (cook at Woodrooffe) 68
Murray (gardener at Belleville) 122

New York 92–3, 203, 218, 248, 288, 309
Newtownbarry House, Co. Wexford
    41–5
Norah 284, 292, 305, 312, 316, 324
Nugent, Frank 199
Nunn, Trevor 307

Ó Cathail, Bob 319
O'Brien, Bridie 195
O'Brien, George, *The Village of Longing*
    96, 150
O'Brien, Georgie 149–50
O'Brien, Jack 194–5, 200
O'Brien, Kate 204
O'Casey, Seán 107
O'Cathain clan 107
O'Flanagan, Dr Kevin 179
Oliver, Robin 313
O'Neill, Jamie 261
O'Reilly, Betty 207

Ormond, Mary 148
Ormonde Cinema, Dungarvan 196
Orpen, Iris 34–5
Osborne, John 219
Osbourne, Jack 168
O'Shea, Milo 166
Osterley Park 228
Owenashad, River 99

Paddy (groom at Ballyrankin) 222–3
Pakenham, Thomas 254
Parsons, Ian 245
A Passage to India (David Lean film)
    305
Perry, Dolly 66–9, 70, 85, 117, 125, 128,
    190
Perry, John 70–5, 167, 181, 204, 228,
    255; homosexuality 69, 71, 73, 99;
    and father Willie 71, 73, 81, 82;
    as collaborator on *Spring Meeting*
    74, 125, 128; wartime service 125,
    126–7, 128–9; and *Ducks and Drakes*
    125–7; and *Treasure Hunt* 159; and
    Dazzling Prospect 218, 219, 220; at
    Bobbie's funeral 263; decline in old
    age 80, 275–7; death of 320–1
Perry, Willie 60, 62, 64, 66, 69–70, 73,
    81–4, 85, 190
Petre, Diana 274–5, 309; *The Secret
    Orchard of Roger Ackerley* 273
Phipps, Annie 244, 245
Phipps, George 243–5, 321, 322
Phipps, James 244
Phipps, Richard 244
Phipps, Sally (daughter of MK): MK
    asks to write biography xiv–xv,
    1–2; birth of (March 1940) 102;
    at Drumnasole as a baby 102–3,
    130, 209; as young child 97, 98–9,
    100–1, 104, 123, 135, 139–41, 143–4,
    146–55; nannies and governesses
    of 102–4, 150–1, 178, 195–6; speaks
    French to John Perry 73; walks with
    Binkie Beaumont 75; at Belleville
    123, 139–41, 143, 149, 177, 179–81,
    185–7, 191; MK's note to over
    Bobbie (1944) 131, 132; and the
    Jamesons 135, 197–9, 207–8; and
    father's death 143–4, 146–7, 185–7,
    190–1; at Ardavoo 148, 150–1, 152,
    153–5, 172; youthful rebellion 157;

Phipps, Sally, writing – *continued*
and Gladys Cobb 166; first visit to
the theatre 167; and depression 178,
225, 226, 310; and Adrian Hamilton
178, 179–80, 181, 225; and John
Gielgud 184–5; and literature 196–7,
317–20; at Dysert 199, 202–3; as
au pair in Rome 211; in London
(1960s) 221, 223–7; and clothes
making 225–6; mature student
at Reading 234; marries George
Phipps 243–5; given Renault by MK
278, 294; introversion and secrecy
284; writing as salvation 285; and
Molly Keane's Ireland (anthology)
288, 317–20; and MK's last media
interview 300, 301
Pickles (dog) 271
Piggott, Lester 233
Pinter, Harold 219
Pollinger, Edmund 246
Pollinger, Gina 171, 246, 263, 317
Pollinger, Murray 246
Pope, Alexander 196
Portobello Nursing Home, Dublin 140
Preece, Nora 236–7, 313
Preece, Roland 237
Printemps, Yvonne 204
Pritchett, V. S. 66, 270
Proust, Marcel 33
Pugin, Augustus 96

Quidnunc (*Irish Times* diarist) 141–2
Quinlan brothers at Tallow 287

Rea, John 144
Reading University 234
The Real Charlotte (Somerville and
Ross) 291–2
Rhys, Jean 248
The Rising Tide (MK novel) 50, 98,
158–9
Ritchie, Charles 235
Robson Lowe Ltd. (stamp dealers) 232
Rock House, Ardmore 134, 136, 137–8,
197–9, 207, 313
Rockport, Co. Antrim 21–2
Roe, Edsil 279–80
Roe, Gwen 280
Roget's Thesaurus 182
Roman Holiday (William Wyler film) 196

Romulus (dog) 17
Roose-Evans, James 304
Rosenthal, Tom 299
Ross, Martin 52
Ross, Mrs 213
Rossmore, Paddy 322
Roth, Bill and Joan 307, 309
Roussin, André, *The Little Hut* 203–4
Rowley, Sibell (Sibbie) 245, 267, 270–2,
275, 286, 289, 300–1, 309
Royal Court theatre, London 219
Runyon, Damon 93
Rushdie, Salman, *Midnight's Children*
254–5
Rutherford, Margaret 24, 218

Sackville-West, Eddie 236, 237
Sandoe, John 278
Sargent, Willie 151
Say It With Flowers (MK adaptation)
203–4
Schaffer, Peter 219, 299
Scott, Bill 147, 171, 174–5, 176, 261
Scott, Maxine 175
Scott, Pamela 147, 174, 175–7, 205
Second World War 98, 106, 114, 119,
123–4, 135, 140, 148, 162, 209, 231;
outbreak of 102–3; Jewish refugees
91–2; and rationing 97, 98, 147, 170;
Ireland's neutrality 102, 125–6, 140;
Bobbie not involved in 117, 132–3,
139, 140; John Perry's service 125,
126–7, 128–9; Guards' Chapel bomb
(1944) 130–2; end of 139
Sheila (housemaid at Belleville) 148–9,
192
Shelbourne Hotel, Dublin 48–9, 141–2,
187, 277, 281
Sinclair, Arthur 142
Skrine, Agnes (Agnes Nesta
Shakespeare Higginson, mother of
MK): background of 4, 252; poetry
of 4–5, 8, 12, 70, 208; return from
Canada 5–6; relations with MK
8–14, 17, 38–9, 55–6, 130, 208–11,
252–3, 301; austere attitudes of
9–12, 38–9, 43, 44, 46–7, 63, 67,
252–3; as social recluse 10, 12, 44,
210, 295; Victorian point of view
11–13, 17, 56, 63, 252–3, 294; and
depression 12, 210; intellectual life

of 12–13, 23; Unionism of 13, 35, 107; intense intimacy with husband 17, 36, 82, 116–17; and social class 19, 51; sisters of (Lou and May) 21–4, 40, 62–3, 66–7, 130, 161, 175, 256; and burning of Ballyrankin 33, 35, 36; letters to MK 208–10; death of (1955) 208, 222; *Songs of the Glens of Antrim* (1901) 8, 208

Skrine, Anthea 213

Skrine, Billie 311, 316–17

Skrine, Charlie (brother of MK) 3, 20, 22, 25–6, 28, 112–13, 129; as excellent sportsman 15–16, 112; marries Theo Thompson 130; MK visits at Ballyrankin 222–3; marries Rosemary Barrett 223

Skrine, Dar 213

Skrine, Godfrey (brother of MK) 3, 15, 18, 26, 27–8, 63, 173, 211, 213, 256, 302; war service 129; and MK's visits to Ballyrankin 129–30, 208; children of 213, 233, 283; and brother Walter 223, 230, 233; death of 316–17, 320

Skrine, John 213

Skrine, Lady Mary Jane (aunt of MK) 32

Skrine, Rosemary (Rosemary Barrett) 223

Skrine, Susan (sister of MK) 3, 5, 11, 24–5, 36, 47, 212; childhood 22, 24, 25, 256; MK's relations with 24, 25, 28; left-wing views 51, 211; parents end love affair of 51; 'bluestocking' existence 51–2, 226; lives briefly with Walter 231

Skrine, Walter (brother of MK) 3, 18, 26, 27, 28, 223, 229–34; wounded in war 139, 231

Skrine, Walter (father of MK) 3, 4, 5–7, 14–16, 42–3, 44, 49, 51; horsemanship 5, 7, 16, 53; intense intimacy with wife 17, 36, 82, 116–17; and burning of Ballyrankin 33, 35, 36

Skrine family: competitiveness and perfectionism xiii, 16, 62, 119–20, 122, 139, 221, 223, 254, 287; emotional reticence/strong covert feelings 3, 15–16, 18, 22, 31; devotion

to duty 5, 28, 230; and horses 5, 7, 16, 26, 27, 52–3, 112, 229, 231, 233; the Bath Skrines 6, 31–2, 47–8, 51; code of behaviour 7, 11, 13, 14–16, 27, 31, 57–8, 294, 295; ideal of courage 7, 26, 27, 33, 34, 38, 52–3, 62; as men of letters 7–8; austere attitudes of 9–12, 38–9, 43–4, 46–7, 67, 252–3; and Victorian values 11–13, 16, 17, 56, 57–8, 63, 252–3, 294; burden of melancholy 12, 27, 30, 62, 69, 119–20, 230; as workers by nature 12, 46, 122, 284; Unionism of 13, 22, 34–5, 107; as brilliant sportsmen 15–16, 26, 27, 112–13; and God 26, 44, 62, 65, 175, 182, 273; Fanshawe cousins in Kildare 28–9; English Aunts 32, 47–8, 51

Slaney, River 29, 36, 56

Slater, Josephine (MK's niece) 283–4

Somerville-Large, Philip 227

Spillane (gardener at Belleville) 121–2

Spinetti, Victor 225

Spring Meeting (MK play) 24, 84, 127, 214, 218, 219, 261; John Perry as collaborator 74, 125, 127, 128; West End production of 74, 81, 88, 89, 142, 182, 183, 279; transfer to Broadway (1939) 90–1, 92

Springmount (house in Dublin) 213

St Mary's Collegiate Church, Youghal 243–4

St Mary's Convent, Youghal 101

Stacpoole, George 312

Stacpoole, Hassard 312

Stacpoole, Michelina 287, 312

Statia (servant at Ballyrankin) 222–3

Sterne, James 274

Sue (dog) 103, 108

Sylvia (governess) 196

Taking Chances (MK novel) 56–7, 59–60, 64, 295

Tallow, Co. Waterford 200, 287

Tessa (dog) 234, 247, 255, 262

Thompson, Ken and Rachel 322

Thompson, Theo (Theo Skrine, sister-in-law of MK) 130, 209–10, 222, 223

Thorndike, Sybil 166–7, 170

Time After Time (MK novel) 106, 263, 264, 268–71

Tipperary, Golden Vale of 190
Tourin (house in Co. Waterford)
    134–5, 144, 156, 198, 206
Trafalgar Terrace, Monkstown 211–14,
    217, 218
de Trafford, June and Dermot 143
Treasure Hunt (MK play) 127, 156,
    159–67, 169, 170–1, 183, 192, 261
Trevor, William 299
Turnley cousins at Drumnasole 38–40,
    102–3, 130, 209
Two Days in Aragon (MK novel) 102,
    107, 127, 156
Tynan, Ken 219
Tysons (store in Dublin) 49

United States of America (USA) 90–1,
    92–3, 203, 218, 248, 288, 309

Vernon, Stephen 241–3, 271, 272–3,
    321
Vernon, Ursula 235–6, 241, 271
Villars (Switzerland) 146–7
Villiers, Barbara 156
Villiers-Stuart, Emily (wife of Ion) 157,
    158
Villiers-Stuart, Emily (wife of James) 185
Villiers-Stuart, Ion 157, 158
Villiers-Stuart, James 157, 185
Villiers-Stuart, Patrick 157–8
Villiers-Stuart, Peter-Patrick 157, 193
Villierstown, Co. Waterford 221, 282–3
Virago 263, 281
Vogue 192

Walker, Mary 288
Walsh, Caroline 313
Walsh, Mrs Paddy 106, 107–8
Walsh, Paddy 97, 106–8
War of Independence, Irish (1919–21)
    xiv
Warleigh (near Bath) 31–2
Watt, Major 49

Waugh, Auberon 300
Waugh, Evelyn: *Helena* 53; *Brideshead
    Revisited* 96, 187, 271
Webb, Alan 166
Welles, Orson, *Chimes at Midnight*
    (play) 217
Welty, Eudora 248–9
Wesker, Arnold 219
West Waterford hounds 147, 190
Westminster, Hugh Grosvenor, 2nd
    Duke of ('Bendor') 154, 241
Wheeler, Anna 281
White, E. B. 308
William Collins (publishers) 18, 120,
    243
Williams, Sippy 131, 132
Wilson, Dr Robert 179, 211
Windsor, Duke of 110
Winkie (dog) 196
Winnicott, Dr D. W. 186–7
Woodrooffe (house in Tipperary) 61–2,
    63–5, 69–70, 75, 76, 81–4, 87, 107,
    190, 195; servants and staff 64–5,
    68–9; attack on during civil war
    65–6; Dolly Perry at 66–7, 68, 69,
    117; and Sivie Masters 69, 77, 78,
    79; MK's love affair with Bobbie
    at 84, 88; In MK's writing 84, 219;
    demolition of 85
Woolf, Virginia 281; *To the Lighthouse*
    152

Yates, Dornford 39, 40, 56
Yeats, Jack 215, 288
Yeats, John Butler 288
Yeats, William Butler 13, 34, 288, 317,
    319
Youghal 101, 141, 243–4, 278
Young Entry (MK novel) 44, 45, 46
Yourcenar, Marguerite 114

Zephi (dog) 221–2, 224
Zoological Society, Phoenix Park 218

ACKNOWLEDGEMENTS

I would like to thank Stanley Price for his valuable advice and for reading this book as I wrote it, chapter by chapter. I am also deeply grateful to Virginia Brownlow, Thomas McCarthy, Joan Roth, Ken and Rachel Thompson, Judy Price, George Phipps, Paddy Rossmore and Bruce Hunter – all of whom read part or all of the work in progress. I thank my agent Caroline Dawnay and her assistant Sophie Scard for their help and encouragement. I give special thanks to Diana Athill, my mother's editor at Deutsch, for her support of the book. I thank the writer Polly Devlin for her deeply perceptive introductions to some of Molly's Virago Modern Classics and for befriending her work both in life and since her death. I am profoundly indebted to Jeanette Woods, who typed and patiently deciphered my manuscript, and to Hazel Allen for helping with computers and for generously giving me her time and assistance. I am grateful to my cousin John Skrine for lending me family papers and photographs. I would like to thank the many friends who encouraged me over the years, particularly Desmond and Olda FitzGerald, Kevin Brownlow, Patrick Villiers-Stuart, Sarah Wiseman, Nicholas Burke, Patrick and Jan Cockburn, Tony Gallagher, Adrian and Charles Dawnay, Rosalyne and Marc Leva, and Joe Meehan, and to Angela Lansbury, who lent me her beautiful and peaceful house to work in.

I thank Denise Long, who kindly sent me the letter John Gielgud had written to her about my mother. I am also deeply grateful to Mary D. Kierstead, Sibell Rowley and Ruth Annesley for giving me the letters they had received from Molly, and to the estates of Diana Petre, John Gielgud, John Perry, Tommie Jameson and Pam Scott. I thank my publisher at Virago, Lennie Goodings, for all the work and care she has put into this project, and I also thank Zoe Gullen and Donna Coonan for their assistance.

I am very grateful to my family and my stepchildren for their encouragement and support.

Above all, I send my love and thanks to my late husband, George Phipps, and to my sister, Virginia Brownlow, to whom this book is dedicated.